# Gothic Romanced

The dark, destructive and monstrous elements of gothic fiction have traditionally been seen in opposition to the rose-tinted idealism of Romanticism. In this ground-breaking study, Fred Botting re-evaluates the relationship between the two genres in order to plot the shifting alignments of popular and literary fictions with cultural theories, consumption and representations of science.

*Gothic Romanced* traces the history of gothic and romantic writings from the eighteenth and nineteenth centuries to the present day. It examines the ways in which these genres were aligned with the historical process of modernity – with the Gothic representing the negative aspects of vice and barbarism that accompanied the changing parameters of civilisation, while Romance clung on to traditional values, manners and feelings. The book demonstrates how these genres have evolved together, alongside cultural shifts and Postmodern theories, blurring the binary between the sacred and the profane.

Botting considers Romance and the Gothic from Mary Shelley, Anne Rice and Alasdair Gray through to *Alien* and *Star Trek*. He manages a fluid and extensive exploration of generic boundaries, including gothic fiction, romantic poetry, literary pastiches, popular horror fiction, cyberpunk and science fiction.

**Fred Botting** is Professor in the Institute for Cultural Research, Lancaster University. He has written extensively on gothic fiction and cultural theory and his books include *Gothic* (Routledge 1996), *Sex, Machines and Navels* (1999) and, with Scott Wilson, *Bataille* (2001) and *The Tarantinian Ethics* (2001).

D1465356

# Gothic Romanced

Consumption, gender and technology in contemporary fictions

**Fred Botting**

Routledge
Taylor & Francis Group

LONDON AND NEW YORK

First published 2008
by Routledge
2 Park Square, Milton Park, Abingdon, OX14 4RN

Simultaneously published in the USA and Canada
by Routledge
270 Madison Ave, New York, NY 10016

*Routledge is an imprint of the Taylor & Francis Group, an informa business*

© 2008 Fred Botting

Typeset in Baskerville by
Book Now Ltd, London
Printed and bound in Great Britain by
TJ International Ltd, Padstow, Cornwall

*British Library Cataloguing in Publication Data*
A catalogue record for this book is available from the British Library

*Library of Congress Cataloguing in Publication Data*
Botting, Fred.
Gothic romanced: consumption, gender and technology in
contemporary fictions / Fred Botting.
    p. cm.
Includes bibliographical references and index.
1. Love in literature. 2. Horror in literature. 3. Science in literature.
4. Popular culture and literature. 5. Horror tales, English—History
and criticism. 6. Horror tales, American—History and criticism.
7. Love stories, English--History and criticism. 8. Love stories,
American—History and criticism. 9. Science fiction, English—
History and criticism. 10. Science fiction, American—History and
criticism. I. Title.
PR830.T3B69 2008
823'.0872909—dc22                                      2007049643

ISBN13: 978–0–415–45089–8 (hbk)
ISBN13: 978–0–415–45090–4 (pbk)
ISBN13: 978–0–203–09071–8 (ebk)

# Contents

# Acknowledgements

Thanks, for the arguments, conversations, suggestions and criticisms helping to shape this book, are due to a wide range of people, from colleagues in various departments at the universities of Keele and Lancaster to the many members of the International Gothic Association. Two invaluable texts were suggested by Anthea Trodd and Jerome de Groot respectively, and Glennis Byron and Dale Townshend provided very useful comments on the manuscript.

The publisher and author would like to thank the following for permission to reprint material under copyright:

Fred Botting, 'Monsters of the Imagination: Gothic, Science, Fiction' from *A Companion to Science Fiction* ed. by David Seed, Blackwells Companions to Literature and Culture (Blackwell, 2005). Reprinted by kind permission of Wiley-Blackwell Publishing Ltd.

—— 'Resistance is Futile' from *Anglophonia/Caliban*. Reprinted by kind permission of the Presses Universitaires du Mirail.

—— 'Romanticism, repetition, reiteration' from *Inhuman Reflections: Rethinking the Limits of the Human* ed. by Scott Brewster, John J Joughin, David Owen and Richard J Walker (Manchester University Press, 2000). Reprinted by kind permission of Manchester University Press.

—— 'Hypocrite vampire . . . ', Gothic Studies, 9: 1 (May 2007). Reprinted by kind permission of Manchester University Press.

—— 'Flight of the Heroine' from *Postfeminist Gothic: Critical Interventions in Contemporary Culture* ed. by Benjamin A. Brabon and Stephanie Genz (Macmillan, 2007). Reprinted by kind permission of Benjamin A. Brabon, Stephanie Genz and Palgrave Macmillan.

Every effort has been made to trace and contact copyright holders. The publishers would be pleased to hear from any copyright holders not acknowledged here, so that this acknowledgement page may be amended at the earliest opportunity.

# Introduction
## Romance never dies

### 'Love never dies'

I was not the only critic to register mild irritation at Francis Ford Coppola's adaptation of *Dracula* (1992) – it marked 'the end of Gothic' at the end of *Gothic*. Annoyance arose only partly at the film's extravagant treatment of Bram Stoker's novel: its overlaying of a distinctly romantic theme seemed to twist the book's nastiness in confused, if not contradictory, directions. Thomas Elsaesser, in a fine critical analysis of the formal complexities and allusiveness of the film, also noted the 'irritation' arising at Coppola's reworking of the myth: appending a romanticised historical frame to the fiction turned the aristocratic bloodsucker's sexuality from 'indiscriminate polymorphously perverse lust' into 'a romance story about star-crossed destinies'. The romance frame, he goes on, 'emasculates the potency of the very notion of the undead, sacrificing the psychic economy of eros and thanatos on the paltry altar of a heterosexual *Liebestod*' (205). Elsaesser's phrasing is telling: in dismissing the romantic sentimentalism of the film, it is hard to avoid resorting to cliché ('star-crossed destinies'), the very clichés, indeed, with which romance abounds and through which it survives. 'Love never dies', as movie posters and publicity for the film declared: the phrase seems to say it all.

Love never dies. With Coppola's *Dracula*, romance, as undead as any genre, seemed to make a dramatic return; a return, as they say, with a vengeance on a genre that emerged in the eighteenth century as its minor offshoot ('the gothic romance'). Romance, as it frames gothic, seems to clean up its darker counterpart, sanitising its depravations; it tries to transform, even ennoble, violent gothic energies as a quest for love in the face of death; it recuperates gothic excesses in the name of the heterosexual couple, occluding the homosocial tensions and cultural anxieties of Stoker's novel and problematising its boy's own imperialism, its prurient revulsions and moral violence. Monsters, in this romantic transformation of gothic, find themselves increasingly humanised while villains become increasingly alluring: repulsion cedes to attraction as horror gives way to romance. Framed by a tragic story which is played out in the confines of a chapel, romantic love is both sanctified and rendered excessive: the cruel destiny which causes Dracula to lose the love of his life, Elzibieta, also prompts him to curse god, renounce religion and become vampire. Vampirism, traditionally associated with instinctual, primitive and animalistic energies, is redefined as an amorous condition, a passion beyond life and death: with Dracula assuming the form of an 'ardent lover' (Dika 390), love, especially lost love, becomes undead, immortal, and thus truer than ever.

Giving Dracula a lover's suffering role diminishes his villainy and monstrosity, and makes him into something of a victim, his wounds demanding sympathy and adding to his allure. In this respect, like Heathcliff, or like those brooding, occasionally callous, silent types of Mills and Boon or Harlequin romances, all he needs is the love of the right woman. And she appears: Harker's photograph of Mina, framed in close-up and clutched by Dracula, is the very image of his lost love. This image, moreover, reciprocates the emotion: the romantic affair is evident in the amorous glances and lovers' trysts over which the film lingers. The romanticism of the film is most striking in the transformation of the novel's scene of Mina's 'baptism of blood' into a consummation of adulterous passion: the horror of religious transgression, Mina feeding at Dracula's breast, unravels, in the film, in a scene of romantic intensity, a passionate entwining of bodies in which both partners – and a voyeuristic camera – fully engage. Mina's voiceover comments on the affair to indicate, as in all good adulterous romances, that the relationship with Dracula is expanding her own sexual horizons. For a film which, visually at least, luxuriates in its Victorian setting, there are few signs of sexual repression among its women. As if in emphasis, rather wooden figures of Victorian masculinity, Van Helsing's 'crew of light', slip into the background as Dracula's and Mina's romance plays itself out to the end, the latter idealising romantic passion in an ultimate and appropriate form: he must die so love can live on, transcendent.

Structurally and thematically, romance seems to provide Coppola's film with complete closure. Its supplementary frame allows the novel to be fully transformed as a romance. Vera Dika's reading of the film as a postmodern 'neo-mythification', bringing gender and representation to the fore, notes the strength of the romantic theme: 'Mina loves Dracula across the entirety of the film with a passion and intensity that is meant to transcend even death' (390). The theme of passion unto death seems to draw on a courtly tradition; at the same time, the romantic myth of transcendence delivers something more modern in the idea that Mina loves Dracula 'completely': the romance is mutual and 'eternal' (394). Love never dies: the fantasy of an individual's completion in his/her union with a beloved other seems to be fulsomely endorsed.

In the respect of a film that draws attention – in close-ups of blood cells – to a different disease (AIDS) than the syphilis of the novel, the romantic argument is harder to sustain. Dika finds it difficult to reconcile 'the idea that love, or desire, should cause defilement and one's own death' with a liberating and positive ideal of amorous union. The idea, in another tacit endorsement of the popular myth of romantic union and natural sexual freedom, is 'a hideous perversion of the human sexual act', but it remains a conflict that the film only inadequately broaches (394). Nonetheless, for Dika, the positive message of the film's reworking of the novel remains: the latter, 'steeped in the mystification of defilement for the sin of sexual desire and the fear of sexual difference', has been transformed 'into a work of innovative and affirmative exultation. Never before has a horror film embodied such hope in the conquering power of love beyond death' (399). From this perspective, Coppola's version has gone further than any other Dracula adaptation in romanticising and liberalising the vampire story. Two decades before, John Badham's *Dracula* (1979) located the story in a longer romantic tradition of '*l'amour fou*' which, embracing *Wuthering Heights* and *L'Age d'Or*, failed to convince Robin Wood of the liberatory potential of the undead vampire-aristocrat. Rather, it prompted a call to 'pass beyond' Dracula: his usefulness as a figure showing how the return of the repressed cannot be contained is, for Wood, countered by the inability to 'purge him of connotations of evil', connotations that keep sexuality in a (repressed) Victorian frame (328). To welcome the return of the repressed and initiate a less Victorian engagement with different sexualities, as Wood advocates, requires forms of representation other than vampire tales.

As Coppola and the screenwriter, James V. Hart, rework the story, and in line with other cultural negotiations of the vampire theme, undead bloodsuckers do not become redundant. In Anne Rice's vampire mythology, for instance, creatures of the night proliferate as decadently attractive beings in a process of romanticisation that, further, enables an association of vampires and cyborgs as figures of liminality, monstrosity and difference busy challenging (Victorian) bourgeois notions of normality and identity (Stone; Haraway 1997). With horror and revulsion jettisoned, romance steps in to provide those 'others' of gothic fiction with a positive charge: they become figures who, in their very difference, throw off older associations and anxieties, and emerge as harbingers of new forms and relationships, their previous threats now tendering a promise. Writing of new technical developments and post-human possibilities, Mark Poster notes that 'the Gothic tale of technology as the being from the dark lagoon is, perhaps, then, narrativised otherwise as a romance with an alien cyborg, a monster who is always already none other than ourselves' (27). The gothic genre's usual trajectory is reversed: a flight from figures of horror and revulsion is turned into a romantic flight towards them, now figures of identification. It is also a flight beyond modern and human frameworks. Further reversals occur as romance comes to the fore: the weight and anxieties of a gothic history give way to a (fantasised) future. In Stoker's novel modern technical innovations, particularly in respect of communications technologies (newspapers, phonographs, typewriters, timetables) provided the apparatus for tracking vampiric incursion (Wicke; Kittler 1997). Now, new media provide the occasion for vampiric identification. Where horror, in throwing up revolting images of decomposition and transgression, maintained Victorian limits and prohibitions, romance moves beyond them.

Although horror cedes to romance, and revulsion to attraction, the romantic reversals of gothic patterns and re-evaluations of the genre's monstrous figures cannot fully cast off their historical weight. In order to engender the intensities of identification and attraction, the very reversal – in transforming cathexes – must retain something of the charge that rendered gothic monstrosities dangerous and exciting: a trace of negativity suggests a reason for continued emotional investment in figures that, to follow Wood's argument, should really have collapsed into obsolescence. In moving beyond horror to romanticise the vampire, Coppola's film looks back as well as forward, acknowledging the pressure of changing cultural and aesthetic contexts, contexts which rupture and pluralise the supposed singularity and unity of any romantic frame. As Elsaesser notes, Coppola's *Dracula* situates itself in the rift between classical Hollywood filmmaking (which emphasises narrative and character consistency along with perspectival and temporal coherence) and a post-classical mode which, breaking and playing with the rules of the former, moves to textual excess, reflexivity and allusion.

The romantic frame, moreover, does not overcome the tensions of the film's structural indeterminacy, but exacerbates them in stretching romance beyond its limits. For Elsaesser, the key element lies in the *mise-en-scène* of the romantic backstory, in Dracula's chapel at the beginning and end of the film: while it appears to sanctify a transcendent love across time – and across the entire film – there are significant elements missing that refuse a simple romantic closure. In the opening, as Dracula, standing over his dead lover's body, utters his fateful curse, he looks upwards: the shot, as though invoking a godlike camera as witness to his despair and transcendent love, is not completed. The absence of a reverse shot seems to place the viewer in a position of mastery at the other end of the vampire's look. But the viewer is duped. Only at the end of the film – back in the chapel (this time with Mina over Dracula's prostrate body) – is the shot completed: Dracula's upward gaze at the start was not directed to some divinity, but to a mural on the ceiling of the chapel, a mural depicting the union of him and his beloved. The romantic couple stands in place of the divinity, a gesture towards a beatified and everlasting romantic love, a timeless relation that – with Coppola's addition of the frame – has determined the plot of the film. The place of the viewer, however, is rendered uncertain by this significant shift in perspective: the voyeurism and specular identification encouraged by classical film is defamiliarised and put 'into infinite regress' since the shot comes to rest on another pictorial image in a film full of painterly allusions (202). Elevated and extended, and then put into focus itself, the romantic frame breaks; the viewer is no longer in a position of mastery, but becomes engulfed by the multiple perspectives of the movie, refusing any safe or singular point of critical distance.

The infinite regress of Francis Ford Coppola's *Bram Stoker's Dracula* is highlighted by the title. Doubly auteurised, the claims to authenticity engender various kinds of textual excess which press upon its formal and interpretative aspects as a romance of origins and a romance of history. While making claims on being a more accurate adaptation, returning to Stoker's novel in more faithful fashion, the film supplements its attention with recourse to the 'actual' history of Vlad the Impaler drawn from Leonard Wolf's *The Annotated Dracula*. Extensive 'authentification' requires textual diversions and renders the film more artificial. Its inclusion of scenes never shot before – like that of the vampire ascending, lizard-like up the castle walls in the early part of the novel – acknowledge the first cover illustration as much as the book itself. The Victorian sets and costumes, too, are absorbed in the authenticating process as another artifice of authenticity: influenced by symbolist painting, expressionist colour, art nouveau. All precursors, as Elsaesser suggests, of abstract art, they serve to gloss the past with appropriate aesthetic references, postmodernising and gothicising at the same time, linking decadent concerns with gender and culture in the 1890s with similar anxieties in the 1990s. In the film, writing is made evident, both literally and metaphorically: letters and journals are read and written, delicate caligraphed pages appearing on screen. Symbolically, a poetic and non-linear set of visual associations allude to a writerliness that overspills frames and draws attention to narrative conventions and cinematic forms: as Harker takes his leave from Mina in an ornamental garden, to begin his journey East, the extreme close-up on one dark eye of a peacock feather fades into the darkness of a tunnel. The cry of the peacock elides the whistle of the train and provides 'solidity' for the visual connection. It also suggests the iris shot of early cinema (Elsaesser 203). But what kind of eye? Evil or otherwise (it is a vampire film)? Another uncertain, if not disarming, gaze.

Coppola's artifice of authenticity tends in another direction with its attention to painterly (rich symbolist and orientalist costumes; the colour and abstraction of the shots), dramatic (dark, curtained sets), fictional and written forms (journals, lushly illustrated *Kama Sutra*, newsprint), indicating a kind of authentic artifice respectful of different modes of cultural and technical production. It is no surprise, then, that one of Dracula's and Mina's amorous rendezvous occurs against the backdrop of an early cinematic screening. Not only is Coppola's *Dracula* a 'highly self-referencing text in relation to movie history', alluding to at least sixty other films, it is also attentive to the technical processes of filmmaking (Elsaesser 198). In making the film, Coppola, with his son, Roman, as special effects advisor, claimed to have used no digital enhancements, employing 'naïve effects' to 'give the film almost a mythical soul' (Coppola and Hart 5). Techniques included extensive use of shadow, reverse running of film, multiple exposures and mirror effects (52). The 'black limbo' of using dark curtains and extensive areas of shadow on sound stages was designed to produce a sense of disturbing and disorientating infinity (42). As it eschews established patterns of classical Hollywood narrative, the film continues to look back to traditional cinematic forms and techniques.

The conjunction articulating old and new, the 'ambiguous nostalgia' exuding from the film, is framed by the vampire film itself, 'prototypical for movie history and for postmodernity' (Elsaesser 198). It is not incumbent on vampires to make sense or represent anything, only to evoke effects: undead, they allow the past to persist in the form of seductive yet spatially disorientating sequences of images that escape conventional temporality and narrative frames. The feeling of 'engulfment' that Elsaesser argues is characteristic of post-classical cinema stems from the rupture of specular framing which allows the viewer some critical distance and perspective. With extensive levels of allusion and reflexivity, with images spilling from their frames, the film becomes 'unreadable' in classical terms: is it ironic, parodic or pastiche (Elsaesser 213)? Does it imply a naïve viewer caught up in the cinematic romance or a sophisticated movie historian mourning the passing of the craft? Or both at the same time?

There is a curious postmodernity, then, to Coppola's *Dracula*'s reinscription of romance, a postmodernity in which history seems to return with a difference. The postmodern romance sees an 'excessive return of past events' (Elam 50). Yet history returns only to be eclipsed in a wash of heritage colour, or another – and increasingly recent – gothicisation of the past (Baldick 1992); to go into reverse, recycling the past as Disney (Baudrillard 1994); or to drag the present into an inertia overwhelmed by the weight of historical images (Virilio 2000). In classical Hollywood terms, the director rewrites Stoker's novel in order that, through love, Mina 'can give the vampire back his soul' (Coppola and Hart 5). But, as a post-classical film, character and narrative are inconsistent. The vampire is monster, villain and lover; the good Victorian fiancée and wife becomes an adulteress and, if not murderer, a merciful killer. With women coming to the fore as active lovers in the film, the novel's male romance is sidelined if not, in Elsaesser's terms, 'emasculated', as a tale of lust, violence and imperial adventure. Where Stoker's novel, pairing Dracula and the professional bourgeois Victorian crew that hunt him, promoted a bloody return to martial romance, the film, curiously, occludes the homosociality of *fin-de-siècle* English culture.

In looking back, in accordance with its longing take on movie history and technique, to an 1890s full of dark passions and quirky instruments, an era associated with sexual repression (they are 'depraved because they are deprived', commented Coppola and Hart, 55), the film seems to evince a nostalgia for the prohibition that rendered sex meaningful and intense (along the lines of A. S. Byatt's postmodern romance, *Possession*, in which the Victorians are seen to be more passionate than their late twentieth-century counterparts). But, in bringing gender and romance to the fore alongside images of decadence, it seems to appeal to an age of lost sexual possibilities and freedoms (their possibility sustained precisely by obstacles and prohibitions), its end marked by the cultural prominence and devastating effects of AIDS. That one lover kills another, given this context, raises further interpretative puzzles: is Mina's a commentary on late twentieth-century sexual relations; is her act one of mercy – a romantic sacrifice of the body in order that love becomes transcendent, or one of self-sacrifice – renouncing female sexual freedom to the duties of marriage and monogamy, or execution? Romances multiply. Beyond the romantic passion of the idealised couple, almost elevated to sanctified heights, romance assumes historical and nostalgic dimensions: for the simplicity of Victorian repressions; for the pleasures of Victorian decadence; for the idealisations of – and fatal obstacles to – eternal love; for some kind of historical origin in the face of textual excesses and indeterminacies; for an overriding narrative frame that, tinged with a credible portion of gothic darkness, can sustain distinctions of good and evil, human and other, despite the reflexive play and ironies of postmodern aesthetic opportunism, that is, a romance of and for meaning.

Pushed to the limit of meaninglessness, romance turns to its subsidiary gothic form, to provide it with some limit, some point at which meaning can be recuperated. As Umberto Eco noted of the title of his own postmodern romance, *The Name of the Rose*, the noun appealed because 'rose' is 'a symbolic figure so rich in meanings that by now it has hardly any meaning left' (3). So, too, romance. It turns to gothic figures: in conjuring up terrors and intense effects, gothic seems to offer curious substance to an almost empty form. At the same time, it is always on the brink of collapsing into its own formulaic devices. 'Dark romance' undermines the separation between realism and escapist romance by disclosing something 'unpresentable', a 'dark or unspeakable desire' associated with feminine excess (Elam 133). Beyond convention and opposition, then, romance provides a screen for something else: its condition, as Eco notes while distinguishing three types of historical narrative, is that 'it must only not take place here and now'. 'Romance is a story of an *elsewhere*' (67). That elsewhere may be past (gothic romance) or future (science fiction), but, as in Coppola's *Dracula*, it remains an 'elsewhere' at odds with the present. As writing or image, moreover, romance remains an undead form: it provides a projective screen while gothic furnishes the dark stain around which meaning and affects cluster and collapse.

In Coppola's *Dracula*, despite the multiplication of diverse romantic trajectories, a single romance remains: like the painting of the lovers on the ceiling of castle Dracula's chapel, still photographs and moving images come to the fore. Romance is manifested in light flickering on a screen in a darkened room, in the excess of visual form and allusion, in the loving attention to technique and apparatus: it is a romance of the cinematic image itself. Even Elsaesser is captivated. Noting how the film manages ultimately to combine diverse viewing experiences and live up to its undead cinematic heritage, he finds 'the true Dracula of cinema' once again risen 'to haunt us all' – 'because who does not want the cinema to be the love that never dies?' (206). Romance seems to survive textual excess, reflexive play and engulfment. Its remarkably plastic and accommodating frame, though exposed, withstands the all-too obvious weight of history and aesthetic convention. Such plasticity is manifested by Daphne du Maurier's *Rebecca*, a novel that both exemplifies the form and is able to expose its underlying – and suspect – gendered assumptions (Light 7). The 'postmodern attitude', coming into play after the avant-garde has reached the limit of an impossibly abstracted metalanguage, consists, Eco argues, in revisiting the past ironically. His example is taken from romance: a sophisticated couple, conscious that Barbara Cartland has been there before and all-too aware of clichéd romanticism, do not resort to nakedly uttering the phrase, 'I love you madly'. The 'solution' lies in saying 'as Barbara Cartland would put it, I love you madly': a message of love will have been sent and received without recourse to 'false innocence' and 'both will have succeeded, once again, in speaking of love' (67–68). Ironised, but romantic nonetheless, romance succeeds in making a statement despite the weight of prior historical utterances and in the face of a general – postmodern – incredulity towards metanarratives.

**Alibis**

Francis Ford Coppola's *Bram Stoker's Dracula* condenses a number of the questions – of contemporary cultural change, of shifts in generic and aesthetic conventions, and of any continuing validity for the category 'gothic' – posed in this book. The difficulty of – and perhaps (romantic) desire for – a coherent critical reading of texts conjoining romance, gothic and postmodern characteristics, characteristics that morph and merge across histories and cultures more than many genres, is also one of the problems addressed in this account of contemporary fictions and films. Such difficulty is highlighted in the title. *Gothic Romanced* begins in tautology and proceeds to perplexity: wasn't gothic fiction a romance form from the start, defined by the writer of the first 'Gothic story', as a blend of 'ancient and modern romance' (Walpole 7–8)? And if it originated as a romance, how can it be romanced again? What would be the point of repetition in aesthetic, generic or cultural terms, even though repetitive structures, plots and themes remain one of the genre's most evident features? The plasticity and persistence of both genres, the contradictions and paradoxes generated by their interlacing and overlaps, the diverse and often ambivalent circulations in changing contexts, raise complex questions for contemporary culture, questions of desire, fantasy and consumption. Romancing gothic, gothicking romance: the process of tracing different generic crossings and diverse cultural effects produces a chiasmus, its 'x' marking the zone of a disturbing Thing that, though productive of a wide range of affects, is also the point where structural, generic and subjective issues coalesce.

Critical historians of genre readily situate the gothic romance as a subordinate form of the more enduring, developed and historically embedded genre of romance. Northrop Frye locates gothic fiction as subsidiary type of romance that exemplifies its more 'popular' and 'primitive' features, marking 'a different social development of literature', rather than being of a worse or better kind (1976: 28–29). Romance originates in two main forms, secular tales of chivalry and knight-errantry, and religious legends of saints (Frye 1957: 34). It further divides in two, presenting 'idyllic' or 'night' worlds above and below ordinary experience. In contrast to romance's ascendant quest, a direction towards transcendence, the sacred or wish-fulfilment, gothic romances manifest a descent into anxiety and nightmare, into realms of shadowy doubles (Frye 1976: 53; 117).

Romance 'is the story of an *elsewhere*' (Eco 67). Hence, the first gothic fictions look back to romanticised feudal times, distinguished from their Enlightenment here and now; to a family past hiding guilty secrets; or to a psychological prehistory (the unconscious) from which repressed wishes and desires return. 'Alibi' also means 'elsewhere': against accusations of criminal activity, one declares that one was in another place at the time the crime was committed. Hence, 'elsewhere' can function as an excuse for or screen to present otherwise illicit or unsanctioned notions, a site for the transgression of social or sexual norms. Another elsewhere emerges: located in a 'night world', opposed to both ordinary experience and the higher realm of idealised quest, it comes to present an other or underside to an enlightened modern culture that liked to see itself in terms of reason, order, morality and progress. In terms of cultural evaluations, gothic fiction finds itself in an antithetical role associated with vices, darkness, passion and excess, very much the negative – even in a photographic sense – against which proper, higher Culture (since the eighteenth century and Romanticism) could define and establish itself, privileging individual imagination and originality against a swarm of lower class, less discriminating readers uncritically consuming formulaic mass-produced trash. Although courtly love played a significant part in the early stages of romantic literature, the eighteenth-century antiquarians who informed the Gothic Revival were more interested in the national and aesthetic implications of medieval tales and ballads, encouraging a taste for medieval chivalry, style and customs rather than stories of love and adventure. As gothic fictions gained popularity in the course of the century, however, critics complained of their stimulation, among undiscriminating readers, of appetites for improbable and idealised amorous and martial adventures, thereby introducing a modern association tying romance to love.

Even in this particular tracing of gothic and romantic differences, their trajectories overlap: popular romances, sentimental love stories, and romantic fictions find themselves in the same bracket as gothic forms, all lower forms or dealing with lower themes, fixed in a devalued cultural sphere and possessing limited aesthetic or moral value. Both genres, moreover, have been feminised: since the eighteenth century the notion that tales of love and adventure were produced and consumed, in the main, by female writers and readers has remained a persistent, if fallacious, cultural fiction. Gothic romance, a subordinate type of romance, was subordinated again almost as soon as it appeared. When Walpole, anonymously, produced his gothic story, the genre of romance was already being derogatively compared to the novel: improbable tales of love and adventure set in the past served no rational, social or moral purpose and only encouraged monstrous flights of fancy that provoked readers to 'go forever out of the way of human paths' (Williams 1970: 162). In contrast, the novel, remaining closer to the laws of nature and society, offered probable representations of a realistic world, with proper and recognisable models of virtue (Clery and Miles). It thus served moral and didactic purposes. Although *The Castle of Otranto*'s appeal to the antiquarian enthusiasms of the Gothic Revival allowed it some success, it was not long before it achieved notoriety as the progenitor of a 'spawn' of fictions giving free rein to a range of licentious passions, vices and anti-social tendencies (Matthias). Gothic romances, particularly as they became increasingly popular in the 1790s, were seen to threaten paternal authority, familial and social order and, even, elicit revolutionary sympathies, with the security of gender divisions and the propriety of young female readers' morals and manners being at the most risk.

Not only critical essays, but many novels (by Jane Austen, Mary Wollstonecraft, Charlotte Lennox) were written warning of the dangers of romance reading, cautionary tales designed to expose the pernicious effects – undiscriminating and irrational identification with heroines, superstitious credulity, emotional overindulgence, unrealistic life expectations and lowered moral standards and priorities – on young female minds. Of a host of writers criticised for lowering standards of taste, morals and behaviour, Ann Radcliffe, the 'great enchantress', was one of the few to retain critical acceptance along with enormous popularity (Miles). Following Clara Reeve in embourgeoisifying the romance (despite the usual feudal and aristocratic trappings), but centring on the plight of the heroine, her stories repeatedly urged against excesses of feeling, immorality and superstition and engineered happy endings of lessons learned, and of marriage, property and status earned. Radcliffe – with her vast popularity and earnings – can be seen as very much the Barbara Cartland of her day, laying out some of the formulas and encouraging the pattern for tales of persecuted, often naïve, sometimes hysterical, sometimes paranoid, heroines, drawn into disorientating environments, threatened yet attracted by dark villains and lost in disturbing yet exciting worlds of amorous and adventurous possibility. And so on, with slight and subtle generic mutations attentive to changing social practices, attitudes and expectations and markets. Through the Brontës, Collins, Corelli, du Maurier and the host of popular romantic fictions packaged as 'Harlequins', 'Gothics', 'Mills and Boon', to the 'Woman's Film' of the 1930s and 1940s Hollywood (Radway; Modleski; Doane). And on.

Although more prevalent and most often misperceived as a specifically feminine form, those dark-toned romances in which love is more prominent than adventure are one strand in the popular development of romance from the eighteenth century to the middle of the twentieth. A line of male, dark romance – subordinating love to adventure – can also be traced from Walpole's concoction, picking up the threads of chivalric warriors and noble, martial adventures and licensing more 'masculine' tendencies towards power and violence: from the incestuous and murderously ambitious raging of Walpole's Manfred, Lewis's Monk, through Godwin's Falkland and Polidori's Ruthven, a darkly romanticised masculinity emerges as a combination of Byronic intensity with a diabolically adventurous exploration of social and sexual boundaries. Passion, brutality, physical and sexual power are displayed as the underside of aristocratic manners and charm. Count Dracula says as much when he bemoans the passing of the 'warlike days' of heroic feudal conflict: supplanted by a period of 'dishonourable peace', 'the glories of the great races are as a tale that is told' (Stoker 43). Those days are recovered, not only with the vampire's incursion into the heart of a bourgeois empire whose virility had been weakened by civilisation, but when the professional men of middle-class England recover their potency and crusading spirit to drive out the eastern invader along with the sexual decadence he stirs up among their women, hunting him down in his foreign lair. Van Helsing's 'crew of light' participate in an imperial romance, like those popularised by Rider Haggard, in which masculinity expands the horizons of its imagined mastery beyond other sexes, to other peoples and their dark continents.

Scientific power, the (male) mind dominating matter, reason and progress mastering (feminised) nature, is also associated with this strand of romance: Frankenstein's fantasy, a flight inspired by distinctly romantic imaginings, overcomes natural limits and creates a new species; in H. G. Wells' 'scientific romances' technical inventions overcome the limitations of time. Romance conjoins gothic and science fiction in these imaginative flights. It can also, in a cautionary mode, flip over into horror: Frankenstein's excessive ambition is realised, mirrored and magnified by the monster he manufactures, his imagined mastery over life itself disintegrating in horror; so, too, with Jekyll's chemical experiments or Dr Moreau's cruel vivisections. Modernity's metanarrative, a framework privileging patriarchal power, reason, scientific progress, is held together fantastically in an opposition of masculine reason and mastery set against the otherness of woman, sexuality, monsters and machines (Huyssen).

One of the key modes through which romance engages questions of mastery, gender and a sense of the proximity of otherness is the sublime. Frye notes that romance 'turns fear at a distance, or terror, into the adventurous' (1957: 37). As an aesthetic encounter with and production of effects of terror, the sublime, according to one of its most influential theorists, Edmund Burke, entwines imaginative mastery with extreme emotional effects. The 'terror sublime' associated with the gothic romance enables the mind to expand and achieve a sense of power (Hogle 2004: 225). Where objects, images and scenes of beauty are contained by their form, proportion and harmonious relationships (softness, smoothness, delicacy), thereby encouraging the relaxation of the beholder and having, for Burke, feminine connotations, the sublime is threatening, dark, masculine. Evoking terror, wonder and astonishment at scenes of grandeur, obscurity and magnificence, the sublime overwhelms the mind with its object, suspending the motions of the soul (1990: 53). 'Hurried out itself' in a confusion of images and nervous tension, the mind experiences power as danger. At this point, utterly divested of mastery, the mind, through passion, recovers itself through the activation of an instinct for 'self-preservation'. The emotions involved move beyond mere pleasure to 'a sort of delightful horror, a sort of tranquillity tinged with terror'. If it does not press too close, causing direct pain or horror, terror provides a vigorous work-out for the nervous system that relieves the torpor of 'common labour' (Burke 1990: 122–23). A double movement characterises the work of the sublime, a subjective dynamism of effects and affects akin to the chiaroscuro – the play of light and dark – that produced sublime atmospheres in painting, architecture and fiction. In crossing boundaries separating self and object, losing one in other, only to restore them, it serves to engender a stronger – albeit imaginary – sense of self. Although described in a conventional division of gendered attributes, the experience is not restricted to men. Radcliffe's heroines frequently enjoy, often too much, its effects, before being returned to the comforts of the marital hearth. Radcliffe, moreover, produced an important aesthetic qualification which distinguished terror and horror as 'so far opposite, that the first expands the soul, and wakens the faculties to a high degree of life; the other contracts, freezes and nearly annihilates them' (149–50). In terror, the mind works in partial darkness on an obscure object, but its activity provides a means for imaginative expansion, for a flight beyond immediate bounds and tensions. The flight engendered by terror is very much the trajectory enabled by romance, a movement beyond . . . elsewhere.

Among those critics from Richard Hurd to Andrew Lang, generally in the minority, who recommended the romance, the characteristics of imaginative freedom and emotional expansiveness were often highlighted. Amid the clamour of critical opposition to the rise of gothic romances, however, the sublime was employed negatively as a way of characterising the genre – and its readers – as a overwhelming flood or a ravenous monster, and thus a threat against which aesthetic and social values had to be defended (Williams 1970). Consuming the genre itself, an unproductive, idle, irrational and immoral waste of time, money and energy engaged in enjoying stories that indulged useless fancies in which sex and death were prominent, seemed to conjure up the spectre of further catastrophic consumption. The sublime – its passions arousing a disturbing combination of dangers, excitements, thrills and imaginative freedoms – enabled links to be made, through gothic forms, to a range of excesses threatening propriety and normalcy: from sexual and vicious appetites, violent, criminal ambitions, destructive mobs, foreign customs and stereotypes, to madness and delusion, the 'elsewhere' of modern reason, order and progress was produced as an imagined, irreversible descent into the 'night world' of romance from which modern culture could always recoil. Popular, ambivalent in its effects, the gothic romance was just about kept in its proper subordinate place as an imaginative exploration of modernity's elsewhere, preserving images of a barbaric past or wishes of immature minds that had – or should have – been superseded. From this perspective, rather than provide a fictional disguise in which more subversive desires and disturbing passions were given outlet, romance's sublime terror allowed otherness to intrude so that it could be expunged or be imaginatively overcome, eliciting and screening out cultural and subjective anxieties with fantasy figures and forms.

Things get messier later in the twentieth century: postmodernism. Postindustrial society brings consumption to the fore. The legitimacy of political formations and social structures is everywhere challenged and the 'grand narratives' sustaining modernity's notions of human progress, reason and order break up: a commodified aesthetic eclecticism gains sway under the rule of money and techno-economic performance and 'anything goes' (Lyotard 1984: 76). Waste, luxurious expenditure, all sorts of excesses, replace imperatives of rational, moral production in consumer economies, increasingly targeting and generating unanchored desires (Goux 1990: 214–15). Hierarchies are levelled, cutting Culture and its canon down to size and scattering the pieces every which way. Subversions, re-evaluations, reversals ensue. Histories become plural, perspectives multiply and genres hybridise. Elsewheres collapse on the here and now. Represseds seem to return at any opportunity, gothic fictions and figures, too.

With its forms and features increasingly visible in literature, cinema, television, art, with a steadily growing body of criticism to press its cause, gothic undergoes both a pervasion and diffusion. In addressing the undersides or uncertain elsewheres of modernity – in terms of sexualities, death, power and consumption – its engagement with darker issues and implications seemed, appropriately enough for the later twentieth century, to speak to those constituencies marginalised, excluded and oppressed by dominant culture and also entertain those disturbing energies and elements repressed by normal bourgeois society. Perhaps a certain frisson, the thrill of sex or death, a tiny touch of transgression, lent it greater allure, a fascination with cultural limits, with all that was forbidden, taboo, other. A hint of resistance – perhaps the possibility of liberation – could be found in extravagant representations of monstrosity and the interrogation of social and ideological limits. But with its darkness dragged into the light, how does the genre stand up to scrutiny? How would its repetitive generic formulas and stock figures adapt? What could be said about its new position in a cultural and critical context in which desire, sexuality, power and otherness were very much on the agenda, a context, too, in which excessive expenditure was turning into the rule of economic and cultural activity? How does one read gothic romances from the late twentieth century? The question becomes pertinent as a gothic canon emerges to render the genre more acceptable and produces a critical establishment more homogeneous in its re-evaluations. The strategy of reversal comes to the fore, the start of a transvaluation of positive and negative terms that identifies monstrosity differently and perceives, often against the grain of texts, not an individuated monstrous other but discourses, practices and systems that make monsters through exclusion and suppression. Starting with the exception that is *Frankenstein*, the position of the monster is rendered more sympathetic: the monster speaks, thereby displaying his suffering subjectivity and disclosing the practices that constitute him as monster in the first place, his exclusion from the realms of name, family or society position him as romantic outsider. The monster offers a challenge to norms, prejudices and values shaping humanity. Monstrosity – as political radicals, like Wollstonecraft and Godwin argued – was a mark of callous or corrupt political and social structures: the monsters made by those systems reflect back on wider, more monstrous formations. A pattern is set: from offering challenges to the assumptions of bourgeois marriage, social norms, patriarchy, aristocratic power, questioning suggests resistance and can readily be seen as subversion.

Unnatural constructions of otherness and abnormality, monsters participate in a wider denaturalisation of ideological constructions of identity, gender, race and class divisions and distributions of power. To the extent, perhaps, that their monstrosity is all too easily generalised and rendered visible as signs of modern humanity: instinctual, repressed, monsters disclose the other side of the psyche; oppressed and excluded, they reveal the monstrosity of the systems of power and normalisation to which all are subjected. Hence, we must learn to love our monster, our own elsewhere, love our (inner) vampire, as our self. A flattening occurs in which 'normal monstrosities' replace 'monstrous monstrosities' (Derrida 1992: 80). Difference, eagerly sought out, is quickly assimilated. In another direction, however, a legacy of a lower, dark, devalued and threatening cultural position still touched by associations of death, sexuality and otherness, a trace of marginality is retained to give gothic re-evaluations their critical-political credibility. Further, in a world without sacred forms or rituals, without metanarratives, the traces of old monsters, romanced for their telling position at cultural limits, begin to tell a grander story: some kind of truth may hide in the darkness of modernity's elsewhere or its unconscious, the secret truth of our selves, a truth more real, because darker and less evident. A dark mirror, monstrosity turns into a screen for transcendent fantasies and the site for a potential reversal of myth and the sacred, infusing the lower 'night world' of romance with its questing ideal and ascendant trajectory.

The levelling of cultural and critical hierarchies in which contemporary gothic romances participate in order to re-evaluate forms of monstrosity also requires some retention of the genre's negativity. A quiet contradiction, an inevitable ambivalence, like the 'post' of postmodernism, remains: earlier forms and effects are never fully jettisoned. The ambivalence is also evident in the cultural legacy of romance and critical assessments of popular romantic fiction's engagement with sexual identity. As escapist fantasy, brief relief from social pressures, a release of subversive desires or a reaffirmation of patriarchal forms like marriage, romance provokes contradictory readings of its relevance, both a reinforcement of and a challenge to dominant social and sexual roles. At times, romance seems little more than an ideological ruse that encourages the willing self-subordination of female subjects, investing masochism with a higher purpose and insisting 'that there never was any pain or renunciation, that the suffering they experience is really the love and recognition for which they long or at least its prelude' (Massé 3–4). Pain and suffering – the true passion of a romantic plot – hold out the promise of a happy ending, desire thus being strung out and framed by the deferrals of fantasy. In romance, however, men become objects of sexual fantasy (Belsey 26) and this, Tania Modleski suggests, constitutes the 'hysterical' dimension of Harlequin romance plots based on courtship: they eventually disclose, beneath hard and cruel masks, that men also have feelings and are thus worthy of love. In contrast, the gothic plot, engages with the paranoia attendant on fitting into sexual roles, from the superegoic and destructive figure of the mother to the threatening and restrictive institution of marriage.

Popular romance seems both critical and supportive of established institutions. For Janice Radway, for whom love is set against the insistence on wealth in bourgeois society, an ideological challenge to the accumulation of capital remains somewhat muted in that the form returns women to the 'exclusive division of the world into the familiar categories of public and private' thereby maintaining and justifying the 'social placement of women' – and the discontent – that encourages romance reading in the first place. Women, for and because of all the fantastic possibilities of romantic adventure, remain at home reading, at a remove from public worlds of work, sexual freedom or active social participation (216–17). Doubleness haunts romance and its readings. Cora Kaplan's account of enjoying the retrogressive assumptions and stereotypes of romantic fiction in a liberal family context notes how the genre encourages various modes of repression and yet moves beyond them: in engaging with 'women's contradictory and ambig-

uous place within sexual difference' it exceeds the simple – and usually negative – forms of identification that female critics like Wollstonecraft and
Austen associated with the romance (144–46). For Kaplan, fantasy has to be
reassessed beyond its opposition to a simple notion of reality. Nor is it
confined to female identity, but forms 'a crucial part of our constitution as
human subjects' (165).

Romance – in drawing out the question of fantasy – discloses a more
complicated relation to the social, sexual and political structures shaping the
markets and audiences that shape its generic alterations, its ideology at times
complementing and at times contradicting prevailing currents. Its 'ideology',
in the sense of a singular and dominant set of ideas or a state apparatus reinforcing class interests, is the very source of the problem: it does not necessarily institute a simple integration of human subjects within prevailing
social and political structures (privileging love over the production of wealth,
say, or at odds with morality, or in bringing amorous freedom into conflict
with familial duty and obedience), although it does reinforce elements of the
individualism integral to bourgeois subjectivity. Nor does romance necessarily sustain a 'protofeminist denunciation' of patriarchy: Fredric Jameson
reads the film *Something Wild* in terms of the legacy of popular romances – the
'Gothics' – as a 'class fantasy' circulating among a distinctly middle class
female group. Privileged and sheltered, the form allows this group to live out
the 'anxieties of its economic privileges and its sheltered "exceptionalism" in
a pseudo-political version of the gothic – under threats of stereotypical
madmen and "terrorists" (mostly Arabs or Iranians for some reason).' This
'pseudo-political' use of gothic forms stems from liberal guilt at the comfort
enjoyed by one class (Jameson 1991: 288).

The form, it seems, folding back on the class that invented it in the eighteenth century, collapses inward and anxiously on an axis of privilege and
shelter. To stave off this implosive tendency, the gothics revert to romance
in an attempt at a revitalisation acted out in ethical rather than political
terms: 'like the private version of the traditional gothic romance, they
depend for their effects on the revitalization of *ethics* as a set of mental categories, and on the reinflation and artificial reinvigoration of that tired and
antiquated binary opposition between virtue and vice, which the eighteenth
century cleansed of its theological remnants and thoroughly sexualized
before passing it down to us' (Jameson 1991: 289–90). Reinstituting binary
oppositions serves to elevate romantic individualism to the level of an ethos,
a 'revitalisation' or 'reinflation' requiring that ideologically dangerous category of otherness to shore up both a set of boundaries and a sense of liberal
selfhood. The 'modern gothic', Jameson continues, 'depends absolutely in
its central operation on the construction of *evil* (forms of good are notori-
ously more difficult to construct, and generally draw their light from the

darker concept, as though the sun drew its reflected radiance from the moon). Evil is here, however, the emptiest form of sheer Otherness (into which any type of social content can be poured at will)' (1991: 290). The gothic romance works with and against the fragmentation and collapse of social and generic boundaries attendant on postmodernist aesthetics: on one level, it restores grand binary oppositions that redefine limits and reinvent distinctions between self and other in absolute categories of good and evil. But this process partakes of (postmodern) artifice and reversal, on a 'construction' of evil that serves as an empty screen on which to project any kind of otherness whatsoever and on the supposition that the easy construction of evil will enable a reflection of good. What is left – as Jameson tersely suggests of contemporary villainy (Ray from *Something Wild*; Frank Booth from *Blue Velvet*) – are figures 'that don't scare anybody any longer', figures announcing themselves as 'the representation of someone *playing at being evil*' (1991: 290). Otherness and evil, fabricated in and as empty form, no longer, in Jameson's questioning of its generic and political limitations, enable gothic romances to escape the postmodern condition of being no more than pastiche or simulation. It is, in this context of collapsing boundaries and waning affects, no surprise that another recent and distinctly artificial construction of otherness, the eponymous protagonist of *The Vampire Lestat*, invokes the grand opposition of good and evil in order to reinvigorate the diabolical meaning of the undead.

The attempt at a definitive and categorical restoration of oppositions and boundaries, discloses both romance's conservative tendency in respect of otherness and its failure to function fully in ideological terms. Jameson's argument, in stressing the political questions at stake in the genre, draws on his earlier engagement with Frye's survey of romance. In that essay, romance offers a transitional and imaginary solution to ideological contra- dictions (Jameson 1975: 158–61). The reading – which builds on Frye's assertion of the genre's polarizing tendencies – notes the adaptability and persistence of romance as both a 'mode' and as myth, to imply that the latter approximates an ideological function. In Frye, romance exceeds ordinary generic status as the 'structural core of all fiction' and draws its strength from the myths or interconnected narratives that generate 'shared allusion' and 'take root in specific cultures' and 'tell that culture what it is and how it came to be' (1976: 15; 9). Providing myths of origin, and delineating the bound- aries of cultural identity, romance, as a 'quest', also directs aspirations to higher or sacred ideals and, avoiding the ambiguities of ordinary life, simpli- fies moral facts (Frye 1976: 51). Romance thus frames reality with fantasy and establishes the boundaries that make sense of self, culture and world. Or, in Heideggerian terms, romance serves as 'that form in which the *world- ness* of the *world* reveals itself' (Jameson 1975: 142). Hence, the importance of myth in romance, both in the mythopoeic sense proposed by Frye and in the terms outlined by Roland Barthes. For the latter, myth operates as a meta-language that provides form and signification that resolves or occludes contradictions, naturalising a bourgeois world as eternal and establishing a 'perpetual alibi' that obviates any need to consider political contexts, material realities or historical change (Barthes 109; 129; 123). Its form 'is empty but present, its meaning absent but full': like the romance, it provides a screen to frame meaning and the world, 'buttonholing' individuals as unified and singular selves rather than subjects of language, politics or culture (124). Myth, moreover, 'is a language that does not want to die' and perpetuates itself and its subjects as 'speaking corpses' (133). Like romance, it never dies: an individual self remains naturally, eternally, at its centre, and fulfilment, naturally enough, remains its aim. Through a myth of romantic union, one's imagined self, its fullness fantasised in relation to its lost, always-to-be-recovered other half, is sustained as life's (rather than ideology's) ultimate and quasi-sacred quest.

Romance is a narrative mode that seems to survive the collapse of modernity's metanarratives, persisting, even in its most clichéd forms, in the face of general incredulity through the ironic self-consciousness identified by Eco: 'as Barbara Cartland would say . . .'. Like the cinema spectator fetishistically disavowing the unreality of the image ('I know it's not real, but all the same . . .'), the viewer or reader is 'no longer able to believe in romance . . . yet still wishes to do so', remaining enveloped 'in the dream of fulfilment', and so perpetuating the 'saturation of contemporary culture with the myth of romance' (Lapsley and Westlake 180). This saturation is increasingly concentrated on an ideal of self. Even for Frye, romance's mythical and sacred trajectories come down to the self and its fulfilment rendered in sexual terms, the quest becoming 'the search of the libido or desiring self for a fulfilment that will deliver it from the anxieties of reality but will still contain that reality' (Frye 1957: 193). The myth of romantic union continues, even in the 'fallen' world of the twentieth century where romantic love has become a cliché (Pearce 135). In the post-war period, romance finds itself linked to 'the production of a sexual self' (Pearce 154–55); from the 1960s, a 'renewed enthusiasm for love as a transformative and enlightening experience' links romance to the political utopias and sexual freedoms that are themselves located in a cultural context invested in expanding individual mobility, horizons and consciousness; in the 1980s, it contracts on a plane determined by economic and consumerist individualism (Pearce 161; 168). Romance's survival seems to stem from its malleability as a mode mythologising the individual self over and above anything else: its empty form, its 'elsewhere', ultimately assuming the shape of a mirror in which self can be discovered, assured, fulfilled, unified, projected. Its empty form, moreover, as it arises in the vacuum left by postmodernity's collapsing structures of meaning and representation, is precisely the gap that a romanticised self imagines it can fill. Yet never completely; never, despite the fantasy, is this self fully realised: the myth of romance, no matter how much it saturates culture and frames expectations, remains just beyond actualisation since, like desire, to completely realise it would be to kill it.

## Dark Things

Something is missing from the contemporary myth of romantic union that idealises and supposedly completes the sexual self. Something else lurks in romance and accounts for its persistence and intensity: darkness, suffering, passion. Romance is not, despite repeated and insistent representations to the contrary, the 'satisfaction of love' or the 'fruitful contentment of the settled couple', but stems from passion and arises 'where love is fatal, frowned upon and doomed by life itself'. Denis de Rougemont's cultural history of romance, charting its decline and deviations from its beginnings in the twelfth century, is aware of contemporary manifestations – of how, in novels, films, advertising, it 'pervades our culture' in the form of an 'idealized eroticism' exacerbated by a desire to escape 'mechanical boredom' (de Rougemont 15; 16). As it falls into a world emptied of sacred myth and becomes profane passion, modern romance is still invoked as an elevating and vital experience, 'something that will alter my life and enrich it with the unexpected, with thrilling chances, and with enjoyments ever more violent and gratifying' (282; 291). This profane idealisation forgets, de Rougemont argues, the misfortune and unhappiness on which romantic passion is grounded and the disturbing and often paradoxical tradition of romance and desire forged by the practitioners of 'courtly love': satisfaction and gratification are sidelined in favour of love itself and love as anguished suffering. Discussing the story of Tristan and Iseult, de Rougemont notes how their love depends on obstructions, laceration and absence for its existence, how it harbours a wish for death as its ultimate completion: this 'purifying ordeal', this sacrificial expenditure of all desires, serves as the basis of a passion that can only fulfil itself and become a 'transfiguring force' by achieving 'absolute unity' in a movement of total negation (41–66). In the twelfth century, the poetic genre has a social function: 'to order and purify the lawless forces of passion' (238). Romance, for all its sacred excesses and intensities, operates as a form of catharsis, drawing out, directing and sublimating unruly passions. Passions remain, the legacy of a 'dark nature' that, death-driven, springs from 'an energy excited by the mind, and a pre-established potentiality in search of the coercion that shall intensify it' (23). Passion, paradoxically, arises in conditions of restraint rather than freedom, demands limits in order that the allure of transcendence is magnified, aiming at the death which kills it.

Celebrated, profaned and in decline almost from its start, romance undergoes numerous cultural reorderings: its mystical, sacred element degenerates into psychology and happy endings are introduced in its novelistic successors. It is not all happy, however: the Romantics cling on to the figure of death – as a 'release' – but passion's intensity is diminished as a 'vague yearning after affluent surroundings and exotic adventures'. The 'real tragic element', after Wagner, diffuses 'in mediocrity' (232). It diffuses further as romantic film: in the 1920s (de Rougemont cites Hollywood in particular) popular cinema attempts an impossible reconciliation – conjoining romance with the happy ending of marriage and thereby turning 'tragic idealism' into 'vulgar nostalgia'. Worse still, romance no longer means the renunciation of happiness, material goods or even life itself, but is rewarded with all sorts of 'worldly enjoyments' (235). For de Rougemont, a decisive contradiction remains: where bourgeois conventions demand the happiness of closure and stability, in romance nothing is allowed to settle. The consequences of this contradiction are extensive, exposing two systems of morality which remain in destructive tension: one upholds the values of the species and the society, sustaining bourgeois norms with the emphasis on marriage and proper – familial and ideological – reproductive practices; the other, literary and artistic, remains bound to passionate ideals imbibed from fiction and film. 'Essentially irreconcilable', passion and marriage pull in opposing directions (277–78): the latter, in popular culture, is caught up with the demand for 'perpetual distraction', for excitements, thrills, gratifications to stave off boredom; it must 'devise fresh obstructions' in order that desiring can continue. In contrast, the settled couple possesses and loses the intensity of love, becoming banal in routine repetitions and daily proximity. Any attempt at unifying passion and marriage – as bourgeois romantic conventions demand – contributes to the breakdown of the latter. The two systems remain in perpetual conflict. One cannot retain the passionate intensity of romance without its darker side, nor can one tame it, order it or homogenise it: it constantly demands something in excess of habit, convention and norm, some – dark – Thing that works as limit and injunction to move on.

While de Rougemont's account of romance foregrounds, somewhat nostalgically itself, the decline of romance's sacred, passionate form, the ramifications of that decline are highly significant in generic and ideological terms, identifying telling contradictions and tensions that set patterns for contemporary consumptions of the myth of romantic union. The conflicting systems de Rougemont identifies, one homogenising and conventional, the other heterogeneously passionate, explain why romance never quite adds up to an ideology in the usual sense of the term: although its self-centredness privileges a certain type of individualism, attempting to provide an outlet for or sublimation of excesses of passion inimical, yet intrinsic, to prevailing mores and interests, its energy is not contained or completed by social structures and conventions. Restless, turning on some Thing excessive, dark and other to civilisation, romantic desire, to sustain itself, aims to go beyond the goods and evils of bourgeois morality, beyond the limits that extinguish desire. If it serves ideology, romance serves it duplicitously, both channelling and activating desire in excess of the conventions that would extinguish it.

A similar pattern operates in terms of generic conventions: once formulas become too repetitive and familiar, they are perceived as mechanical and boring. Without difference and variation, generic codes become obvious and predictable. Excitement, interest and affect wanes. Desire moves on, in search of innovation, stimulation and reinvigoration. Romance, idealised, replayed and rendered conventional, turns into a reiteration of banal sentiments and tired clichés; the consumer of words or images turns away, bored. From its formulaic inception, gothic fiction similarly surfs the edge of failure, a 'terrorist novel writing' predictably repeating a list of stock, staged and improbable devices, settings and events (Anon 1796). Gothic, its artifice of terrors, shocks and all-too familiar figures of otherness, wears out its own conventions to become a 'boring' and 'exhausted' genre no longer capable of scaring anybody (Jameson 1991: 280). Gothicking the romance and romancing the gothic manifest attempts to revitalise tired genres. Gothic, in adding, or returning, those elements of darkness and misfortune to the romance, injects something else, something different, into an evacuated form, renewing intensity and revitalising desire with objects and plots that seem more dangerous, real and credible; romance, furnishing grand oppositions and limits to be transcended, allows gothic to glimpse, as it wallows in its own superficially gloomy depths and sham figures, something more meaningful, elevating its night world to a reflection of higher human quests, hinting at something of the sacred. Even abjection is 'edged with the sublime' (Kristeva 1982: 11). A double supplementarity comes into view: romance adds to and surpasses a bourgeois moral system; gothic supplements romance. The additional adding to – and displacing – of one supplement by another introduces an unstable, possibly limitless process of desiring and substitution.

As a result, the second supplement, gothic, needs a bit of the other, that is, romance. In a recent interview, the most notorious camp goth shocker in US music, Marilyn Manson, discussed his divorce, depression, new love and vampire identifications. Distinct seams of romance, both sentimental and darkly passionate, inflect his comments. As 'something that can be killed by stabbing it through the heart', the vampire is subjected to a rather sentimental form of romanticisation: love hurts, love bleeds. Its darker aspects do not disappear, however: 'the idea of consuming someone, whether it's literal or metaphorical, is quite romantic', Manson, goes on, straying into the realms of passionate intensity. Such intensity, it is suggested in an appropriately romantic vein, is lost in the settled couple, his previous relationship crushed by the 'conventions of marriage'. Sentiment and passion, cliché and sacrificial excess, conjoin in his final 'definition of romance': 'somebody has to be willing to hold hands and jump off the cliff with you' (cit. Vernon 14–18). The sweetness of the banal romantic image of holding hands almost undermines the intensity of the ultimate romantic sacrifice. Nonetheless it leaves the English interviewer contrasting his public image in the US with an acknowledgement of a certain 'sweetness' to his character and a recognition of the 'amused affection', in the UK, that goths generally evoke.

Romance requires darkness. In a lecture contemplating the 'Secret Life of the Love Song', Nick Cave, goth rocker turned paragon of liberal, *Guardian*-reading (dark) romanticism, criticises the haste of 'compulsive modernity' and the 'hysterical technocracy' of modern music because it coldly and blandly effaces the romantic core of the genre. For Cave, the love song is 'never simply happy' but 'must first embrace the potential for pain'. Unlike those untrustworthy songs that litter programming and exclude the ache of love, the true love song does not 'deny us our human-ness and God-given right to be sad'. Cave continues:

> The writer who refuses to explore the darker regions of the heart will never be able to write convincingly about the wonder, the magic and the joy of love, for just as goodness cannot be trusted unless it has breathed the same air as evil [. . .] so within the fabric of the love song, within its melody, its lyric, one must sense an acknowledgement of its capacity for suffering.
>
> (Cave 7–8)

Sadness, darkness, suffering give the love song greater conviction and credibility, and confer greater authority on the artist's divinely creative imagination. In its 'darker regions', the heart discloses, through pain and suffering, an almost sacred sense of humanity, a passion able to elevate the love song from abjection to the sublime heights of wonder and joy. An almost theological dimension emerges in which, through the pieties and penitence of romantic passion, through the encounter with evil, good emerges more strongly.

The excesses of romance are plotted more darkly still in Cave's previous incarnation as singer and songwriter with *The Birthday Party*. 'Deep in the Woods', written in the vein of a blues song of lover-murder (another song about killing my baby down by the river), turns the fairytale dangers of forests into the setting for a macabre remembrance and re-enactment: sung from the position of the mourning lover (also the killer), the wood itself becomes murderous antagonist, eating the woman's body and dumping it in the mud. There is revulsion at the image of worms carving into her skin, belly and shoulder (a hint of Graveyard poetry's *memento mori*) and a disgusted recollection of the previous night's embrace. More than a murderous confession or salacious enjoyment of violence, the song enacts the extreme of romantic passion, loss and absence: in death she has achieved the position of 'the one and only', the decomposition of her material being prelude to amorous sacralisation. So special is she that, as if to complete romantic union, the lover-killer prepares, with the trees as agreeable witnesses, to turn the knife on himself. Having sacrificed her for love, he, too, must die. At this point the tone and tempo changes dramatically: the slow, grinding sparseness of guitar, bass and drum and the aching dark growl-moan of the vocal give way to a vibrant romantic outburst declaring – apparently contemptuously – that 'love is for fools'. Pathological violence, it seems, exposes the murderous frailties underlying the fantasy of human sexual relationships. Ecstatically. Love renders the lover special, no matter how solitary or wretched, the uniqueness of his suffering underlined by his being called to be utterly apart from everyone else (the metaphor of rain falling on his house but no others is employed in the song). But there is a joyously determined pulse and dark humour to the rhythm and rhyme, reinforcing the subsequent acknowledgement that, although love is for fools, 'God knows, I'm still one'. Yet, love's condition is not sacred: the gutters are awash with love's ugly and lonely children – all victims and detritus of serial love/killling (Cave 58–59). A song of self-recognition, of loss, loneliness and abjection; a song of violence, mutilation, excess, passion – but with love.

Deep in the shops, a desire is consuming. . . . Romance, in the inevitable cliché, manifests itself as a consuming passion. Just as the genre, in its exhaustions and formulaic renewals, excites, gratifies and sates interest, bringing desire to the fore, so consumer culture comes to depend, not on a fixed and limited notion of human need, but on the uncertainty of desire itself (Goux 1990: 221). And desire's condition is always to want more, an endless exploitable excess, or as Angela Carter phrases it, an 'inexhaustible plus' (206). Following eighteenth century critical characterisations of the genre as ravenous, unconstrained and thoroughly appetitive, Frye's comment on popular romance identifies a 'proletarian element' that just keeps on generating desire: 'never satisfied with its various incarnations', romance reappears again and again 'hungry as ever, looking for new hopes and desires to feed on' (1957: 186). A vampiric image lurks within romance's consuming effects, stimulating and exhausting desire in an endless cycle of dis-satisfactions. In never being able to satisfy or kill off desire, romance reproduces the incompletion required for more. The double bind, or open circuit, is noted by Radway in her account of the ambivalent political effects of popular romances' political effects: it addresses female concerns but never quite answers them, except in fictional form. Returning to the division of public and private, romances ultimately serve 'to justify the social placement of women that has led to the very discontent that is the source of their desire to read romances' (217). Playing on the desire that stems from a discontented social position, romance offers the imaginary satisfactions that promise gratification before dumping readers at the point they started – discontented . . . and desiring. A successful marketing ploy, it has a touch of Oscar Wilde's cigarette, the 'perfect pleasure' of which is to leave the smoker wanting more. In consumer culture, the subject that is constructed in relation to images and commodities remains wanting: subjective lack (the basis of desiring) is not denied, but, repeatedly – and vainly – in a barrage of alluring images, is displayed as a deficiency that 'can be made good' (Lapsley and Westlake 180) – with more consuming. Like the myth of romantic union, the powerful myth of individual plenitude is repeatedly called upon, circulated to saturation point, but actualised only as an image.

In the 1980s, the resurgence of cinematic romances – like *Romancing the Stone* – offered a new twist in the genre, to the extent that its female subjects were no longer punished for being active, independent and in possession of themselves and appeared to be neither dupes of the myth of true love nor fully liberated models of individuality. Wealthy, adventurous, successful in love and at work, the films presented 'images of women who can have it all (like the subjects of Michelob Light beer commercials)', forming 'an ideal female subject of post-industrial consumer society' (White 42). As ideal models – like any other advertising image – these characters are not the same as subjects of consumption, but serve to make an unattainable lifestyle more desirable – because, of course, it is unattainable. The onscreen ideal offers an image of completeness and manifests the gap between it and the viewer, a gap romantic fantasy and identification alone can cross: desire, framed and directed by this identification, channels consumption towards associated images, stories and commodities, as in the marketing of the woman's film of the 1940s. A dynamic of discontent-desire continues. Screens of desire – the advertisement or romance – stimulate possibility and disappoint it, the frame or genre operating a mirror that depends on an alternation between fullness and emptiness: excited, caught up in the romance, the subject experiences the fullness of involvement, affect, satisfaction, then, as formulas become too familiar and obvious, it finds itself let down, exhausted and empty. Emptied, however, screens can be filled again. And so on.

Evacuation and plenitude define the predicament of the 'disordered shopper', a being sustained in an alternation between abject inidentity and fantasised fulfilment, a condition that depends on lack which is 'sought out and produced by any body', irrespective of gender, in a pattern of desire, consumption, evacuation (Lieberman 245). In line with justifications of postmodern capitalism, that expenditure, luxury, waste and excess are its norms, the consumer is not restrained by dictates of reason, morality, need or usefulness (Goux 1990). This is why romance survives in a context incredulous towards metanarratives: the latter regulate and police it, where romance feeds, and feeds on, desire. Without direction or limit, there is no final consumption, in the sense of fatal expenditures, of the total sacrifice of material things, the utter consummation or destructive using up that intensifies, completes and kills passions. Contemporary consumption, as Lieberman notes, is managed on the basis of credit – the 'never-never' deferring final payment and thereby postponing any closing sacrificial gesture. Without this limit, desiring has no anchor and can go on expending itself in search of its, ultimately unsatisfying, objects. As de Rougemont observes of the cultural pervasion of romance, the process of reinvigoration, desire and dissatisfaction, of evacuation and plenitude, escalates and accelerates to conjure up the intensity of passion: the stories, images and commodities promising life-altering experiences and enjoyment must be ever more violent to be gratifying.

There is, it seems, no end to lack-desire-consumption in contemporary culture. Pleasure and consumption, rather than pain or prohibition, 'have become our punishment' (Lotringer 177). Writing a supplement to the history of sexuality, Sylvère Lotringer's study of sex clinics in the US makes the observation that love – 'one of the most formative myths our culture has secreted' – comes, with the collapse of myth, to be replaced by sex as the mode of 'socializing desires' (177). Moving beyond Victorian notions of repression and sexual secrecy, sex becomes an imperative, a right, and an everyday social activity. With the sex trade, high street sex shops, toys, DVDs and Internet: 'everywhere sex is taken casually as legitimate entertainment' (7). Becoming 'fully externalised', an everyday ritual in the absence of other social rituals, sex is just a mode for people 'to talk about themselves', a form for 'the presentation of self in everyday life' (171). There are serious consequences as sex becomes increasingly free from prejudice and superstition, as a mysterious and unknown realm is 'turned into another Disneyland' (8). However, an apparently healthy – in psychological and physical senses – normalisation of sex, a liberated casting away of its Victorian baggage, discloses an obscene side to culture: in 'exposing everything as sexual' it extinguishes the excitement and interest once attached to sex (172).

Lotringer argues that the general pursuit of a Reichian line of argument – a restoration of natural functions, rational management and rights to orgasm, 'simply sent sex spinning all the more helplessly in the empty play of the culture' (9). This 'overexposure' has significant effects on a society in which sexuality, rather than death, has a more predominant role in cultural formation (20). A succession of new perversions and excesses need to be discovered to recall the prohibitions that make sex – and identity – interesting. Unpicking the boundaries between normality and deviance allows a general emptiness to appear: where perversions are an invention of norms and norms are defined only in relation to the perversions that exceed them, without deviance no fantasy of normality can be sustained. And the spinning continues, revealing absence rather than sexual or subjective plenitude, hence the need for 'sacred monsters' (Lotringer 12–19). Few, however, make the grade. So the search goes on. It may have an end, however: the clinical practice of treating perversions by giving the patient more and more of what he wants ironically takes excess to a limit: 'boredom therapy'.

## Double supplement

Love, as everyone knows, is vain: it is both narcissistic and futile. 'For what is love', asks Lacan, 'other than banging one's head against a wall, since there is no sexual relation?' (1982: 170) Lacan's remark does not reject the idea of romantic love, as many have done, as simply a stupid delusion or intoxication, but offers a very different explanation of the underlying structure of the myth of romantic union, one that accounts for its persistence in terms of the language and fantasies shaping subjectivity. It locates love's multifarious drama among wider questions pertaining to the effects of sexual difference and desire in cultural systems: love 'supplements' the (absence of) sexual relationship (1998: 45). Discounting the illusion of love as a self's completion or fulfilment, Lacan contends that it is not a 'sexual other half' who is sought out in love. Instead, love manifests the 'search by the subject, not of sexual complement, but of that part of himself lost forever, that is constituted by the fact he is only a sexed living being, and that he is no longer immortal' (1977b: 205). Subjectivity is produced in the movement from real to sexed being introduced by language and cultural practices: at birth, a child has no sense of itself or its differences from others, no sense that life leads to death, and no speech: it feeds, excretes, sleeps and grows. Socialisation and language – naming, weaning, potty-training, codes of dress and address – introduce the differences and divisions necessary to the consciousness of individual, gendered identity. Biological functions are thus retrained according to cultural regulation, separating the child from what she or he used to be and requiring that the child leave behind something of itself in the process of renouncing immediate satisfactions and accepting cultural codes. A different sense of unity fills the gap: in order to fit into the circuits of social understanding, mores and norms (the signifying conventions and channels of desiring Lacan calls the symbolic register or Other), the child must see him or herself as a whole and separate individual, rather than an un-self-aware assemblage of various bodily needs and functions. This is accomplished in the imaginary register with the help of a mirror: the reflection offers the only way a child can see itself as whole and, on that basis, assume a position as a single individual, a person able to say 'I', that is, to position her or himself in the circuits of language and culture (Lacan 1977a).

A gap remains in this fundamental and necessary misrecognition: the child only sees its embodied shape in inverted form, as an image located in another place. Its unity remains imagined even though, in assuming that sense of identity, it speaks and acts in the world as if it were real. The sense of imaginary unity also has to accede to the differences of culture, to obey and internalise its rules and prohibitions, to bend its wishes into the structures that determine acceptable outlets and objects for desire. To become a subject of culture is both to give up something and to become someone. Given that identity is sustained in relation to other people and enabled by systems of communication and meaning, the sense of unity is both required and threatened by the Other: it is not a property internal to the self, but stems from outside, in a system of signifiers and their possible but uncertain meanings. Love forms part of a demand for love directed to the Other, a demand that the imaginary sense of wholeness be recognised and the gap between self, image and language be filled. In this respect, love remains in the field of narcissism: 'to love is essentially, to wish to be loved', a wish that difference, separation and death be overcome, disclosing 'it is one's self that one loves in love'. But the mirror only offers an image at a remove from the subject and thus functions as limit marking the 'inaccessibility of the object' (1992: 151). Love is thus 'impossible', the gap, although occluded in the imaginary, remains: one is never oneself, but defined by others and the Other. Likewise with desire: it is not internal to the individual but is articulated in systems of signification. 'Love demands love', demanding it '*encore*' (1998: 4). The gap introduced by this incessant demand (more is never enough) opens a path for desire, and is only arrested – imaginarily and temporarily – if the subject discovers some Thing that can fill it, that can take the place of the missing part of the subject.

Another name for the gaps that define a subject in relation to itself, other and culture, is 'lack', the counterpoint to desire that defines subjectivity as a 'lack in being' or a 'want-to-be'. Lacan, linking desire and language, develops Freud's use of the Oedipus myth and its account of the child's encounter with lack as a disturbing confrontation with sexual difference (which parent has or has not a penis), to focus on the symbolic institution of gender roles. The former seems to be consolidated by the latter: socially, the father is construed as a more powerful figure and becomes a metaphor of the authority, language, rules, laws and roles to which the child – already bearing the father's name – has to accede in becoming an individual subject. The mother – and the love and satisfactions she provides – must be renounced since incest is taboo and she already 'belongs' to daddy. Through the ruses by which early wishes persist into adulthood, the renunciation is never complete. A symbolic circuit is introduced which directs desire through appropriate channels of punishment (castration) and fantasised reward: to regain mummy's love which daddy already has, the male child must become like daddy to win the love of another who happens to be like mummy. Desire operates in terms of displacement, looking for substitutes of that original lost object of love. The split is noted by Freud in his essay 'On the Universal Tendency to Debasement in Love' where he traces a peculiar resistance in the sexual instinct to achieving sexual satisfaction. He offers an explanation based on the prohibition against incest: the true object remains lost, displaced by surrogates in an 'endless series of substitutive objects' that never deliver full satisfaction. Instinct's loss of complete satisfaction, 'as soon as it submits to the first demands of civilization', is culture's gain: sexual sublimation produces the 'noblest cultural achievements' (Freud 1977: 258–59). Loss is thus productive of desire and culture, and all subjects, all incomplete, lacking, relational beings, take their bearings from it.

According to psychoanalysis, there is very little, if any, of the other person involved in amorous relationships. The 'missing part' of oneself – lost, sought out, missed again – remains elusive in actuality and as a conceptual category: a 'Thing' or '*objet petit a*'. Distinguished from objects in the usual sense of material things, Thing or *a* are lost, partial objects and absent, immaterial, excessive qualities that have real and structuring effects as remnants or leftovers of the libidinal intensities sublimated by cultural processes. Idealised, the loved other can assume the place of the missing part and fill the gap in the subject, imaginarily satisfying and halting the displacements of desire. But that gap remains, the loved one never quite completing the imaginary circuit or matching up to the lost object: '*I love you, but, because inexplicably I love in you something more than you – the* objet petit a *– I mutilate you*' (Lacan 1977b: 268). The other side to love, the point at which narcissism's fragile ego breaks down, is fraught with violent, dissatisfied intensities. The object *a*, which articulates symbolic and imaginary registers, filling the gaps between subject and Other, never fully screens off the lack or the fundamental, unsymbolisable absence – the real – that underlies them. In this respect, as screen, filter or protection, *a* forms the basis for all sorts of phantasmatic projections and defences: 'the real supports the fantasy, the fantasy protects the real' (Lacan 1977b: 41). In the blank space of *a*, fantasy projects objects that hold the passions and overwhelming excesses of intense energy (*'jouissance'*) at bay, providing formats in which they can be managed and thus protecting subjects and culture with a frame that allows them to continue desiring. Fantasy, like the sublime and sublimation, provides access at a distance, in a more tolerable form. In screening off a terrifying absence associated with lack and castration, fantasy serves as a frame in which subjectivity can continue desiring: 'the whole realization of the sexual relationship leads to fantasy' (Lacan 1998: 80). Fantasy circumscribes, for men at least, all sexual activity and hides the absence of a sexual relation: it allows them to project their own lack and the intensities of *jouissance* onto women, thereby preserving the culturally pervasive assumption that they are powerful, complete, in control and disavowing the 'castration' they have already undergone by virtue of submitting to the 'phallic' signifier of paternal culture.

Romance is a form of fantasy in this sense, circumscribing reality with the illusions – the sense of imaginary plenitude – that allow subjects to function normally. Courtly love constitutes a 'highly refined way of making up for the absence of the sexual relationship, by feigning that we are the ones who erect an obstacle thereto' (Lacan 1998: 69). Lacan has clearly paid attention to de Rougemont's lessons in love, where obstruction and prohibition are paramount in the production of passion. Romance, in its earliest form, exemplifies structures of desire and fantasy. The 'dark Lady' of romance is not a real person but is an effect of aesthetic sublimation, an object 'elevated to the dignity of the Thing'. She is not a sexual or narcissistic complement but a 'terrifying, inhuman partner', a bit of a machine, an arbitrary and inaccessible figure associated with the cruel and unforgiving codes she forces her knight to live by. Inaccessible, she is all the more desirable. As lady, and so beholden by ties of marriage to her lord, who is also the knight's master, she embodies the phallic and symbolic codes of chivalric relations, and subjects the lover to a range of tasks and trials that may be rewarded by only the slightest 'mercy', a small token or look that becomes the most important sign of love. As lady, she is also a woman, a screen for the knight's projection, focus of the libidinal intensities that – in relation to prohibition – turns her into Thing. Simultaneously holding out and holding off the possibility of sexual consummation, she fuels the fantasy that union would be satisfying, complete, total. Her position is both object and Other in the fantasy frame: as Thing, she fills in the missing part, screening off the horrifying absence and intensities of unruly *jouissance*; as signifier of law and prohibition she dispenses the punishments and rewards that are taken, with delight, as cause for her subject's continued – imaginary – enamoration and, further, constitute a symbolic regulation and sublimation of, otherwise disruptive, desire (Lacan 1998: 150–63; Žižek 1994: 90–98).

Romance undergoes many alterations over eight centuries, while continuing to provide a form for fantasy and desire. As culture and its forms change, so the circulation of romance and its receptions alters. Commenting that passionate love has become an 'increasingly ridiculous thing', Lacan goes on to note a major alteration in its mediation: 'we undoubtedly play upon this alienated and alienating process, but in an increasingly external manner upheld by an increasingly diffuse image. The thing, if it no longer takes place with a beautiful woman or with a lady, is accomplished in a darkened cinema with an image on the screen' (1993: 252). While suggesting that popular media, in reiterating images of love, have turned its sublimity into something ridiculous, Lacan's statement also implies that the psychological dimensions of passion have been drawn out and diffused in images, and that these screen images have replaced the Lady to the extent that they take over her function as Thing, flattening, even short-circuiting, symbolic structures of prohibition and deferral so important in sustaining passion and desire.

Significantly, Lacan makes this comment on romance and the screen in his seminar on the psychoses. Psychosis, in psychoanalytical terms, is caused by a disavowal or rejection of the paternal metaphor articulating symbolic structures. Without paternal prohibition to arrest the play of desire and confer meaning, the subject, allowing any figure to serve as its apex of identification, is cast adrift in a 'swarm of images' (Lacan: 1977c). Psychosis, a postmodern condition linked to schizophrenia, takes the form of a breakdown in the signifying chain that looses a plethora of disjointed and disorientating flows (Jameson 1991). The romance enjoyed in the cinema seems to follow this pattern, throwing up a succession of images that captivate and carry away the viewer in an imaginary plenitude sustained by a dual, rather than ternary, relation. Fantasy screen and media screen collide, eclipsing or flattening the triangular distance inscribed by a symbolic perspective, and pressing more disturbingly on the viewing subject: while it may heighten sensational enjoyment, the fascination with, flattening and proximity of the image – both real and unreal at the same time – also troubles differentiations between reality, image and fabrication. It follows the patterns of simulation which inaugurate a different kind of seeing, one beyond believing, appearance, representation or reality-testing. Where the overexposure of sex announces the absence of a sexual relation to a culture deafened by the noise, the screening of romance points the absence of any representational relation.

Modern symbolic distinctions, the triangulation based on Oedipus, find themselves superseded by simulation's narcissistic and digital dimensions in which a dual relationship comes to the fore: the captivation of Narcissus and the image he, fatally, loves as himself occludes any other aesthetic or critical horizon (Baudrillard 1990b: 173). Narcissus returns to a simpler identification with the screen and a greatly reduced version of the romantic subject. He presents a figure for the mimetic play that precedes subjectivity with alternations of ego and object. In its rapid oscillations, 'in the dizziness of rebounds', narcissism appears 'as a screen over *emptiness*' (Kristeva 1987: 23). The media screen has more extensive effects on a pre-subjective condition that is full and empty, posited and lost: Narcissus names a situation of 'drowning in a cascade of false images (from social roles to the *media*), hence deprived of semblance or place' (373). Divested of precise body or image – diffused in images – Narcissus is cast into exile, 'an alien in a world of desire and power, he longs to reinvent love'. It is a longing we all share, Kristeva implies, since 'we are all ETs' (1987: 382–83). The use of a benign and diminutive alien as her example draws out the proximity – even in-difference – between self and other reduced to the point of being barely distinguishable partners. The love Kristeva wishes to reinvent, however, is associated with care not passion, but it is still very much a love collapsed upon on its own cinematic image.

Narcissism never quite closes on itself, not even in death since death has been foreclosed by the undeath of the image. Passion – 'born of a fatal desire for mystical union' – was once regarded 'as open to being surpassed and fulfilled thanks to the *meeting* with some *other*', an encounter that admits 'this other's alien life and ever distinct person' and introduces the chance of 'unending alliance' and 'real dialogue' (de Rougemont 322). But the only openness that now remains lies in the screen's emptiness, and its readiness for projection. Where love is tied to the image, dialogue and otherness are foreclosed along with the monstrosity that announces the possibility of a future. The supermediated version of narcissism Kristeva proposes sees self close ever more tightly on its image to the extent that it becomes itself only as the image of an alien: it does so in the disclosure of the screened emptiness it assumes as its own, the space where it can continually become another image of a creature that once occupied the realms of fantasy: a monster, perhaps, or a ghoul, or a zombie. Or a vampire.

Replacing ET with a vampire – as in Coppola's attempt at reinventing love by locating romance in the canines of horror – makes little difference, it seems, even though the love it aims to renew is rife with sublime and darker passions. Without monsters, however, it can only fall back on the image, the simulation, of romance. The end of *Dracula* closes the romantic fantasy frame by inverting its opening: Mina drags her lover's body to the chapel's altar to kneel over it, and she is the one who wields the knife and draws blood. After decapitation, the close-up of his face is lit warmly to emphasise that humanity has been returned to him. His eyes stare upwards, even in death, if blankly. Mina's look follows his dead stare, and the camera follows hers to rest on the two-dimensional pictorial surface of a painting of the lovers on the ceiling of the chapel. The camera dwells on this image, a moving medium captivated by a still picture. It is the final shot of the film. With Dracula dead, love can survive, sacred once again. But romance is not re-sanctified, only the image of romance, its passion forever frozen. The image, still within film's movement, is framed as the object of Mina's gaze: she and the spectator are one, lovers both, staring at romance's screen. The nostalgia that exudes is not nostalgia for romance in general, but for the form that takes place in a darkened room with an image on the screen, a cinematic Thing already, in 1992, on the point of disappearance.

# 1 Romance, ruins and the Thing

## From the romantic sublime to cybergothic

### Virtual imagination

*Neuromancer* reformats the matrix of romance and romanticism. The novel relates a quest romance – the penetration of a gothic stronghold and the destruction of a cloned and cryogenically frozen corporate dynasty – and a romantic search for union between two immensely powerful artificial intelligences. Its near future is dominated by technologies of communication and control, by corporate power, and the consumption of biotechnical enhancements and prostheses. Information is transmitted and received in an unmediated neural space, while memories are revived as ghostly holographic images, simulations undistinguishable from their lost origins. Humans have the capacity of 'dreaming real' (Gibson 1984: 168), and death is surpassed biologically and digitally: personality can be stored in data banks, overcoming the boundaries of life and death. Cyberspace offers other great romantic syntheses. Humans are no longer restricted by time and space, 'jacking in' to the matrix (plugging one's brain directly into the datascape) allows mind to transcend matter virtually as a 'bodiless exultation' (Gibson 1984: 12). Subjects in cyberspace experience consciousness anew, the empire of the eye enabling total vision: 'divided like beads of mercury . . . his vision was spherical, as though a single retina lined the inner surface of a globe that contained all things, if all things could be counted' (Gibson 1984: 304). The cyberspatial matrix, it seems, presents the specular subject with complete imaginative plenitude.

The matrix is sublime: in its play of light and dark, imaginative possibility and shadowy powers, the infinity of data takes the form of a cityscape with its awesome towers of ICE ('intrusion countermeasures electronics') and immense spires of gleaming data. This awesome realm overcomes Romantic antitheses of mind and body, self and Nature, in a virtual dimension which allows the processing subject – the 'console cowboy' – to wander as freely as any poet. The sublime space of the matrix also takes the subject beyond consciousness in another sense: to encounter the brain death of the flatline, and to the point where distinct identity vanishes in the totality of abstracted information: 'beyond ego, beyond personality, beyond awareness he moved . . . grace of the mind-body interface granted, in that second by the clarity and singleness of his wish to die' (Gibson 1984: 309). The synthesis of mind and body, self and other, obliterates all separation in a singular – and fatal – fusion. The locus of this fusion, the Other, is the matrix itself:

> Cyberspace. A consensual hallucination experienced daily by billions of legitimate operators, in every nation, [. . .] a graphic representation of data abstracted from the banks of every computer in the human system. Unthinkable complexity. Lines of light ranged in the nonspace of the mind, clusters and constellations of data. Like city lights, receding [. . .]
>
> (Gibson 1984: 67)

This graphic abstraction realised neurally in the brain also calls up the dreamspace of the Romantic imagination, mind and totality united like a digital aeolian harp. But, like dreams, they fade, too absolute for human subjects to sustain.

In the novel, the actual subjects – the thinking, speaking, shadowy agents of the plot – are not human at all, but two Artificial Intelligences, 'Wintermute' and 'Neuromancer', engaged in a struggle to conjoin as a new entity. Wintermute is 'live mind', machinic, chill rationality fused with the desire for new synthesis, a process Neuromancer resists (Gibson 1984: 315). The latter is characterised in terms of personality, creation, immortality, a necromancer of the nerves calling up dead and perfectly simulated beings. In this neural romance of artificial personality, the living-dead bits of infor-mation stored in the matrix's data banks are able to combine to form a new being, a higher consciousness transcending that of humans. A spectacle of ultimate fusion, a perfect Hegelian synthesis, is set out as an absolute tran-scendence resulting from the union of Wintermute and Neuromancer. In a discussion at the end of the novel between Case, the human protagonist, and the new entity, the totality of the transcendence is made plain: 'I'm the matrix', it says, 'Nowhere. Everywhere. I'm the sum total of the works, the whole show' (Gibson 1984: 316). This form of divinity is not naturalised as a human image of absolute being. At the end of the story – as the new entity reaches towards the cosmos – humans remain earth-bound: transcendence or synthesis is not theirs; the romance of the machine heads elsewhere, incomprehensible, sublime, absolutely Other.

*Neuromancer's* ending, for all the technological thrills it has to offer, delivers a distinctly inhuman conclusion: its enthusiastic imagination of the digital delights of the near future shadowed by negatively sublime and distopic figures of eviscerated urban spaces, ruined and wretched bodies, shattered identities. The euphoria and exultation of neurotechnological transcendence is mirrored by destruction, ruination and anxious vigilance. In the novel, humanity sees itself on the edge of extinction, continually threatened by the machines that threaten and exceed its powers. There is even a specialist police force (the 'Turing cops') that attempts to control the growth and power of artificial intelligence. They arrest Case for what is no less than species treason: 'you have no care for your species. For thousands of years men dreamed of pacts with demons. Only now are such things possible' (Gibson 1984: 173). Recognising the inhuman implications of artificial life in anxiously archaic terms, they present the future as a gothic romance in which realisable monsters of the imagination fly beyond human power. In this flight of a machinic romance, utopia and distopia collide, leaving humans behind. Another repetition of romanticism, it sees the human subject teetering, sublimely, on the brink of another romantic dissolution.

## Crisis, romanticism, repetition

The ongoing technoscientific revolution, for its advocates and detractors alike, continues to promise economic, social and political upheavals as great as those produced by the liberal revolutions that transformed Europe and America in the latter part of the eighteenth century. Amid the revolutionary rhetoric accompanying the bicentennial and millennial fervour of the end of the last century, visions of the future diverged along a spectrum whose poles were painted in impossibly utopian and grimly distopian colours. Both poles, nevertheless, coincided in the pervasive sense of crisis and reinforced the ambivalently joyful and horrified apprehension of unimaginable, and hence repeatedly imagined, changes. The host of shadowy things lurking within and at the outer limits of future visions came to resonate with an apocalyptic tone; their imminence occasioned an unspeakable urgency attendant on the motions of a crisis that seemed to reach sublime proportions. Here, the reiteration of romantic discourse disclosed something unpresentable at the core of modernity's self-narration. Indeed, around figures of crisis, the strange subject of modernity again began to unfold, prompting questions of representation, history, agency – and romance.

Since Jean-François Lyotard first delineated the postmodern as 'incredulity towards metanarratives', locating it in respect of an unspeakable irruption prior to and in excess of modernity's self-presentation, the question of history's future anteriority rather than its determined progress has led to a reconfiguration of the relationship between romanticism and the present (1984: xxiv). Describing postmodernism as a 'late-flowering Romanticism', Patricia Waugh discusses the 'break down' of distinctions between critical and functional knowledge in the face of an all-invasive capitalism which heralds a 'new Dark Age' of barbarism and irrationalism (1992: 1–7). The subject of romanticism, in at least two senses, remains in a state of crisis. It is, moreover, a crisis repeating a crisis at the heart of romanticism. As an academic subject, 'current scepticism about the distinctiveness and value of literature, the canon, criticism and its theory reworks that original Romantic crisis' (Hamilton 1995: 19). On a broader scale, the crisis involves questions of commercial hegemony and ideological contestation, an echo of the social, political and poetic issues reverberating from romanticism's revolutionary moment. For Edmund Burke, shocked by the 'great crisis, not of the affairs of France, but of all Europe, perhaps, of more than Europe', the romantic reverberations of the French Revolution wonderfully and absurdly disclose a disturbing monster of unimaginable change:

> everything seems out of nature in this strange chaos of levity and ferocity, and of all sorts of crimes jumbled together with all sorts of follies. In viewing this monstrous tragicomic scene, the most opposite passions necessarily succeed and sometimes mix with each other in the mind: alternate contempt and indignation, alternate laughter and tears, alternate scorn and horror.
>
> (Burke 1969: 92–93)

As oppositions collapse and revolve, tearing the social and political fabric of Burke's late eighteenth-century present, an epochal shift ambivalently, monstrously, glowers on the horizon. Such a crisis, moreover, sublime and yet strangely integral to romanticism, seems to determine the modernity of the last two hundred years in a manner that accords with Jean-François Lyotard's diagnosis of 'the postmodern condition': 'postmodernism thus understood is not modernism at its end but in the nascent state, and this state is constant', thereby posing a real question of presentation, the imagination and the subject's nostalgia for presence (Lyotard 1984: 79).

A similarity can be identified between the contemporary 'commercialist hegemony' of global liberalism and its absence of ideological conflict and the post-Waterloo period: they are conjoined in the scenario of 'imperial break-up, ethnic crack-up, and commercialist mop-up' (Christensen 1994: 453–54). The horror associated with this repetition suggests that Frances Fukuyama's account of 'the end of history' may be accurate. The apocalypse has already happened, the 'good news' has spread to all, to redeploy Jacques Derrida's critique of Fukuyama's 'evangelism' (1994: 57). Apocalyptic millennialism, according to Steven Goldsmith, not only underpins the romantic politics of liberal revolutions, but reappears in contemporary concerns about political and aesthetic representation. Not only do literary critics and cultural commentators mobilise romantic questions to address the end of modernity, many of the claims surrounding the digital revolution are propelled by a similar romantic rhetoric, as a cursory glance at the title of cyberculture's most famous fiction suggests. *Neuromancer*, although written on nothing more advanced than a electronic typewriter, romanticises technology in a way that actually informs, rather than simply reflects, the perceptions and practice of cyberculture, most notably in the way it has provided the definition of 'cyberspace' for both those employed in hi-tech industries and those outside the technical elite. In cyberspace, moreover, romanticism is reiterated: the body, called the 'meat', is cast aside as the non-space of the mind is filled by a dazzling array of computer-generated images enabling the discorporated subject to roam freely in the heady realms of virtual reality, intoxicated by the speed and sublimity of the datascape. This induces, for Gibson's human protagonist, a sense of 'bodiless exultation', a feeling of awesome power, of transcendent consciousness: the synthesis of mind and body occurs in the hallucinatory matrix of cyberspace. And synthesis, in the novel, is actualised in a new, but no less Hegelian, form: two opposed artificial intelligences fuse to create a consciousness of god-like proportions. Citing Frankenstein's monster as a precedent to the process of human deification, one critic notes how the 'mystical aura' shrouding Gibson's machines 'creates a cybernetic sublime' (Olsen 1991: 284). For another, cybernetics involves 'the crystallisation of the Cartesian cogito into material objects and commodities' and a 'sublime vision of human power over chance' (Csicsery-Ronay 1991: 186). Fictional in origin but technologically realised with breathless rapidity, the unbound imagination that outruns reality returns to an electronic earth to inform the new sciences. Prometheus provides one role model for the cyberpunk (Leary 1991: 245). The romantic humanism of Terence McKenna, biotechnologist and philosopher, also replays a new Prometheanism of Frankensteinian proportions as he imagines the culmination of a philosophical quest as the outcome of accelerated technical and scientific capabilities: for him, the discovery of being itself is imminent, a discovery that will free life from matter (Rushkoff 1994: 19–20).

Romantic and revolutionary tones recur among manifestos of the 'new edge'. Introducing the *Mondo 2000 User's Guide to the New Edge*, Rudy Rucker calls the adventurous, unnameable and enormous movement associated with narco-biotechnological change the 'Great Work'. This, he goes on,

has something to do with people getting more and more mixed up with machines, . . . it has to do with the end of old-style politics. A wave of revolution is sweeping all of Planet Earth. Incredible: The Soviet Union is no more. How many more years can it be until the revolution comes back here to the United States, back to where it started?

(1992: 13)

Coming home, the revolution returns to the origins of American, and perhaps modernity's, freedoms. But the dissolution of eurocentric imperialist tyranny itself becomes the strange cause of another global, incomprehensible, sublime and apocalyptic expansion. In the future, so the story goes, machines will have the same kind of rights liberalism once exclusively reserved for humans. Noting the shifting democratic ground and the unstable boundaries between natural and artificial entities, Chris Hables Gray proposes 'The Cyborg Bill of Rights' in which liberalism is extended to include the freedoms of electronic speech and electronic privacy and citizenship is ascertained, not by recourse to nature, but through a 'cyborg citizen Turing test' (1995: 254–55). Given that many humans, as well as machines, fail this test, such cyberliberalism falls well short of a standard of universal suffrage.

The romanticism recited in technological utopianism has, like the romantic imagination, an inverted image. Robert Markley identifies how, in accounts of new technology, cyberspace is perceived as 'a habitat of the imagination' infused with a 'rational magic' akin to poetry. Late capitalism and romanticism conjoin in 'holistic, transcendent and sublime' metaphors:

> The transition from a rhetoric of technocorporatism to a romanticism filtered through *Star Trek* is less abrupt than it seems. The rhetoric of cyberspace characteristically invokes the pleasure and power of an imaginative world made whole . . . with an emphasis on fullness, plenitude and mystical unity.

(1996: 3)

But, Markley continues, the conjunction, at the level of commoditised informational exchange, 'equates poetry with an escape from the history that has brought these technologies into being'. The transcendence of material history, the technological production of the escape velocity required for the final flight into a fully imaginative and creatively whole sphere returns to the aesthetic, political and historical conditions of its production: romanticism is doubled and bound. Nor is it the human self that attains a plenitude and wholeness beyond history. The totality that emerges no longer appears human: in *Neuromancer*, the union of two artificial intelligences produces a synthesis in excess of humans, an excess associated with (and beyond, since the artificial intelligence that emerges in the story makes contact with extraterrestrial life) the totality of the network itself. Humans, despite the imaginary and virtual fulfilments of cyberspace, are left in the subordinate realm of matter, mortality and history. What Vivian Sobchack criticises as the 'bumper-sticker libertarianism' of cyberpunk rhetoric, it seems, has little to do with a liberal humanist subject (1993: 580). The slogan, 'Information wants to be free', indeed, situates information, rather than humans, as the desiring subject of technolibertarianism. While 'information fantasies have entered social practice, many tinged with a distinctly apocalyptic fire', the visionary impetus only fuels a move into a fully prostheticised and automated digital space in which subjects are divested of all the corporeal remnants of humanity (Davis 1993: 596). The new Jerusalem emerging from this contemporary marriage of heaven and hell distinguishes an apocalypse of an entirely different order, an apocalypse in and of machines. The plot of Neal Stephenson's *Snow Crash* (1992) turns on the archaeological excavation of an ancient code which not only breaks down any computer system but also, via the terminal screen, erases the faculties of human programmers. The contagious viral metaphors contaminating both computers and their users escalate to produce 'apocalyptic visions' linking physical and systemic disin-tegration (Lupton 1994: 565). *Fin-de-siècle* anxieties about the bug waiting to explode every system and download devastating economic and social conse-quences in the 'real' world, suggested that the apocalypse that once lay only in the realm of symbols, metaphors and imaginations found itself brutally literalised in the very digits that inaugurated the new millennium.

Sublime and apocalyptic visions, of course, participate in a darker romanticism. In contemporary terms, moreover, darkness encroaches ever closer on the illuminating imagination: the spiritual, psychological and imaginative journey of earlier romantics, intent on 'opening up new hori-zons for the living', is superseded and evacuated in Gibson's fiction, 'leaving behind decaying goods and a residue . . . of mostly nameless rage' (Glazer 1989: 158). In a similar vein, noting how infinity's void is filled out by human constructs and levelled in the interface between human mind and machine, Jack Voller outlines a reversal in the evolution of sublimity from an exalted plenitude to the postmodern revelation of pervasive emptiness (1993: 20–21). It is significant, then, that the material landscape of cyberpunk fiction is one of devastation, decay, social and structural disintegration:

> The ruined city is for this reason the appropriate place to leave the body behind: operating as a kind of cemetery space, the urban ruins of cyber-punk signify a transfer of interest from physical exterior to electronic interior. Inhabiting a ruined environment becomes an objective correl-ative to entering a disembodied space (cyberspace).
>
> (Sponsler 1993: 263)

The devastation of the primary locus of modernity, the city, functions analo-
gously to wild, deserted landscapes of sublime nature: once the evacuation
of natural sense was attended by an imaginative overcoming of a crisis in the
faculties; now the entry into a virtual realm is predicated on the displacement or effacement of materiality. Boundaries between subject and object,
between interiority and exteriority, between imaginative transcendence and
material immanence, however, are not restored on the cyberspatial plane:
they are supplanted and recoded in the same process, rendering the future
both utopian and distopian in shape.

The communicational technologies that surround and transform the
globe are romanticised as angels by Michel Serres, message-bearers and
visionary vehicles of a new millennium. In place of the world of work,
production, pollution and crisis, there emerges a new paradisiacal, liberal
utopia, a world devoted to 'knowledge, culture, welfare, art, conversation'
where everyone partakes of 'the life of angels' (Serres 1995: 55). The new,
universal city emerges from the wastelands of post-industrial decay: a city of
light, virtual speeds, technological angels, it 'bears a striking resemblance to
the symbolic heavenly Jerusalem of antiquity' (Serres 1995: 69). Here, things
are fabricated with information, the universe shaped by the wind of a
romantic *psyche* and materialised in software; 'the word becomes flesh', the
'*techno*' replaced by '*logos*'. At present, however, things remains in a state of
transition, in a purgatorial space 'between the hot hell of old-style labor
processes and the speculative paradise of new technologies' (Serres 1995:
71). An age-old historical pattern is repeated, apocalyptic, revolutionary,
destructive and creative:

> The Trojan Wars, the sack of Rome, the destruction of Alba, Jerusalem
> and Athens, the fire of Alexandria, the taking of Constantinople . . . In
> history and its founding texts, Europe was built on the ruins and
> destruction of these primitive cities. . . . The earthquake in Lisbon, the
> fire of London, the sun of Hiroshima . . . Is this history being perpetu-
> ated? Which America was the basis for the disappearance of the primi-
> tive pre-Inca citadel of Machu Picchu? Over what ruins does the new
> and universal now fly?
>
> (Serres 1995: 77)

No creation without destruction; no change without devastation. No angels
without dead bodies, hence their predominance on television; hence, also,
the pervasive visibility of poverty, misery, destitution across the ruined
globe. These figures, 'the wretched of the earth', are, for Serres, 'messengers
of an extraordinary state which is unknown to us', 'phantoms' piercing the
illusion of everyday reality and thereby heralding an other world. Where

Serres sacralises the wretched and the abject as ghosts of a future past as much as messengers of states to come, cyberpunk simply jettisons them, meat to be discarded, the obsolescent, inefficient bodies supplemented and then made redundant by machines. The ruin of modernity's city and the evacuation of its bodies become the basic condition of the leap into the mercurial sphere of communications. In a less optimistic vein, Paul Virilio (1995) discusses the abjection and human detritus involved in the substitution of virtual reality for actual reality: workless and disempowered by technological reconfigurations, the (industrial) body, too, undergoes interior evacuation, a colonisation and supercession by means of the interplanetary, space age technology that has been turned inward. For him, the dark divinity of technofundamentalism delivers only the relentless inhuman immanence of an utterly machinic power.

There are at least two modes of repetition articulated in contemporary reiterations of romanticism. One appears in the romantic terms employed in technoscientific rhetoric and the evident romanticisation of the delights of cyberspace. But the sense of crisis, along with the images of ruin and devastation underlying visionary leaps into a virtual future, also replay a thoroughly romantic scenario. In their account of German romanticism, Jean-Luc Nancy and Philippe Lacoue-Labarthe note how a 'triple crisis' established the conditions of romanticism: a social and moral crisis pertaining to the relationship of the bourgeoisie to culture, a political crisis most visible in the French Revolution, and the Kantian critique itself. The German Romantics, however, were involved in something more than the reflection and reproduction of a crisis in literature alone: their project opens up 'a general crisis and critique (social, moral, religious, political . . . ) for which literature and literary theory will be the privileged locus of expression' (Lacoue-Labarthe and Nancy 1988: 5). In this respect, they argue, 'we still belong to the era it opened up':

> A veritable romantic *unconscious* is discernable today, in most of the central motifs of modernity. Not the least result of romanticism's indefinable character is the way that it has allowed this so-called modernity to use romanticism as a foil, without ever recognizing – or in order not to recognize – that it has done little more than rehash romanticism's discoveries.
>
> (1988: 15)

The rehashing of romanticism repeats the popular idea of a revolt of reason against the state. The liberal and revolutionary impetus of modernity is dominated by the assumption of 'a romanticism of libertarian and literary rebellion, literary because libertarian, whose art would incarnate insurrection'. But this rehashed romanticism has its 'reverse side' in which the 'literary absolute' disclosed by the literary-libertarian momentum 'aggravates and radicalizes the thinking of totality and the Subject. It *infinitizes* this thinking, and therein, precisely, rests its ambiguity' (Lacoue-Labarthe and Nancy 1988: 15). The ambiguity, moreover, comes from the crisis at the core of the simple rehashing of romanticism as modernity's 'foil', from the interrogation attendant on the infinitisation that proceeds from the ambiguity of the literary absolute.

Romanticism is repeated on a straightforward plane; its crisis, too, is reiterated, provoking an ambivalent constitution and disruption of assumptions of political priority and subjective agency:

> we are all, still and always, aware of the *Crisis*, convinced that 'interventions' are necessary and that the least of texts is immediately 'effective' ['*operatoire*']; we all think, as if it went without saying, that politics passes through the literary (or the theoretical). Romanticism is our *naïveté*.
>
> This does not mean that romanticism is our error. But rather that we have to become aware of the necessity of this repetition compulsion.
>
> (Lacoue-Labarthe and Nancy 1988: 20–21)

As repetition turns into repetition compulsion, a very different sense of the relation between romanticism and modernity evinces itself. Indeed, the implications of repetition compulsion extend, through an account of the significance of Kantian critique, to the questions posed of the subject, and the gap constitutive of subjectivity, in psychoanalysis.

The crisis which shapes romanticism in terms of the naivety of agency and political priority appears in the gap linking aesthetics and philosophy. In Kantian critique 'an entirely new and unforeseeable relation' articulates them, enabling the 'passage' to romanticism. The movement, however, does not occur by way of a solid and directly negotiable connection: 'in reality, an abyss opens up where a bridge should have been built and, if some connections are woven – between art and philosophy, for example – they also appear in the paradoxical figure of disconnection [*deliason*] . . . '. The effects of such a dis-connective abyss leave the subject as the 'I' of an 'empty form' to disclose an object ungraspable except within the limits of intuition alone (Lacoue-Labarthe and Nancy 1988: 29–30). The subject of Kantian reflection is not equated with the reflection of imaginary wholeness produced in a 'mirror stage'; it evokes 'no "jubilant" assumption of the subject, no self-awareness as awareness of substance'. Instead, it

> connotes only a pure referral or reflecting back, obtained by a simple optical pattern and presupposing, moreover, the mediation of an inert,

dead body, of a blind tain. Insofar as reflection operates in the judgement of taste as the freeplay of the imagination (that is, as a function of
synthesis in its *pure* state, producing no object whatsoever) it brings
about the unity of the subject only insofar as the subject sees itself in the
image (*Bild*) of something without either concept or end.

(Lacoue-Labarthe and Nancy 1988: 31)

The abyssal relation articulating aesthetics and philosophy discloses an
abysmal subject. Defined neither by object nor image, and only misrecognised in the naivety of imaginary jubilation, the subject finds its counterpart
in the figure of the 'blind tain', the unseen and unreflecting basis of reflection.

## Sublime Thing

In his reading of Kant's *Critique of Judgement*, Lyotard develops the question
of the subject and the formless figure of the abyss. What is felt in the sublime
is the 'disproportion' and 'incommensurability' of the faculties of reason and
imagination: an 'abyss' repelling and attracting the imagination 'is enjoined
to present the absolute'. Hence, the sublime leaves no room for the notion of
a 'subject of synthesis' understood as a container or agent of experience
(1994: 24–25). What is felt in the sublime, Lyotard concludes, is a 'differend'
that 'makes the raw magnitude of nature a sign of reason while remaining a
phenomenon of experience' (1994: 234). Even as the reading of the sublime
is framed in his own terms, Lyotard has occasional and apologetic recourse
to psychoanalysis. Sublimity, he observes, 'is only the irruption in and of
thought of this deaf desire for limitlessness. Thinking takes "action", it "acts"
the impossible, it subjectively "realizes" its omnipotence. It experiences
pleasure in the Real. I ask the reader to forgive me for using terms of the
idiom of Freud and Lacan to situate this violence' (1994: 55–56). A sovereign expenditure akin to *jouissance* describes the heterogeneity and violence
of the sublime, a process in which thought, even as it acts to imagine a superior state, also evacuates, loses or unknowns itself.

In the dynamic theory of forces disclosed in Kant's version of Burkean
delight, Freud's pleasure principle is invoked to argue that delight 'arises
"indirectly" as a feeling with two conflicting moments: the "vital forces"
experience a momentary check, *Hemmung*, an inhibition; they are held back,
repressed. When they are released, they "discharge" – this is the *Ergiessung* –
all the more powerfully in the following moment' (1994: 68). Charged by the
incomprehensibility of the sublime as an impediment to the possibility of
thought, delight moves from 'transitory anguish' to powerful expenditure.
The economy of the sublime, its double momentum of attraction and repul-

sion, turns on some 'thing' which, Lyotard suggests, 'arouses such ambivalence' (1994: 68). Reflections on modern art take their bearings from this 'thing' as what takes thought beyond nature, 'the thing before which thinking retreats and toward which it races'. For Lyotard,

> there is some 'thing' that leaves thought dumbfounded even as it exalts thought, this object is not one of nature, or, rather, its nature is not that nature, the 'writing' (*Chiffreschrift* ... ) of whose forms is able to be immediately 'read' by the feeling of the beautiful. The 'thing' cannot belong to a nature that lets the imagination of genius search its 'writing' for something further with which to present more forms than the writing presents, and with which to form another nature.
>
> (1994: 69)

The 'thing', dumbfounding and exalting thought with an excess to presentation, forms a space, a locus of production and writing. It is, at once, a locus that, since not of nature, can be associated with mind, but only insofar as 'the objects of these ideas precisely never give an adequate presentation of themselves in a form that would be adapted, *angemessen*, to them' (1994: 69). Using the example of the hideousness of the raging ocean arousing sublime feeling, 'it does so', Lyotard comments, 'insofar as it refers thought negatively to a higher finality, that of an Idea'. 'This gesture of thought', he continues, 'averts the "horror," as Burke would say, the hideousness of the present, that subverts it and turns it into admiration and respect for an unpresentable Idea – this gesture is called "subreption"' (1994: 69–70). And *subreptio*, in canon law, he notes, describes the obtaining of privilege through dissimulation, an 'abuse of authority' (1994: 70). It is done, moreover, for 'a glimpse of the Idea, the absolute of power, freedom' and depends on an unpresentable object, on something 'formless'.

The thought of the thing, in which thought never corresponds to nature nor remains purely of the mind, thought aroused by some Thing unpresentable, formless, excessive, is addressed in Jacques Lacan's seminar, *The Ethics of Psychoanalysis*. Beyond sense, that is, beyond perceptual and cognitive faculties, as well as beyond symbolic structures of meaning, *das Ding*, in the terms Lacan develops from Kant, constitutes a crucial and strange articulation and separation of registers, locus of repetition and in-humanity. As thing, *chose* and *causa*, it functions as the cause of law, the place establishing the possibility of law (1992: 43). But the Thing is also sublime in that 'it is impossible for us to imagine it' (1992: 123). Significantly, the impossible object called the Thing is distinguished from *Sache*, from those objects whose reality is determined by symbolic structures. Articulating the domains of the real and the signifier, the Thing situates humans between registers: in this respect it pertains to the experience of the uncanny, 'characterised by its absence and strangeness' (1992: 63) and associated with the *Nebenmensch*, the double, who is both familiar and alien, a source of division and difference in judgement (1992: 52). The Thing is not, however, simply or absolutely exterior to the subject; nor is it part of an integral inner core: neither and both at the same time, its position is paradoxically defined by Lacan as an 'intimate exteriority' or 'extimacy' (1992: 139). It is

> at the center only in the sense that it is excluded. That is to say, in reality *das Ding* has to be posited as exterior, as the prehistoric Other it is impossible to forget – the Other whose primacy of position Freud affirms in the form of something *entfremdet*, something strange to me, although it is at the heart of me, something that on the level of the unconscious only a representation can represent.
>
> (1992: 71)

The absence and strangeness of the extimate Thing provides a space for the shaping of identity and anxiety in relation to an object that assumes the weight and destiny of otherness in the form of a 'terrifying, inhuman partner' (1992: 150). A screen for the projection of phantasms, anchoring point of symbolic sense and identity, the Thing, nevertheless, remains a 'vacuole', a gap or tear around which signification reconstitutes itself in terms of the subject: 'it is around *das Ding* that the whole adaptive development revolves, that is so specific to man insofar as the symbolic process reveals itself to be inextricably woven into it' (1992: 57). Inhuman, in respect of an absolute alterity associated with the primary Other and the symbolic systems governing humanity, the Thing remains in-human, a kernel occupying the gap integral to the specific existence of any split subject.

The Thing, developed by Lacan in his *Ethics*, begins to assume the form and function associated with his later and most important psychoanalytical innovation, the *objet petit a*. At the extimate core of the psychic economy, both Thing and *a* determine the modes of expenditure that Lyotard, employing Freudian notions of dynamic forces, identifies in the sublime. Where pleasure, in respect of beauty, circulates so as not to disturb the reality of the subject, the sublime operates through an inhibition and tension that generates the intense pleasure of discharge. Pleasure follows what Lacan, after Freud, calls 'an inertia principle', the homeostatic circulation of energies bound by the order of the signifier. But, inimical to the signifier, the object *a* lies at the centre of its circulations, absently structuring the expenditure of its economy: the real, 'beyond the *automaton*, the return, the coming-back, the insistence of the signs, by which we see ourselves governed by the pleasure', presents itself 'in the form of that which is *unassimilable* in it', that is, as noise, accident, trauma and in excess of the homeostatic apparatus of the pleasure principle (1977b: 53–55). The gap, the scissions appearing in signifying systems and determining their repetitions, forms the locus of the unconscious and the place where *a* appears. In this sense, the inhuman Thing remains utterly in-human and as such radically alters conventional conceptions of the human subject perpetuated in ego psychology and humanist (and post-humanist) discourse. For Lacan, the Cartesian *cogito* is distinguished as a 'monster' and 'homunculus' in opposition to the subject who is 'constituted as secondary in relation to the signifier' (1977b: 141). Split, this subject is marked, differentiated from the animal s/he once was, and ought not to be confused with the object *a* which nonetheless establishes the basis of imaginary identity. In the space of *a*, between the real and the symbolic, imaginary figures are projected as duplicates of subject, but not as a substitution of *imaginatio* for *cogito*. As an effect of misrecognition the 'reflected, momentary, precarious image of mastery' means that the subject 'imagines himself to be a man merely by virtue of the fact that he imagines himself' (1977b: 142). Although *a* allows for the projection of so many imaginary identities, it discloses an entirely different subject divided between desire and the drive: in relation to the anchorage of *a* the subject moves along the chains of signification associated with desire, but desire is orientated in relation to lack and the gap constitutive of the movement of the drive. Here another subject appears, a 'headless subjectification', an acephalic subject in excess of any imaginary articulation (1977b: 184).

In *The Ethics of Psychoanalysis*, Lacan discusses the relation of the Thing to the *Wunsch* that discloses a universal and particular law of desire outside the normativity of pleasure and pain that defined the limits of the late eighteenth-century constitution of the human subject. Appearing in the 'depths of a subject in an irreducible form', the Thing which allows for the 'discovery of the thought of desire', it seems, is born before psychoanalysis and can be phrased in Wordsworthian terms as 'the child is father of the man'. But the romantic recourse to childhood, Lacan notes, although inaugurating the field of infantile sexuality and psychic development that psychoanalysis explores, serves only as a historical 'vanishing point' with reference to the shifts and tensions which shape the question of the human subject (1992: 24–25). Psychoanalysis, Lacan underscores elsewhere, does not merely repeat a romanticised unconscious associated with dark, repressed desire: it opens up the question of it and its subject in terms of a gap, a constitutive rather than simply inverted darkness (1977b: 24). It can be called 'extimate darkness', a darkness linked to the emergence of the Thing, a darkness evinced in Wordsworth's poetry which subsequently assumes a more disturbing aspect within the Romanticism of later writers. For Wordsworth, the dark and disconcerting Thing which appears quite traumatically in early parts of *The Prelude* ultimately serves as the basis for a paternal identification and subjective reconstitution. But the extimate darkness around which the poetic subject is structured remains both a locus of subjective dissolution and sublime imagination, its gap determining the desire for boundless human plenitude with an interior limit and cause inassimilable to the progress of mind.

In the first book of *The Prelude*, the external landscape gives form to a disturbing and transformative inner experience. Having stolen a rowing boat and delighted in the transgressive pleasures offered by maternal nature, the young Wordsworth encounters an image that, sublimely, interrupts his innocent, and illicit, enjoyment. Superegoically, a 'huge Cliff, black and huge', 'like a living thing, Strode after me' (1805, I: 409–12). The castrating threat hallucinated by the youngster proves decisive. He flees the scene, but not its effects:

> and after I had seen
> That spectacle, for many days, my brain
> Work'd with a dim and undetermin'd sense
> Of unknown modes of being; in my thoughts
> There was a darkness, call it solitude.
> Or blank desertion, no familiar shapes
> Of hourly objects, images of trees,
> Of sea or sky, no colours of green fields;
> But huge and mighty forms, that do not live
> Like living men, moved slowly through my mind
> By day, and were the trouble of my dreams.
> (1805, I: 417–27)

The procession of strange, inhuman forms, alien to the object-world of human reality, occupies the extimate darkness, the inner evacuated space of subjectivity. The troubling darkness returns, in association with mountains, later in *The Prelude* to serve as the space that, in evacuating quotidian subjectivity and sense, enables the poetic turn towards imagination and visionary power.

The more mature Wordsworth, having learnt from his disturbing early experience, is better able to cope with the sublime effects of mountains. In Book VI, Wordsworth's account of his ascent of the Alps is laced with excited anticipation of the sights that await him. Instead, the travellers become enveloped in the mist and he is mortified to discover that they have crossed the Alps without enjoying the pleasures of the summit. With this moment of awful revelation, disappointed desire delivers a darkness whose sublimity comes from within as much as without. Indeed, it is elevated, in the fuller passages from the 1850 version, to become the basis of the transcendent imagination:

> Imagination – here the Power so called
> Through sad incompetence of human speech,
> That awful Power rose from the mind's abyss
> Like an unfathered vapour that enwraps,
> At once some lonely traveller. I was lost;
>                    (1850, VI: 592–96)

The sense of being lost, the abyssal disorientation, registers an encounter with something beyond language in the paternal absence of vaporous embrace. The loss, however, is momentary, the negativity sublimated a few lines later into an understanding of the Imagination's relation to the glorious power apprehended beyond speech, a recognition that sustains hope and desire on another level. This is the passage's moral and the recognition of a glory that comes with the revelation of the 'invisible world':

> Our destiny, our being's heart and home,
> Is with infinitude, and only there;
> With hope it is, hope that can never die,
> Effort, and expectation, and desire,
> And something evermore about to be.
>                    (1850, VI: 604–7)

The negative moment is transformed by the higher power of the imagination: the space of darkness causes it to arise in new form and discover an immortal truth of being, as being in desire and hope. From a sense of desolation, subjective dissolution and mental ruin, from being subjected to the incomprehensible machinations of dark interior and exterior forms, from having all selfhood threatened with annihilating otherness, the subject of the imagination triumphs in the momentary identification of a position of knowledge, security and symbolic superiority.

Arguing that 'the essential claim of the sublime is that man can, in feeling and in speech, transcend the human' (1976: 3), Thomas Weiskel analyses the way it utilises the image of the abyss to establish a paternal or symbolic relationship to that which exceeds phenomenal experience or rational thought. In Wordsworth, the sublime connotes more than identification with the father, and moves towards the transcendence associated with the paternal metaphor or phallic signifier:

> Visionary power is associated with the transcendence of the image and in particular with the 'power of sound'; yet it depends upon a resistance within that transcendence of sight for sound. In the Wordsworthian

moment two events appear to coalesce: the withdrawal or the occulta-
tion of the image and the epiphany of the character or signifier proper.
                                                        (Weiskel 1976: 175)

The paternal signifier, of course, is that which directs desire and sustains
hope: it also enacts a dialectical negation and conservation of antithetical
darkness. Overcoming darkness, a creative power manifests itself as the
transcendent force of poetic signification. As Weiskel notes, the 'epiphany'
of the signifier 'intimates death (the apocalyptic destruction of nature and
the natural man)' and allows for the emergence of creative power (1976:
189). Indeed, visionary power, in very much the same terms as are used to
describe the crossing of the Alps, is bound up with great poetry.

A 'ghostly language of the ancient earth' remains within the glorious
power of poetic language, marking an ambivalently creative and disturbing
locus of darkness within the movements of words:

> Visionary Power
> Attends on the motion of the winds,
> Embodied in the mystery of words.
> There darkness makes abode, and all the host
> Of shadowy things do work their changes there,
>                                         (1805, V: 619–23)

In the 1850 version of *The Prelude* the winds are 'viewless', underlining the
sense of power beyond perception. The difficulty in apprehending this
power, exacerbated by the intricate turnings of the syntax, lies in its uncertain location among winds, shadowy things and a mysterious language with
darkness at its centre. The sound of words and winds announces the *spiritus*,
the breath, breeze and psyche animating Romantic poetry, the very shell
whose sounds produce 'a loud prophetic blast of harmony', as well as foretell
apocalyptic destruction at the beginning of the book (1805, V: 94–98).
Creation, it seems, is predicated on a destruction or process of ruination.
And while darkness allows for dialectical overcoming in the achievement
of symbolic poetic authority, its extimacy suggests a power fundamentally
in-human.

The ambivalence of the dark power at the heart of English Romantic
discourse takes later poetry in quite different directions. Most notably,
Byron's 'Darkness' sees its global imposition as an event without any glimpse
of transcendence and with absolutely no future for humanity. Closer to
Wordsworth, Percy Shelley locates power in terms of the evacuation of any
paternal authority: it serves as the basis for an impossible idealisation. In 'To
Wordsworth', a sonnet of love and mourning, a Wordsworthian language of

nature and the politicised figure of the Romantic poet dissolves to leave death in their place: Wordsworth, though he still lives, is addressed as though symbolically dead, a betrayer of poetic ideals. The sonnet becomes his unflattering poetic epitaph. Mortality, and the internal distance it opens up within the subject also, in other poems by Shelley from this period, inhabits the perception of nature. 'Mont Blanc', for instance, appears to reinforce a dialectical understanding of the synthetic bonds uniting mind and nature: the sense of an 'everlasting universe of things' flowing through the mind provides an intimation of a Power comparable to the bursting energy of the River Arve. But the mind that is entranced by sublime vision and passively holding 'unremitting interchange' with things is drawn beyond the ghostly cave of poetry to a more apocalyptic vision: Mont Blanc is glimpsed as the omnipotent ruler of a desolate and icy wasteland, 'a desert peopled by the storms alone' (1923, l. 67), a barren, ghastly and ruinous realm of rocks and glaciers:

> A city of death, distinct with many a tower
> And wall impregnable of ice.
> Yet not a city, but a flood of ruin
> Is there, that from the boundaries of the sky
> Rolls its perpetual stream;
> (1923, ll. 105–9)

The city that is not one confounds distinctions of stasis and motion, just as ruin seems to roll endlessly on. Indeed, the opposition of life and death is also confounded by the unthinkable otherness of the place, having overthrown 'the limits of the dead and the living world' (1923, l. 112). The power that is suggested by the sublime vision of the mountain, however, is not resolved into a suitably transcendent solution: it remains as much absent as present, truly beyond comprehension. The poem can only end with a question, a question about existence, the imagination and vacancy.

The ruins of Mont Blanc are not simply ruins; their devastation opens onto some Thing utterly unknowable and inhuman:

> Thou hast a voice, great Mountain, to repeal
> Large codes of fraud and woe; not understood
> By all, but which the wise, and great, and good
> Interpret, or make felt, or deeply feel.
> (1923, ll. 80–83)

The voice, however, remains unheard, despite the interpretations and intuitions of the great and good. Nonetheless, the lesson given by the mountainous image of the absolutely Other constitutes a central element in Shelleyan politics: time and a Power beyond human understanding and mastery mean that political schemes and governmental tyranny are but vain and fraudulent impositions on a Nature beyond their grasp. The political moral associates change with a superhuman energy. Shelley follows the republican and enlightened message advanced by Constantin François Volney in his *Ruins*, in which human tyranny, vanity, irrationality and frailty in the face of nature is charted through recourse to the remnants that mark the decline of every civilisation in history. In Shelley's 'Ozymandias', the same message is ironically reiterated: 'Look on my works, ye Mighty, and despair', declares the tyrant Ozymandias, but around the words his monument to his own imagined omnipotence lies in ruins, shrouded by the silence of the desert. Time and nature have turned his pronouncement upon him.

The presentation of ruins as sublime testaments to the work of an inhuman, incomprehensible and darkly natural Power is taken to an extreme in Mary Shelley's *The Last Man* as it charts the end of humanity as a global event, an anti-apocalyptic consumption of romantic-humanist fantasy by a relentless plague. A familiar futuristic vision of democratic ideals describes a republican Britain in which human transcendence of the material world has been enabled by sound politics and technological advances. But the earthly political utopia is devastated: the revenge of Nature on enlightened liberal political culture takes viral form to destroy both individual and social body from within. In contrast to *Frankenstein*, which presents the monstrous dissolution of Romantic individuality and creative aspiration as a solitary failing, *The Last Man* locates monstrosity in an excessive, inhuman but feminised Nature: benevolent nature, 'our mother and our friend', becomes a menace, a monster, a merciless, indifferent mistress demonstrating that 'though she prompted us to assign her laws and subdue her apparent powers, yet, if she put forth a finger, we must quake' (Shelley 1994: 232). Nature, here, exceeds sublimity: the inverted image of romantic-humanist fantasies of transcendence, beyond recuperation or mastery, it, or she, leaves the human figure in no position of dignity or imaginary power.

In Frances Ferguson's account of *Frankenstein* and the 'nuclear sublime', Kantian aesthetics provide a framework for understanding ambivalent investments in fabulous texts concerned with the end of the world: countering the assumption that the sublime offers a sense of unique consciousness, Shelley's first novel reverses the 'dream of self-affirmation'. What emerges from this reversal is akin to the plot of *The Last Man*, written as it is, in the form of a prophecy, and thus, to no one: 'to think the sublime would be to think the unthinkable and to exist in one's own nonexistence' (Ferguson 1984: 7–8). Death, the subject's non-existence, emerges as the ambivalent condition for sublimity, the possibility of utter dissolution simultaneously establishing the basis for the solitary elevation of self. 'Solitude', Ferguson states, 'comes to be cultivated as a space for consciousness in which the individual is not answerable to others, and the waste landscape becomes the site of value because one can make it a peopled solitude, anthropomorphizing rocks and stones and trees, without encountering the pressures of a competing consciousness' (Ferguson 1992: 114). Transcendence proceeds from an overcoming of otherness and the popula-tion of ruined or empty spaces with figures of the solitary mind. In this light, Ferguson's unattributed citation from Wordsworth's lyric, 'A slumber did my Spirit seal', appears significant. In the poem, the movement from a slum-bering, not-yet human state of existence to one of transcendent conscious-ness occurs through the recognition of the female other's death. Unrepresented, the moment of death allows the subject to attain a position overlooking the entirety of the mutable globe.

Things are quite different in *The Last Man*. No transcendence succeeds the encounter with death. There are no enlightened political consolations like those of Volney's with regard to the ruin of imperial civilisation nor any sense of positive change associated with Power. Instead, Shelley's novel pushes mutability to the extreme limit of its inhuman logic. The Nature in excess of humanity conforms to what Bataille calls 'base matter': active, eternal and dark, the 'monstrous archontes' of base matter exceeds good and evil. 'External and foreign to ideal human aspirations', base matter 'refuses to allow itself to be reduced to the great ontological machines' erected by them (Bataille 1997: 162–63). Base matter evacuates both idealism and materialism. An acephalic figure replaces the human subject: Bataille's 'last man' exists within and in excess of the closed Hegelian dialectic, a figure of unemployed negativity refusing all philosophical, economic and political systems. In *The Last Man* humanity is reduced to being nothing more than a 'monstrous excrescence of nature' (Shelley 1994: 467). Divested of all value, relationship, meaning, the excremental last man appears as the consummation of Romantic solitude: the master of all he can see, his enjoyment is both sovereign and redundant: although his conscious-ness alone is paramount, nothing remains to offer any recognition. Solitary, but not sublime, the figure is mirrored by the 'impossible book' that performs the ultimate humanist gesture of seeking 'to live the death of all humanity' (Johnson 1993: 258). Utopian and arcadian, apocalyptic and anti-apocalytpic, the novel's levelling of democratic politics and its cruel a-romantic consummation leaves an acephalic figure at the end of a history that has never, despite the best efforts and aspirations of poets, philosophers and scientists, been quite human. Modernity, from its inception, it seems, has depended on an end to history, its very life requiring a terroristic, sublime expenditure that only ever ambivalently constitutes the subject. The novel thus charts the impossibility of the Romantic subject in relation to the unpresentable Thing of the sublime, an abyss that, for Lyotard, founds and unfounds modernity.

A strange modernity permeates *The Last Man*, something familiar to an age used to imagining global annihilation. The end of history, according to Mary Shelley in 1826, occurs in 2100. For Francis Fukuyama, writing *The End of History and the Last Man* in 1992, the collapse of any serious ideological competition to liberal democracy, marked by the dismantling of the Berlin Wall and the end of the Cold War, announces the end, the culmination of humanist progress as all humans are completely and satisfactorily recognised by political institutions. The only things left for contemporary subjects are the commodified pleasures and consumerist desires guaranteed by the freedoms of market and opportunity. An end to a romantic story appears in the closure of liberalism's triumphal progress to the political and economic liberation once demanded in revolutionary tones. Fukuyama's modern humans are the last man, in a supplementary position to the end of history: 'jaded by the experience of history, and disabused of the possibility of any direct experience of values', self-absorbed, directionless and wanting risk to stimulate waning desire (Fukuyama 1992: 306; 328–29). Yet Mary Shelley's novel had already posed the question of what happens after the end of history: having imagined democratic liberalism at its peak, her end of history is extremely literal. The one who is left remains only with an otherless, errant and unsatisfiable desire: as he prepares to leave the citadel of human civilisation and sail off around the world he says 'neither hope nor joy are my pilots – restless despair and fierce desire of change lead me on. I long to grapple with danger, to be exiled by fear, to have some task, however slight or voluntary, for each day's fulfilment' (Shelley 1994: 476). Hollowed out, the subject seeks thrills and excitement, something to do, some object of and in desire to direct his itinerant path. This figure is no moral or rational being required to work by the dictates of production, scarcity and need: all his material needs are satisfied in abundance. Desire, despite the plethora of commodities and spatial freedoms, is condemned to wander the deserted globe in search of new objects of satisfaction. So, too, with Fukuyama: modern subjects confronted with the void at the end of history are left to utter the escalating demand for more, subjects of consumption, nonproductive expenditure and waste.

## Virtual repetition

Baudrillard's America, land of accelerating and disappearing desire, symbolises the ruinous state of contemporary western culture: 'it is a world completely rotten with wealth, power, senility, indifference, puritanism and mental hygiene, poverty and waste, technological futility and aimless violence'. And ruin, generated internally and expelled on a global scale, continues to resonate with a quietly apocalyptic air: 'and yet I cannot help but feel it has about it something of the dawning of the universe' (Baudrillard 1988: 23). The new dawn, however, promises to return the world to a nascent state, shedding all the appendages of human culture and its human-ised nature: 'heir to the deserts', American culture is not opposed to nature but discloses something like its base matter, a general desolation inhabiting all life and 'the emptiness, the radical nudity that is the background to every human institution'. The desert exposes a world 'outside the sphere and circumference of desire'; confounding all distinctions and meaning with its sterility, it is 'a sublime form that banishes all sociality, all sentimentality, all sexuality' (Baudrillard 1988: 63; 71). Its sublimity, moreover, assumes an extimate form as a 'natural extension of the inner silence of the body', 'of its capacity for absence, the ideal schema of humanity's disappearance'. All America exists as a desert, culture's 'wild state' sacrificing 'all intellect, all aesthetics, in a process of literal transcription into the real'. Articulated in terms of the absent-present space of the in-human Thing, flowing out and into the indifference of the Real, culture and nature begin to dissolve: Death Valley, 'the sublime natural phenomenon', and Las Vegas, 'the abject cultural phenomenon', 'mirror each other across the desert, the one as acme of secrecy and silence, the other as acme of prostitution and theatricality' (Baudrillard 1988: 67–68). All signs of humanity, all manifestations of desire, sexuality, sense or reason evaporate in the dry heat and midnight chill of a realm of utter indifference.

While the desert remains a background noise in which all signs are consumed and desertified, America is glimpsed through another process of evacuation, one suggested in Baudrillard's injunction to grasp the secret of the city by beginning with the cinema screen and moving outwards to the city (1988: 56). Hyperreality becomes the counterpart to the indifferent desert-real. Images, signs, simulations consume all traces of humanity in an entirely alien order, thereby disclosing the radical indifference at the heart of all cultural systems. Machines of vision and speed, technological supple-ments supplanting any illusion of human sense, are the instruments of this obliteration. For Nick Land, outlining the implications of machinic processes, 'the high road to thinking no longer passes through a deepening of human cognition, but rather through a becoming inhuman of cognition, a migration of cognition out into the emerging technosentience reservoir, into "dehumanized landscapes . . . emptied spaces" where human culture will be dissolved' (Land 1993a: 217). The citation from Gilles Deleuze is significant in that anoedipal machinic desiring puts an end to 'great fiction of transcendental philosophy' based on Kantian judgement (Land 1993a:

224). Critique, realised in the immanence of machinic process, leaves transcendentalism behind as a 'theological relic' that mirrors the ruins of culture (Land 1993b: 472).

The machinic unconscious eviscerates bodies, evacuates subjects, voiding judgement and law, extinguishing human history:

> Where Kant's transcendental subject gives the law to itself in its autonomy, Deleuze/Guattari's machinic unconscious diffuses all law into automatism. Between the extreme fringes of these two figures stretches the history of capital. The eradication of all law, or of humanity, is sketched culturally by the development of critique, which is the theoretical elaboration of the commodification process. The social order and the anthropomorphic subject share a history, and an extinction.
>
> (Land 1993b: 472)

In machinic desire, humanity encounters the end of history. The computerised matrix imposes a future in the form of 'a planetary scale artificial death – Synthanatos – the terminal productive outcome of human history as a machinic process' (Land 1993b: 474). Capitalism provides a model of the process in which productive economy, supposedly in the service of human interests, is bypassed by the insurgence of machinic desire from a future that utterly rewrites history as the inhuman history of the machine:

> Machinic desire can seem a little inhuman, as it rips up political cultures, deletes traditions, dissolves subjectivities, and hacks through security apparatuses, tracking a soulless tropism to zero control. This is because what appears to humanity as the history of capitalism is an invasion from the future by an artificial intelligent space that must assemble itself entirely from the enemy's resources.
>
> (Land 1993b: 479)

Superseding human values and agency with the speed of digital exchanges, the informational commodities of global capitalism become the only rule, thereby placing desire in line with desiring. Neither subjective nor pathological factors apply, nor do the terms of a humanised moral, economic, political and rational order:

> The obsolete psychological category of 'greed' privatizes and moralizes addiction, as if the profit-seeking tropism of a transnational capitalism propagating itself through epidemic consumerism were intelligible in terms of personal subjective traits. Wanting more is the index of inter-

lock with cyberpositive machinic processes, and not the expression of private idiosyncrasy. What could be more impersonal – disinterested – than a *haut bourgeois* capital expansion servo-mechanism striving to double $10 billion? And even these creatures are disappearing into silicon viro-finance automatisms, where massively distributed and anonymized human ownership has become as vacuously nominal as democratic sovereignty.

(Land 1993b: 478)

Machinic desire, describing the hypercharged and rapid digital exchanges between automated relays, is also the point of articulation in which every last vestige of a human order is rewired according to technocapitalist requirements: humans are plugged into TV commercials, shopping channels, on-line ordering services. Wanting more, the excessive and escalating imperative of consumerism, quickly draws humans into electronic circuits and screens, spitting out any hint of dignity, value or autonomy along the way.

'Cyberrevolution', with its 'machine plague' (Land 1993b: 475), turns the sublime social and political upheavals of modernity inside out: liberalism and humanity are evacuated by the technological developments of the economic form in which they were created. The warring antipodes of humanist idealism and materialism are apocalyptically overthrown by the new, virtual and immanent materialism of machinic process. The machine apocalypse, however, seems to manifest the other side of romantic imaginings and its sublime subject, instantiating itself in the very void disclosed at its heart. Indeed, a romantic unconscious, disclosing the empty Thing in place of the subject, appears as the very image of machinic process, driven by the alien and acephalic force of a radically indifferent Other. Perhaps, romanticism, its unconscious and its subject, has never been human. Perhaps it has always been machinic. At the same time, Baudrillard's and Land's sublime glimpse of the ruination of human culture and the subject at its centre seems to present a distinctly romantic stance with their interminably final gestures made to an inhuman future displaying the sovereign gesture of the last man. Or perhaps, the sublime threat of the machine reinvigorates an illusion: on the point of annihilation by terminating machines, a sense of humanity is retroactively evoked in imagined opposition to the awesome Thing of nonexistence.

But history may have terminated already, as Baudrillard contends in *The Illusion of the End*, now moving in reverse over its ruins. All the 'non-degradable waste' of obsolete empires and grand narratives is reprocessed in 'the synthetic form of heteroclite history', so that, worse than the end of history, '*history will never come to an end* – since the leftover, all the leftovers – the

Church, communism, ethnic groups, conflicts, ideologies – are indefinitely recyclable' (Baudrillard 1994: 27). Here, history is completed in its endlessly recycled form by the 'mind children' who will surpass but not erase humanity: Hans Moravec's vision of superintelligent computer-generated machines running all the corporations and institutions of the global economy leads to the complete digital simulation of human culture and history, preserved with minute accuracy in the data banks of the future (Platt 1995). Where hope once relied on the reality of the apocalypse, the evanescence of that reality and the possibility of revelation means 'our Apocalypse is not real, it is virtual. And it is not in the future, it is *here and now*' (Baudrillard 1994: 119). The virtual apocalypse, neither religious nor transcendent, accommodates itself quietly to the familiar surfaces of the present. The immanence of technological praxis does not overcome reality, its idea sublimely grasped. Instead, in networks of innovation, circulation, exchange and replication, it produces itself and a host of objects in every act of communication and inscription, overwriting the void of reality with rapid relays of images. This literalisation at work in the virtual apocalypse means that everything can be realised, recoded and replicated. More than simulation, it involves a process of making real: the abyssal space of the Thing becomes the basic and invisible condition of terminal screens, filled out in the superficial depth that comes from the motion of endless image-objects. With the capacity to master or construct realities, capitalised technoscience assumes, in place of judgements based on reality, justice or rights, the role of sole authority, the future's only programme. And what is stake, it seems, is not so much the often proclaimed dignity, freedom and value of human life, but the in-human Thing without which all may be machine.

In *Neuromancer*, the meat – the accursed share of technological redundancy and thus the residually human, organic part – continues to talk: 'it'll change something', the novel suggests. The meat, however, is the leftover discarded in the death-driven romance of cyberspace. Romance heads for the stars without human body or form. Sublime power is glimpsed in its utterly inhuman shape. The future slides into darkness. Gothic shapes return, spectres of fear and anxiety: cybergothic.

As gothic cedes to cybergothic, the genre's cultural role in screening off an ultimate, formless horror with familiar figures of fear is turned on its head: gothic shapes occlude a darker and more destructive romantic flight, a return, not from the past, but from the future. Drawing on the images of ruined urban centres, wasted bodies and wired minds from cyberpunk fictions and film (*Neuromancer*, *Blade Runner* and *Terminator*), 'cybergothic' describes the machinic economic and biotechnological systems that have escaped the control of human agents and institutions: 'v(amp)iro finance' pushes economic functioning to a sexually and financially promiscuous degree; productive and efficient to an extent that exceeds any human grasp, there is no control mechanism at work to regulate human production, reproduction and consumption (Land 1998: 80; 86–87). Replicants, terminators, clones, cyborgs – in this new world order – may assume dark gothic costumes as latter-day monsters or vampires but they do so, not to shore up the collapsing machinery of modernity and provide the illusory and vain comfort of familiarly horrifying images, but to infiltrate and destroy modernity's defences: gothic shapes provide only the disguise that allows an inhuman future to assemble itself in the ruins of modernity, 'the future of runaway processes derides all precedent, even when deploying it as camouflage, and seeming to unfold within its parameters'(Land 1993b: 476). The disguise points in two directions: to a past – modernity, already in ruins – and to a future embraced as fantastically apocalyptic, sublime, inhuman, destructive and romantic all over again.

# 2 Romance consumed

Death, simulation and the vampire

## The gothic crisp

[. . .] skidding, half-falling in a scramble-slide over slick stones and the pulp-dust of rotten masonry [. . .] crash-landing among the soggy litter of cardboard and butts, broken bottles, crushed cans and crumpled polythene packages strewn over the floor of the hollow beneath the ruin. Panting and choking in the stale air of the dingy, subterranean sanctuary, he carefully withdrew his precious prize. In the gloom, the dark bag was invisible. By touch alone, he traced its form. So light, almost without substance. The hard sheen of the surface compressed slightly under the pressure of supplicant fingers. A movement inside, or so it seemed. He shivered.

Dark diamond of exquisite desire.

On his knees, he pushed towards a patch of light, eager to feast his eyes upon the object that had so long eluded him. The square puffed packet was utterly black. Its glossy surface reflected nothing, seeming to suck all light into itself.

A shudder forced him from his reverie. He had no idea of how long had he been staring absently yet with such intent. Now plenitude beckoned. He pinched the sides and gently pulled the sealed seam apart, releasing a deep whisper. In an instant a fetid breath, a stench so vile and viscous, oozed out to envelop his heaving frame with the sensation of a chill, excrementally rank slime. Momentarily he paused to shake revulsion from desire. He peered within: utterly black. Slowly, he inserted his right hand, two fingers creeping to withdraw a single wafer pinned between their tips. It was like nothing he had ever seen: its ethereal thinness had an ivory pallor that was almost transparent, though he could see nothing through it. It existed as no more than a blur in his field of vision.

And now the wafer moved near his pursed lips. It slid between his teeth to lie on the dryly expectant tongue. He closed his mouth to bite, on almost nothing. He waited. Then his whole body became suffused with alternating currents of lurid heat and needling ice. Every taste he had ever tasted along with an unimaginable multitude of other flavours pulsed through him. His eyes rolled back on waves of sickly delight; his body convulsed in suffocating torrents of delicious nausea. His mouth gaped wide in an ecstasy pleading for more.

It clamped shut on its own hollow darkness.

From an inner crevice that seemed to surround him, something began crawl and twitch. A body – his body – sucked on itself, expanding and contracting in a glutinous cacophony. Limbs, then torso, ballooned; bones shrank and shrank, cracking and crumbling away. An incredible agony consumed him, moved beyond him, flying toward a florescent darkness. He watched as if from elsewhere. The palpitating sac puffed out its parts and shrivelled back, as if squeezed by an enormous unseen hand. Stretched membranes, no longer discernible as arm or leg, puffed and shrivelled, stiffened and trembled, becoming darker and slimier after every pulse. It seemed as if they were about to burst and drape the walls in their black and glowing ooze. But suddenly the hollow was as it had been before, gloomy and littered and damp, and with only an additional crumple of black cellophane beside the wrinkled, filmy patch of darkness.

(Marshal 63–64)

So climaxes the curious short story entitled 'Wafers of death'. Published as part of a collection of short stories in 1999 by a small press, the tale is as improbable a fiction as any in the gothic tradition. Thoroughly immersed in familiar gothic motifs and themes, what is striking and particularly improbable about the story is the manner in which it combines all-too common features from the genre's past with a very contemporary setting and an unusual central object of mystery – one as far removed as possible from any gothic associations. The story's ending takes place beneath the ruins of a church; the fleeing protagonist, a victim of his own excessive curiosity, like any eighteenth-century gothic heroine, finds himself to be a participant in a supernatural communion, his mysterious quest culminating in an atmosphere of gloom, darkness and apprehension. The religious overtones, after the fatal taste of the sacramental wafer, assume a more corporeal focus, spiritual terror succeeded by bodily horror as the protagonist enjoys an almost orgasmic dissolution, a joyfully anguished disintegration of physical boundaries in death. The act of consumption which leads to dissolution recalls the 'racking pangs', the 'grinding in the bones' and 'deadly nausea' of Jekyll's transformation into Hyde (Stevenson 83), or the 'dark and putrid mass, seething with corruption and hideous rottenness' that describes the final stages of chemically-induced decomposition in Arthur Machen's *The Novel of the White Powder* (233).

From eighteenth-century terrors and enlightened ruins to decadent and regressive nineteenth-century excesses, the story combines sacred and sexual anxieties, conjoining moral prohibitions and transgressions with abhuman pleasures and horrors. With the obscene transformation at the close, moreover, fears of alien possession and awful mutation are also conjured up. However, the story centres on the quest for a particular and mysterious bag of potato crisps. It begins with excited whispers in a secondary school classroom, with reverent speculations on the existence and marvellous properties of a mythical bag of crisps. The trail warms up amid various strange occurrences until, in the competitive heat of the chase, one teenager snatches the packet and flees to enjoy his prize alone. While this might seem an odd and unsuitable context in which to situate a gothic story, the setting seems canny enough in its recognition of the way in which the genre has developed in recent years. The teenage milieu of the story complements the baby boom audience addressed by post-war B-movie horror, a genre and marketing match neatly pastiched in a scene from *Scream* showing a classroom debate on the stock conventions and predictable formulas of horror cinema. High school teenage horror forms the basic ingredient of one of the most popular gothic television series of the last decade: *Buffy the Vampire Slayer* failed at the movie theatres but succeeded on the small screen, its high-kicking heroine and her gang of misfit slay-groupies, staking and beheading their way through countless demons, monsters and undead and through plots archly self-conscious of their generic precedents.

The gothic treatment of teenage angst, sexual uncertainty and social alienation, then, informs the location of 'Wafers of death'. In particular, the scene of fatal consumption appears as little more than the secret den where the rites of illicit intoxication are performed: the leftovers of the packaging of cigarettes, alcohol, solvents, pills and powders litter its floor as the more portentous signs of contemporary ruin and degradation. The story thus draws upon parental and social concerns directed at the problematic position of the teenager and, dressed up in gothic melodrama, presents its warning against the dangers of chemical excess. But, in its recycling of gothic images and entangling of social anxieties, the story attempts a broader and more critical articulation of cultural concerns. Consumption itself is set up as a site of horror. The crisps that are overdressed in mock-gothic garb and hyperbolically invested with such lethal and supernatural properties are one of the most banal and ubiquitous and insubstantial items of consumer enjoyment. To invest such innocuous commodities with overblown powers is to emphasise their symbolic status at the expense of the laws of probability and thereby stretch credulity beyond any fictional limit. Nonetheless, this exercise in evacuating and then reconstructing the meaning of objects and signs lies at the heart of consumer society, with advertising, marketing and branding repeatedly capitalising on the power of simulation to sell goods and stimulate desires (Wernick; Goldman and Papson). If the packet of crisps in the story were to be branded, it would come under the registered trademark of the 'Death' brand, which purveyed cigarettes and vodka with black labels bearing the image of a skull and crossbones. Death crisps only take this logic to a ridiculous, yet telling, limit.

Death, sex, consumption. Their conjunction, in gothic traditions, is as long-standing as it is entangled. From the first gothic story – Walpole's *The Castle of Otranto* – illegitimate desires for bodies, property and power were circumscribed by the increasingly dominant commercial imperatives of the eighteenth century. Though looking back to a fantasised feudal past, the fictions were thoroughly immersed in the anxieties of the present, with sexual excesses, terrors, horrors and death forming the screen on which economic and social tensions were projected and displaced. In conjunction with the taste for sensibility, the gothic fiction of Ann Radcliffe disclosed ideological tensions and new alignments of social values and economic practices. Sensibility serves to 'underwrite both laissez-faire capitalism and the self-regulating society the English bourgeoisie desired' (Poovey 311). As a society defining itself in terms of morality, utility and reason, the dangerous excesses threatening social order were identified with unrestrained passions. Heroines manifest a susceptibility to passion, its dangers marked out by disobedience towards paternal authority and dutiful conduct: their curiosity and lack of rational control leads them into an immoderate and vicious world of darkness, horror and villainy. The latter brings forth the new anti-social dangers of a 'masculine passion of unregulated, individualistic, avaricious desire'. Hence, a single woman's value, in a combination of symbolic and economic registers, is 'tied to both sexual purity and endowed property' (Poovey 323). The moral and material bourgeois order fantastically resolves its tensions through a providential reward of virtue and, often fatal, punishment of vice.

Gothic fiction and its new formations of character are uncertainly positioned between a 'traditional genealogy-based model of identity', associated with aristocratic decline and a 'market-based model' in which relations are more fluid and mobile, in tune with the patterns of trade and commerce (Henderson 226). Indeed, surfaces and appearances rather than interior and private developments disclose economic pressures such as the move from use-value to exchange-value and circulation of paper currency over gold. Hence, gothic forms ought not to be judged according to Romantic standards as a *bildungsroman* 'gone awry' but as a genre that 'traces problems in the perception or "consumption" of other people rather than the work involved in personal growth'(Henderson 240). In an unstable economic context in which social relations and sexual identities are grounded less on land and genealogy and more on paper, in markets and on surfaces, consumption, though a necessary part of commercial and productive circulation, becomes a site of concern because it threatens to exceed the rationality and morality forming the basis of bourgeois order. Adam Smith, whose justification of the selfish circulations of the new economy itself finds a quasi-supernatural guarantor in the 'invisible hand' that ultimately shares out some of the benefits of wealth, notes the lack of limitation that defines consumer desire: while the desire of food is limited by the size of the stomach, 'the desire of the conveniencies and ornaments of building, dress, equipage, and household furniture, seems to have *no limit or certain boundary*' (cit. Adriopoulos 745). Consumption assumes the form of a spectre exceeding the restraints of morality and reason. The appeal, beyond need or use, of fabrics, clothes, ornaments, all sorts of household objects and goods, implies the emergence of consumerism, with the 'middling classes' beginning to buy larger quantities of goods that expressed 'individuality, self-differentiation and luxury'. It is problematic, however, to assume that this easily prefigures 'modern patterns of consumption' (Styles 540). The complex conditions involve economic, aesthetic and ideological factors, requiring not only new material and social practices but shifts in taste and expectation. For Colin Campbell, 'autonomous, illusory hedonism, combined with the ranking of pleasure above comfort' defines modern consumerism (48). Sensibility, with its emphasis on the perception and presentation of individual aesthetic appreciation and emotion, plays a part in the new ethic shaping consumers because 'objects which advertised their taste' were 'also indicative of their moral standing'. Where aristocratic customs, attitudes and style also inform consumerism, its emphasis on honour rather than pleasure and passion checks the development. Instead, the romantic idealisation of character is required: its 'sensitivity to pleasure' stimulates and legitimates autonomous and illusory hedonism 'by providing the highest possible motives with which to justify daydreaming, longing and the rejection of reality, together with the pursuit of originality in life and art; by so doing it enables pleasure to be ranked above comfort and counteracts both traditional and utilitarian restraints on the expression of desire' (Campbell 53–54).

The tension between moral regulation and markets is manifested within and in reaction to gothic fictions. Luxurious consumption, material ambition and selfish desire provide the hallmarks of villains whose aristocratic dress covers up their more venal bourgeois vices. The emerging order thus projects its less appealing qualities onto the class it supplanted, while at the same time assuming, to a lesser extent, more virtuous traits of gallantry, honour and manners as its own. Heroines, moreover, must learn the moral and economic value of virtuous behaviour by confronting the effects of irrationality and impropriety that their curiosity and lack of discrimination brings about: the terrors and horrors, the threats of death and violation at the hands of rapacious villains, ensure the purging of vice and excess and the return to a bourgeois propriety, its rules and polite codes of behaviour, that links personal worth to the value of one's property. A moral lesson, particularly in Radcliffe's fiction, checks the obvious dangers of passionate, consuming excess. In imagining and resolving excessive consumption, fiction suggests that the actual extent of consumption is less than its imagined dangers. Desire, or passion, in excess of reason and morality, is presented as a major threat in a genre that is repeatedly criticised for its stimulation of consuming excesses. Attacked by critics for its excitation of antisocial desires and immoral appetites, gothic fiction sexualises consumption: female readers and writers are regularly blamed for arousing romantic passions, indulging wanton sensation and encouraging licentious pleasure beyond the control of reason and propriety (Williams 1970). Reading fiction is seen as a useless indulgence, a dangerous waste of time: it misdirects energy towards improper identifications and vicious ideas and thereby corrupts character and destroys social bonds. Consumption, then, appears in moral, economic and corporeal senses as waste, corruption and destruction: using things up in excess of need or rational purpose, it is a luxurious squandering of resources that eats away at the health of the individual, family and society. It leads to that ultimate horror and final consumption, death (Porter).

Towards the end of the nineteenth century, and in the wake of its massive expansion of industrial modes of production, the mass consumption of standardised commodities becomes more apparent as a social phenomenon, though it remains nonetheless subject to scrutiny and criticism. A stronger, sexual connotation to consumption, in the sense of *consommation*, or the intense expenditure of energy, is also brought to bear. In her reading of *The Picture of Dorian Gray*, Rachel Bowlby traces the links between the aesthete and the consumer, the Wildean aphorism and the commercial advertisement: 'he lives the dream life of the aesthetic consumer, culling momentary impressions and satisfactions from a world which withholds nothing and offers everything. His continual search for "new sensations" involves treating the world as a source of subjective gratification to be enjoyed and used up' (156–57). The proximity of art and consumption, both privileging pleasure and desire, occurs in a context in which identities are both aestheticised and commodified, and subjected to the fluid and shifting patterns of consumer existence. Such decadence, of course, threatened the disintegration of social bonds, the insistence on pleasure weakening the social fabric to the extent of portending the degeneration of civilisation as whole. The aesthete, the homosexual, the 'New Woman', embody the challenge to social and sexual mores and the subversion of all stable boundaries (see Senf; Craft; Pick; Dyer). Femininity, represented in vampiric terms, focused the anxieties of masculine sexual, symbolic and material economies: 'woman, having been consumed in the marriage market, then having become consumptive as a wife through lack of respect, exercise, and freedom, took her revenge by becoming a voracious consumer' (Dijkstra 355). The vampire, with its foreignness, animality, unnaturalness, depraved appetites, condenses fears of decadence and regression, of a culture consumed by the return of all that it has repressed. *Dracula* does not, however, only look back to the pre-historical, atavistic or mythic energies threatening to consume civilisation. As both Dijkstra and Jennifer Wicke note, the novel has a prospective dimension, demonstrated by its absorption with numerous features of mass culture and its media. Photographs, shorthand, phonographs, guide books and timetables indicate the pressures of technological innovation and consumption. Circulating, undead, like photographic images, Dracula's correspondence to mass culture is displayed in his 'protean' and mutating form, his invitation into the home the start of a process contaminating the leisure class (Wicke 476). His disciple, Renfield, also manifests the '"phagous" nature of consumption' (Wicke 478–79). While the disruptions of the vampire, like other figures of deviance and danger, are expelled or exorcised, thereby restoring the norms of familial life and reforming the boundaries of life and death, the undeath of the image as it circulates through mass culture remains much less easily confined. With the circulation and consumption of images, neither sex nor death defines an inviolable limit, nor do they harness the force of prohibition or taboo.

At the end of the twentieth century, the alignment and significance of sex, death and consumption begins to suggest a different set of meanings and values to those which gothic fictions of modernity drew upon so greedily. The realignment concerns the boundaries that gothic figures marked out in the realms of social taboos and anxieties; the limits transgressed and charted by figures of terror and horror. Once considered 'the most private of things', 'the realm of life in which we are most ourselves', sex is now advertised with abandon (Dyer 56). No more than a simple norm of social interaction, it is encouraged rather than prohibited in the circulation of images and signs. Everywhere visible and sought out, its thrills succumb to a waning of interest (Lotringer; Heath). Hence, the appeal of death as a final taboo: an ultimate limit, the darkness of which cannot be penetrated, the finality of which draws a line of horror and law. But the frisson of this limit, replacing the thrill of sex, offers opportunities for transgression and speculation and profit, a site to be capitalised on. As the cook observes in Peter Greenaway's *The Cook, the Thief, his Wife and her Lover*, black food warrants a premium: a souvenir of death to come, it is a commodity for which the consumer must pay a higher price. Here lies the appeal of the death brand: that which is most disavowed extracts the greatest profit; one pays for what cannot have, exchanging one's money for that which is beyond exchange. There is a perverse short circuit at work, however, in which sex, death and consumption assume a new status on a different plane: the taboo which restores the limit of prohibition, thereby invigorating the frisson and the tenacity of desire, renders death a commodity. Death, once at the impossible horizon of desire, the very gap of unattainability in a culture in which every desire is catered for and instantly gratified, finds itself on the shelf with all the other goods on display. This is the paradox of the death brand: in reactivating desire through the restoration of an ultimate limit (to be imaginarily crossed in consumption) the advertised spectre of death is relocated in the circuits of exchange and marketed like any other commodity. Death is feasted upon and simulated at the same time, stimulating and deferring desire which trails, ultimately unsatisfied, through an endless chain of consumables. Emptied of the affect (like sex) that comes with the charge of prohibition or taboo at the same time that such intensity is capitalised upon, death is rendered a hollow object of exchange, over which almost gratified desire, ever-unsatisfied-ever-to-be-satisfied, aimlessly trails. The real thing, of course, is missed, hovering phantom-like in the future.

Divested, like sex, of its horrifying limits and erotic charge, death is repositioned. No longer does it mark an absolute consumption, a final using up or expenditure of energies. The excesses – of vice, unreason, sexuality or decadence – from which gothic fiction variously recoiled for over two hundred years of modernity no longer establish cultural limits: they become incorporated. Indeed, 'postmodern capitalism', having eschewed the regulating principles of reason, morality or utility, encourages wasteful expenditure and luxurious indulgence, capitalising upon uncertain desires to enjoin consumption without limits (Goux 1990). In this world of consumption, death is situated both at the end of the system, marking its 'term', and as the 'extermination' that stalks it: death is 'in-scribed' and 'ex-scribed' in systemic functioning; it 'haunts it everywhere' (Baudrillard 1993a, 5, n. 1). The locus of consumption is internalised in the expenditures and excesses of the postmodern economy, dependent on a ghostly figure of exhaustion, its operations generated by the spectre of being used up. An empty figure for 'general equivalence', death forms the strange basis for economic circulation in an age of simulation and hyperreality, ensuring the 'reversibility' and exchangeability of all things and signs (Baudrillard 1993a: 146). Positioned in this way, death announces that 'the principle of simulation governs us now, rather than the outdated reality principle. We *feed* on these forms whose finalities have disappeared. No more ideology, only simulacra' (Baudrillard 1993a: 2). '"Natural" death' becomes banal: there is no exchange, no interest. Only when the 'phantasm of sacrifice' is approximated in 'the violent artifice of death' – a car crash, for example – is there any degree of fascination: the disruption of the system, its derailing or breakdown, briefly and spectacularly unmasks the absence over which simulations circulate (Baudrillard 1993a: 164–65). Naturalised to the point of banality, death's only value is as artifice. Otherwise, Baudrillard argues, taking his cue from Victor Hugo in the nineteenth century, the 'hygienic' imperatives of contemporary culture enact a sterilisation of death, cleansing it and, at the same time, rinsing its traces throughout the cultural sphere:

> the make-up of death: Hugo's formula makes us think of those American funeral homes where death is immediately shielded from mourning and the promiscuity of the living in order to be 'designed' according to the purest laws of standing, smiling and international marketing.
>
> (Baudrillard 1993a: 180)

Cleaned and made up, the dead in these homes become the most placid of vampires in the indifference they introduce between life and death: retaining 'the appearance of life', the corpse 'still smiles at you, the same colours, the same skin', seeming 'himself even after death'. This is a 'faked death, idealised in the colours of life', a death '*naturalised* in a stuffed simulacrum of life' (Baudrillard 1993a: 181). The life once simulated by the undead becomes the simulation of life already subjected to the general orders of simulation. The symbolic tremors and revulsions once caused by the figure of the vampire seem, in a culture in which symbolic limits and prohibitions barely pertain, to mark only the erosion of all boundaries, but without horrific intensity.

The naturalised, sterilised dead, still smiling in the comfort of their (funeral) homes, quietly disturb contemporary subjectivity. Instead of mourning, the ritual activity through which the loved dead one's absence is introjected and the symbolic fabric is repaired, the subject is left in a state of melancholy:

> the unconscious is subject in its entirety to the distortion of the death of a symbolic process (exchange, ritual) into an economic process (redemption, labour, debt, individual). This entails a considerable difference in enjoyment: we trade with our dead in a kind of melancholy, while the

primitives live with their dead under the auspices of the ritual and the feast.

(Baudrillard 1993a: 134–35)

Quietly pervasive, death leaves the subject gently disquieted, overcome by a haunting melancholy. Symbolic processes are evacuated, their injunctions and rituals, along with the dead, neutralised, and their limits effaced by the generalised exchanges of postmodern consumption and simulation.

The implications of this shift from an order of production to one of simulation are extensive, as Baudrillard's provocative writings contend. Without a symbolic framework to differentiate between signs and meanings, to discriminate values and limits and to direct desires, anything goes: 'we have transgressed everything, including the limits of scene and truth'. Fundamental distinctions are voided: 'no more black magic of the forbidden, alienation and transgression, but the white magic of ecstasy, fascination, transparency. It's the end of the pathos of the law' (Baudrillard 1990a, 71). The carefully policed cultural substrates that harboured the intensities of desire and transgression lose their force without the charge of law's prohibition: the very loci of darkness and taboo where sex, death and the gothic prospered throughout modernity lose their definition as the line distinguishing them and symbolic law is erased in the movement of freedom and marketing. For Baudrillard, it is liberation that causes a reversal and flattening of all boundaries, subjecting them to a crossing and blurring associated with 'trans': transaesthetics, transsexuality, transeconomics (Baudrillard 1993b: 17). Liberation, indeed, once it bypasses the charge of prohibition, transgression and negativity, engenders a pervasive neutralisation of symbolic boundaries and intensities. The relationship between sex and death is no exception:

> Speaking of death makes us laugh in a strained and obscene manner. Speaking of sex no longer provokes the same reaction: sex is legal, only death is pornographic. Society having 'liberated' sexuality, progressively replaces it with death which functions as a secret rite and fundamental prohibition. In a previous, religious phase, death was revealed, recognised while sexuality was prohibited. Today the opposite is true. But all 'historical' societies are arranged so as to dissociate sex and death in every possible way, and play the liberation of one off against the other – which is a way of neutralising them both.
>
> (Baudrillard 1993a, 184)

Sex, liberated to death, is neutralised; death, made-up like life, is naturalised. Both are voided and rendered banal, except, perhaps, when combined in the violent and artificial intensity of the crash when flows of economic and signifying circulation are briefly, but spectacularly and shockingly, interrupted. In the crash, or, rather, in its traumatic afterlife, there remain the ghostly traces of the thrill attendant on crossing a (sexualised or erotically fatal) limit.

Death, like sex and consumption, is absorbed on the same, general plane of simulation. The ridiculous banality of the 'gothic crisp', of course, makes this point as it entwines an entire, gothicised history of consumption with a commodity that tells the story of simulacra and simulation. There can be little in the realm of consumption that is more (chemically) artificial a foodstuff than the crisp, few things so obviously simulated in terms of flavour and so far removed from nutritional substance. Indeed, the development of crisps neatly illustrates the orders of simulation identified by Baudrillard in *Symbolic Exchange and Death*. Following the model of the 'counterfeit' that attends the move from the Renaissance to the industrial order of production, the crisp, via new investments in consumption, finds itself inscribed in the shift towards the realm of simulations and the hyperreal (Baudrillard 1993a, 31–50). Baudrillard delineates the successive orders of the image (through which simulation envelops representation) thus: first, as 'the reflection of a basic reality', then masking and perverting 'basic reality', then masking 'the *absence* of basic reality' and, finally, bearing 'no relation to any reality whatsoever' – 'its own pure simulation' (Baudrillard 1983: 11). In terms of potato crisps, thin discs of oily vegetable liberally garnished with chemical flavourings, there are four related clusters. 'Plain', 'Ready Salted', 'Salt and Vinegar', 'Cheese and Onion', 'Smoky Bacon' reflect the basic (snack)food reality of chips – with salt and vinegar added, and sandwiches filled with cheese and onion or bacon. The next cluster refers not to food but to flavourings of food, that is to the masking or perverting of the taste of food. Examples include 'Prawn Cocktail' (the sauce is important), 'Worcester Sauce', 'Bovril', 'Marmite' and 'Tomato Sauce' flavours. In the third category – that which masks the 'absence' of basic reality (forgetting for purposes of illustration that all crisps as simulations actually emerge in this space), comes, uniquely, the 'Hedgehog flavour' crisp. Discounting legends about baking it in clay, there is no general social convention sanctioning the consumption of the hedgehog, if edible at all, and hence no basic reality to which the crisp flavour refers, thus no possibility of assessing the verisimilitude of the taste. Instead, in pointing to the absence underlying the repertoire of crisp flavourings, 'hedgehog flavour' discloses their general artificiality and points to the emergence of the 'pure simulacrum' of crisp self-referentiality. Here, simulation takes over, the 'Salt and Lineker' variety being its prime example: alluding to an earlier variety in the play of names, the principal reference is to a famous English international footballer, Gary

Lineker, now turned television personality and presenter. The celebrity, famed for his geniality, turns malevolent crisp stealer in numerous commercials; the crisps he endorses, moreover, are those that bear his name. A self-referential chain of simulation expands around the celebrity and 'his' crisp flavour (though there are no endorsements guaranteeing that they even approximate to the taste of the person himself): manufactured in Leicester, the home of the crisps is also home to Leicester City, the side supported by Lineker, for whom he played and who now wear the crisp maker's name across their shirts. The reflexive circuit of simulation is extended further: 'Salt and Lineker' were the first of a new genre of crisps imbued with celebrity football associations: 'Cheese and Owen' bring the new outstanding striker in English football, Michael Owen, into the chain.

Were it not for the 'gothic crisp', such a chain of simulations would be ridiculously distant from worlds of darkness, desire and fear. But, it seems, gothic images are themselves caught up in such a banal play of simulations, unable to generate the intensity and frisson once accorded their indulgences in sexual and morbid horrors. Disabling transgression in its liberation of all desires and taboos, the plane of consumerist simulation conjures up and renders banal all images of otherness. Gothic is disneyfied, along with everything else as western history draws to a close, its leftovers repackaged and recycled. According to Baudrillard, the Disney brand, founded by a man who has been cryogenically frozen in the hope of staving off death, exemplifies the way that simulations erase all otherness, all difference, all temporality. A place 'where all past and present forms meet in playful promiscuity, where all cultures recur in mosaic', Disney is not imaginary but presents

> a prefiguration of the real trend of things – Disneyworld opening for us the bewildering perspective of passing through all the earlier stages, as in a film, with those stages hypostasized in a definitive juvenility, frozen like Disney himself in liquid nitrogen: Magic Country, Future World, Gothic, Hollywood itself reconstituted fifty years on in Florida, the whole of the past and the future revisited as living simulation.
>
> (Baudrillard 1994: 115)

Gothic, significantly, is prominent in Baudrillard's list of Disney attractions. Its function, too, in the late twentieth century can also be defined in terms of Disney: where, as an example of hyperreality, the latter serves to 'conceal the fact that it is the "real" country, all of "real" America, which *is* Disneyland', so the former, with its dark horrors and desires, screens the possibility of a real world of sex, of death, of catastrophic consumption, outside of simulation, occluding the way that such a world is already a nostalgic projection, an anoriginal fiction (Baudrillard 1983: 25).

Gothic fiction, its devices and modes of production, is bound up with the development of simulacra and simulations. According to Jerrold Hogle in a series of essays exploring the development of gothic signification, the genre emerges as a 'counterfeit', situating itself between a Renaissance and a commercial era, nostalgic and prospective in its outlook. The first fiction, Walpole's *Otranto*, draws on *Hamlet* and employs its signs 'as partially empty recollections of former statuses (being still *nostalgic* for absolute grounds themselves) and as announcements of "natures" that could seem recoined, rhetorically transformed, or simply masked (counterfeited into a "questionable shape") by new displays of social position that reused signifiers of older ones' (Hogle 1998a: 188). Fakery surrounds *Otranto*, its story, its history of production and its setting (Hogle 1994). Walpole's neo-gothic makes reference to 'an antiquated belief-system, as in the reference to his ghosts to portraits, effigies, outdated emblems of sin'. Its origins lie in 'the already broken, empty, and (often) fake nature of the icons he adopts and refashions' (Hogle 1998a: 189). The counterfeited past of the fiction thus enables a move from the 'bound' order of medievalism to the 'unbound' fluctuations of the eighteenth-century free market, cloaking the latter in fake images of the former in the way that Walpole blends ancient and modern romance 'to promote more market success' (Hogle 1998a: 190). Later variations of gothic writing move progressively into the realm of the simulacrum that is associated with the emergence of industrial modes of production. Hence, *Frankenstein* 'continues this "Gothic" ghosting and remarketing of the counterfeit, even to the point of showing the ghost of the counterfeit turning into the simulacrum of industrialized reproduction', as it turns from alchemy to science (Hogle 1998a: 191). *Dracula*, written eight decades later, is located in a context of bourgeois sign-production in which a nostalgia for 'older sureties of reference' vies with a textuality 'conscripted into capitalistic exchanges of signs for signs' where selves are presented 'in outward figures that are reproduced mechanically' (Hogle 1998b: 210). From its opening, Stoker's novel simulates a range of (stock) gothic precedents in its settings and aristocratic villain. But the theatrical background to its composition emphasises its entanglement with new orders of simulations, including new media: theatre, simulation and 'recast Gothic' are all 'especially pointed enactments of the Western progression in human self-projection from the use of the sign as counterfeit to the simulation of simulacra of counterfeits of the past' (Hogle 1998b: 217). The layers of self-reference to a tradition of counterfeiting and simulation, absorb gothic fiction within a play of images and self-reflections whose trajectory moves further and further from illusions of reality even as it engages more closely with the simulations that increasingly give shape to the experience of modernity.

Since its inception, a modern invention, gothic fiction has fabricated its figures and phantasms, counterfeit ghosts and terrors conjured up as the other side to reason and enlightenment. As gothic fiction enters a world of simulation, its artifices are redoubled in the screens of simulation. A world of simulations does not, then, dispense with ghosts, phantasms, vampires, doubles. On the contrary, they proliferate among the exorbitant effects of simulation, throwing up recycled shapes of haunted modernity as well as its ghosts. Around the screens and psyches of the present there float figures that are the leftovers of a thoroughly liberated world, ghosts of transgression, death and darkness, faint, phantasmatic, fake assurances of a realm beyond simulation. But these ghosts do not stay in their allotted place. The world of simulations is multiply haunted, with entertaining ghosts of the 'disney-gothic' variety circulating freely with figures of anxiety and alienated subjectivity: these ghosts return from the past giving old form to new fears; they leap forward to dress an uncertain future; they mark the transitional states between economic and social formations. Old gothic un-familiars, dressed in heritage attire, thus call up spectres of reality and history already absorbed by disneyscreens of simulation; but the technological and economic forces of the hyperreal disclose tears in the screen of reality, gaps to be populated by yet more ghosts.

The epochal shifts in economic production and consumption give rise to hauntings in the realm of goods and things. The shift from feudal to industrial production presents commodities in the form of use-value, the move forward, towards industry and markets, legitimated with a retrospective gloss. This double perspective frames 'Nature' with 'a ghostly existence as use-value at the core of exchange-value' (Baudrillard 1993a: 2). With the incursions of simulation, commodities are defined in productive terms according to the logic of exchange value 'the better to hide the fact that it circulates like a sign and reproduces the code' (Baudrillard 1993a: 31). Here, the relationship between money and commodities assumes a spectral form (Žižek 1997: 103). Gothicised, the new economic order appears quite familiar: with the help of technology, it sucks the life from human bodies. Capital, furnished with new tools, still feeds like a vampire, in the manner that, according to Marx, it has done since the nineteenth century (Marx 1976: 342; 1973: 646). New mechanisms of capital turn all consumers into vampiric feeders. Technoscientific changes posit a new relationship and a new identification in which the vampire is less the metaphor of a cruel and voracious system and more a figure for a humanity struggling to find an identity for itself. Donna Haraway's vampire – in a world in which biotechnologies and capital challenge the very bases of human existence – presents a more sympathetic if troubled outcast posing questions of racial and sexual transformation for a humanity becoming cyborg, reprogrammed and redefined by networks of information and genetic knowledge (Haraway 1997: 214–15).

For her, new questions of social and familial bonds have to be raised, new issues of psyche, mortality and identity posed:

> It is time to theorize an unfamiliar unconscious, a different primal scene, where everything does not stem from the dramas of identity and reproduction. Ties through blood – including blood recast in the coin of genes and information – have been bloody enough already. I believe that there will be no racial or sexual peace, no liveable nature, until we learn to produce humanity though something more and less like kinship. I think I am on the side of the vampires, or at least some of them. But, then, since when does one get to choose which vampire will trouble one's dreams?
>
> (Haraway 1997: 265)

Mortality, reproduction, kinship, tied by blood to nineteenth-century modes of (social) (re)production, no longer have the vampire as their horrific antithesis. Informatics (the alignment of genetic and information technology with networks of capital) requires an identification with the vampire as a liminal and uncertain being. For Baudrillard, 'our entire culture is full of this haunting of the separated double' and thus demands a different image for the subject: 'a vengeful vampiric double, an unquiet soul, the double begins to prefigure the subject's death haunting him in the very midst of his life' (Baudrillard 1993a: 142). The subject of consumption and simulation finds him or herself in the unreflecting vampiric mirror, absorbed by the screens of hyperreality. These screens pervade everyday existence with their calls to correct consumption and promotion of dietary and fitness regimes. Undead images overcome the inevitability of death, as Anne Rice observes: 'in the United States, now, there are people who really think that if they jog, eat the right food, take the right vitamins and wear the right clothes and meditate, they're not going to die. And whenever anybody has died, they just didn't do those things' (Rice 1999: 178). With the discovery (and patenting, no doubt) of the 'Methuselah gene' controlling aging, the line that wavers due to the presence of the double, will find itself erased: humans cross over to the realm of the undead. Vampires are made flesh via genetic therapies and scientific screens. Western practices, indeed, display vampiric characteristics in their political and economic relationship to the developing world: for Baudrillard 'humanitarian interference' in the affairs and disasters of Southern hemisphere states takes the form of a 'bloodsucking protection' (Baudrillard 1994: 67). Vampirism is indistinguishable from western consumption: 'Vampires, old or new, are cannibals feeding on the world around them, acting out in their own persons the bloody support system that sustains our lives – my shoes made by sweated labor in Brazil, my meat from castrated and constrained animals' (Zanger 26). In other forms, too, a world of once phantasmatic ghosts is actualised technologically, the clone enabling a 'materialization of a double by genetic means' (Baudrillard 1993b: 116). In hyperreality, it is not only boundaries of self and other, or life and death that are rendered uncertain: the double, a figure of interior states in modernity, assumes a material form and the world becomes palpably ghostly.

Once exiled and outcast as figures of horror, deviancy or decadence, the monsters, ghosts and doubles of the gothic tradition find themselves absorbed and recycled as common images of a contemporary condition that is itself shifting and uncertain, having lost its secure ties to the natural or social body, in the form of sexuality or death, kinship and blood. The recycling, moreover, contributes to a further disneyfication of gothic figures, a double simulation in which the attempt, retrospectively, to situate a realm of fear, darkness and transgression outside simulation, is brought more fully within the orbit of simulation and its lightly disquieting shimmer of strange sameness. Pervasive, almost normal, the mildly anxious circulation of gothic images attests only to the general dislocation experienced in the move to a life on, or determined by, the omnipresence of screens, an absorption of, or consumption by, flickering doubles whose difference is difficult, if not impossible, to ascertain. Gothic fictions, at the end of the twentieth century, perform a double, contrary function: exhuming the traces, calling up residues barely charged with intensities, horrors, repulsions that would restore limits and re-mark boundaries, their vague spread only signals the disturbances and insecurity of a world without limits, one consumed by general deviations and excessive expenditures, caught up in flows of unending simulation.

## Hypocrite vampire . . .

In 1976, the year that *Symbolic Exchange and Death* appeared in France, Anne Rice published *Interview with the Vampire*. For all its francophilia, moving from the rougher pleasures of transplanted French culture in New Orleans to the decadent delights of nineteenth-century Paris, there appears little that directly or self-consciously connects the vampire story to the emerging hyperreal world. The narrative form displays few of the features associated with postmodernism, the aesthetic by-product of post-industrial society. Little generic play is in evidence in the monotones of its confessional, autobiographical mode, and little sense of a parodic stance emerges in course of retelling the passions and ennui attendant on the vampire's adventures. As a blend of the romantic tale and the vampire story, the novel offers itself as an unreflective pastiche of genres that reached their peak in the 1790s and then the 1890s, to have their currency subsequently renewed through the appeal of popular cinema. The uncritical recycling of popular genres, along with the world-weary posture of its narrator, however, testifies to the 'waning of affect' displayed by postmodern aesthetics, a waning that stands in curious historical comparison to genres notorious for their stimulation of sensation and thrills. What Jameson describes as 'that boring and exhausted paradigm, the gothic', certainly seems to have run out of steam with *Interview* (1991: 10; 289). A similar point is made by Lestat in the second volume of Rice's series: romance is gone, evil is not what it used to be, vampires have become redundant.

If the novel formally fails to excite interest, the fact of it – and perhaps its popular success, tells another story. In rewriting the vampire tale, expanding vampire mythology and extending its geography, however, Rice turns it into an account of modernity, modernity, that is, on the cusp of the postmodern. At this point, the cultural conditions and theory of simulation outlined by Baudrillard have a significant impact on understanding Rice's reinvention of the vampire story as a simulacrum whose network of associations extend in retrospective and prospective directions. The novel performs the doubleness of simulation, combining a nostalgic simulacrum of a lost past and a narrative reconstructed as a simulacrum in the empty space of the present and its media. *Interview*'s account of modernity is framed by the scene of its enunciation in the present. In a grubby hotel room the vampire begins and ends his story in the presence of a fascinated young reporter. The setting for the narrative does not only highlight a scriptural technology, the speech that will become writing in the second volume (when *Interview*, the story goes, has become a bestseller in the fiction lists) but is recorded on magnetic tape to be broadcast on radio. Vampire fiction is disseminated through various different media, turning the unheard voice of vampiric ghost-writing into the ghostly telepresence of modern communications. The voice that is never heard in the story, moreover, recalls the phonographs of Stoker's novel. The long association between vampirism and technology is extended in the second volume to include the telepresentation of a form that is never seen: Lestat broadcasts his image via television and video to startling effect (indeed, technology's range and power delivers the loud awakening that provides the start for the third volume). Unheard voices, unseen figures in the narrative allude to the spectral shapes and ghostly sounds that circulate, undead, among twentieth-century media.

*Interview*, however, is more absorbed with traditional ghosts as its narrative restarts in the late eighteenth century. The romance, from this point, is tinged with Romanticism. The personal history of his development as vampire is recounted by Louis, reborn, or unborn, in 1791. Told in the first-person, with Louis' speech in quotation marks (Dyer 65), the story positions the reader on the side of the vampire, encouraging a phantasmatic readerly identification that, in the novel, seduces the reporter with the desire to become one of the undead (though the story and the way it is told communicates little of the vampire appeal). The focus of vampire subjectivity opens what was once a repulsive object of horrified speculation into a creature of extreme sensitivity and pathos. As Margaret Carter comments, the narrative position 'reflects a change in cultural attitudes towards the outsider', a Romantic effect that, in various contemporary fictions, turns the threat of the vampire into an attractive quality (27–29). The story thus blurs the line between a world of human subjects and terrifying, supernatural monsters. As with Mary Shelley's Romantic monster, the conferring of a voice within the text, endows the vampire with feelings, motives and, of course, a strange humanity. Strange, indeed, because Rice's humanised vampire still feeds, albeit reluctantly, on human blood. Here, vampire mythology requires adaptation: vampire lore moves closer to a natural justice in that victims are supposed to be chosen from the murderous, criminal and undeserving classes of humankind. Strangely, then, in its respect for life and justice, vampirism supplements the law, parasitically operating as its agent in picking off the detritus of society. With his qualms about taking human life, torn between the instincts of an unnatural animal and the taboos of cultivated humanity, Louis is rendered a more complicated being and more sympathetic as his diet – rats, for instance – becomes more repellent: his sovereign undying humanity is measured by its proximity to abjection. More human in their corporeal powers and sensory and mental acuity, Rice's vampires, like Shelley's monster, remain touched by suffering, superior to and yet more wretched than the life around them.

The narrative plays on the traditional position of the Romantic outcast to gloss the vampire subject with all the characteristics of selfhood. Family losses and responsibilities, impossible loves and homosocial attractions, colour in the callous pallor of the vampire. Existing on the borders of society, the lone predator becomes a solitary wanderer seeking companionship and security, intensely aware of his difference and fascinated by the frailty and mortality of the humans around him: 'our eternal life was useless to us if we did not see the beauty around us, the creation of mortals everywhere' (Rice 1977: 111). His alienation and disquieted solitude, his love of beauty and knowledge, along with his humane concerns endow him the qualities of a Romantic self, tortured by self-consciousness and a questing spirit. Louis' views, presenting undeath as an opportunity for cultural development and the vampire as the aesthetic connoisseur, sit uncomfortably with his nature, as an ironic comparison with the child-vampire, Claudia, suggests: 'I should never be as grown up as she until I knew that the killing was the serious thing, not the books, the music' (113). His cultural aspirations and humane sympathies contradict the conventions associated with his identity in a curious, ironic inversion of values and meanings. His relationship with Claudia, quasi-lover and protector, misreads her innocence as that of a Romantic child-woman (in the manner of Wordsworth or De Quincey): she is neither a figure of painful loss, of unnaturally early death nor a fallen but redeemable figure of sympathy, but a 'demon child' and a 'magic doll' confounding dividing lines between innocence and diabolism, supernature and mechanical artifice. Louis, moreover, presents himself as a victim of the cruellest tyranny: his maker, Lestat, allows him little knowledge of his vampire nature and exploits him to pay for a life of luxury, material plea-sures and sensual indulgence. With the child-vampire, Claudia, Louis rebels. Believing they have killed their persecutor, they use their freedom to embark on a journey of self discovery. They leave New Orleans and start a European tour in search of their origins and others of their kind. The tour, of course, takes them to the Romantic wilderness of Transylvania where they encounter only the disappointing forebears of the vampire species – zombies whose rise from death takes the form of walking but barely animated corpses.

The European tour ranges not only across famous locations in a geographical and fictional vampire tradition: its temporal and historical dimensions, given the vampires' lack of a lifespan, allow vampirism to become entwined in and reflect upon the development of modern culture. Paris forms the centre of this cultural tour, exerting a magnetic force, to which Rice's narratives repeatedly return. In *Interview*, it is the place where Louis and Claudia find the creatures they were looking for and the place to which Lestat returns. Years before, it is revealed in the sequel, it served as the location where he began his career as a vampire. Born to the impover-ished provincial aristocracy in the period before the French Revolution, Lestat enjoys the last days of the luxurious existence of the *Ancien Regime* before beginning his own travels. He nonetheless leaves a legacy – the Theatre of Vampires – which forms the principal venue for the main adven-tures in *Interview*. Paris is distinguished for its epochal significance in cultural and political terms. It emerges as the aesthetic capital of modernity, a capital, appropriately enough teeming with openly visible but unrecognised vampires. In its urban mix, the crowded streets of industrial and commercial progress are sidelined in favour of the pleasures of an artificially illuminated night-time, where the vampire not only stalks the darker alleys in search of prey but inhabits luxurious hotels and frequents popular theatres. A solitary existence is counterpoised with a nocturnal bohemian social life as, in this amorphously nostalgic nineteenth century, Romantic individualism meets aesthetic decadence.

The vampires in Paris enact the other life of modernity. In their own theatre, they perform sensational dramas for crowds who have left the world of organised industrial mass production and bourgeois commerce to seek brief and spectacular pleasures in the flickering lights of the nocturnal city. Theirs is a true masquerade, concealed openly within a performance of vampirism for a crowd seeking sensational entertainment. Yet they are what they represent, a bohemian theatrical community whose decadence and nocturnal existence feeds off the world of the city. Armand, their leader, keeps boys who, spellbound in their devotion to him, enjoy an exquisitely delicate existence on the edge of life and death. Armand, however, remains at a remove, not only from the realm of mortals, but from the small community over which he presides. His indulgences have left him with a weary air, his passions seeking some new object, some new mirror in which he can recognise himself. Louis, with his solitude, his alienation and his curiosity, fills that role. The two, as they roam the streets and converse in their hideaway on the nature of vampiric (un)life, provide a pseudo-philosophical focus for the novel, their homoeroticism and status as outsiders allowing them to reflect on the masquerade by which they can 'pass' as humans.

Wandering among the streets of nocturnal nineteenth-century Paris, the solitary vampire comes to assume the shape and role of the *flâneur*. 'it was my desire to escape the theater then entirely, to find the streets of Paris and wander, letting the vast accumulation of shocks gradually wear away', says Louis, oppressed by the atmosphere of the vampire community (259). Noting that Rice's text re-views *Dracula* through Walter Benjamin (though Charles Baudelaire seems a more likely source), David Punter observes that 'the vampires who stroll its night-time, gaslit streets are nothing but the very image of the *flâneur*' (1996: 162). The 'labyrinth of the city', for the *flâneur*, becomes a 'labyrinth of merchandise' (Benjamin 1983: 54). For the vampire, of course, it is a labyrinth of edible goods. Neither inside nor outside the life of the city and its crowds, its defining, differential figure, the *flâneur* is, Walter Benjamin underlines, no 'philosophical promenader' but 'takes on the features of the werewolf restlessly roaming a social wilderness' (1999: 418). With a literary genealogy that sees the 'hunting-grounds' of Cooper's novels turned, by Poe, into the urban scene of crime and detection, the *flâneur*'s nearest relative is 'The Man of the Crowd', 'someone abandoned in the crowd' yet intoxicated by its jostling stream (Benjamin 1999: 439; 1983: 41 and 55). The impermanence of the city's movement and its alluring and multiple distractions is absorbing. But it is also draining:

> An intoxication comes over the man who walks long and aimlessly through the streets. With each step, the walk takes on greater momentum; ever weaker grow the temptations of shops, of bistros, of smiling women, ever more irresistible the magnetism of the next street corner, of a distant mass of foliage, of a street name. Then comes

hunger. Our man wants nothing to do with the myriad possibilities offered to sate his appetite. Like an ascetic animal, he flits through unknown districts – until, utterly exhausted, he stumbles into his room, which receives him coldly and gives off a strange air.

(Benjamin 1999: 417)

Desire, activated by a restlessness combined with an array of distractions, overshoots its objects and leaves appetite unsatisfied. For Belsey, Rice's tales 'put on display the relentless imperatives of unsatisfied desire' (88). Something more is required. The vampire Louis, for all his instinct to feed on human life, remains an ascetic figure, looks for more than a regular blood supply to sustain his immortal existence. Hence his, and Armand's, appreciation of the ennui that attends immortality, his fascination for human finitude that continues, ironically, to haunt vampiric speculation and a desire sustained in the face of its extinction.

Few vampires, Armand notes, 'have the stamina for immortality'. Frozen in time at the moment of their un-birth, vampires, themselves evanescent and artificial creatures of the night, want 'all forms of their life to be fixed'. Living, or un-living a paradox in that vampirism is itself bound up with decadence, corruption and dissolution, 'everything except the vampire is subject to constant corruption and distortion'. Resistant to the change that everywhere surrounds the undying being, death presents itself as the only source of meaning and stability when 'immortality becomes a penitential sentence in a madhouse of figures and forms that are hopelessly unintelligible and without value'. Wanting the very limits and boundaries that seductively drew the vampire beyond life means that the ultimate object of desire becomes its end, an end to desiring: 'he simply wants no more of life at any cost' (306). The despair and anguish of Louis' Romantic post-mortality is shown by Armand to be inherent in their condition. But the intensity of feeling is worn down by repetition and the banal existential commentary postulated by the thoroughly dis-illusioned Louis:

> It was as I'd always feared, and it was as lonely, it was as totally without hope. Things would go on as they had before, on and on. My search was over. . . . It was futile to leave him to continue, futile to travel the world only to hear again the same story.
>
> (257)

The exotic, intoxicating possibilities of vampirism, the worlds of desiring it promises are undone by the very thing that allows desire's flight: death. Without death, desire roams hopeless and futile, doomed to repetition rather than final satisfaction. For Louis, immortal life only exposes an absence at the heart of things. He discovers that religion and myth are 'fantastical lies', mere illusions that cede to an equally 'fantastical truth'; 'that there is no meaning to any of this' (258–59). Having left death behind, the vampire has exhausted meaning along with desire: his hunger remains at the level of instinct; he is condemned to feed without the consolations of any order that would provide meaning and limit to his activity.

The modern subject assumes the form of a vampire. Like the *flâneur*, its condition marks an apotheosis in subjectivity: no longer social or anchored in a symbolic framework, identity wanders aimlessly, intoxicated and repelled by the urban crowds and glittering streets and stores. The vampire's disillusioned romanticism and its dissatisfied decadence, moreover, anticipates, with its radical freedom of existing beyond death, an alienation and lack of essence in tune with existentialism. The novel not only looks back at modernity to chart the manner in which the aesthetic and spiritual subject of Romanticism becomes the decadent asocial aesthete of the *fin-de-siècle*: it looks forward – within its own timescale at least – to incorporate an anxiety more apparent in the twentieth century. Permitted by the anachronism of the vampire, the conflation of periods and their attendant aesthetic codes and subjective shapes distinguish an attempt to define, on the basis of other distinctive cultural-historical positions, another 'spirit of the age'. Indeed, a discussion between Armand, the 400-year-old vampire, and Louis rather clumsily tries to mark out the latter's significance as a new everyperson and establish the novel with some vague credentials as social commentary: 'I'm not the spirit of any age. I'm at odds with everything and always have been! I have never belonged anywhere with anyone at any time!' Armand contradicts him: 'This is the very spirit of your age. Don't you see that? Everyone feels as you feel. Your fall from grace and faith has been the fall of the century.' Such a fall, with its allusions to a romanticised Lucifer, could have taken place in the late eighteenth century, though Armand's words are uttered in a fictional nineteenth. He goes on to contrast the alienated individualism of Louis with other vampires:

> 'They reflect the age in cynicism, fatuous sophisticated indulgence in the parody of the miraculous, decadence whose last refuge is self-ridicule, a mannered helplessness. You saw them; you've known them all your life. You reflect your age differently. You reflect its broken heart.'
>
> (310)

Again, the multiple reflections provided by vampires make the reference of the statement obscure. The other vampires, it seems, possess features that could apply as much to a late twentieth century wallowing in the absence of metanarratives as to the end of a nineteenth century threatened with decadence. Indeed, the cynicism and sophistication vies with parody and self-ridicule to situate the reference in the non-localisable hyphen of post-modernity. From there it implodes: the statement becomes self-referential as a commentary on the very figures who speak in the novel.

Of which age is Louis the spirit? And what does it mean, moreover, to propose an ageless creature such as a vampire as the 'spirit of an age'? The vampiric reflections offer their usual and strange mirror to modernity, a composite modernity of recycled styles and postures. Multiple, these reflections are also amorphous and thereby offer a blank space of projection and misrecognition in which any image or spirit can be glimpsed. Rice, it seems, intensifies and diminishes the traditional negative appeal of the vampire as a marker of cultural anxieties and uncertain limits. But, in the standard gesture of twentieth century reversals, the identification becomes sympathetic and positive, a figure for a human condition, for an anguished, alienated individual. In an interview in *Lear's Magazine*, discussing *Interview*, Rice stated that the novel is about 'grief and guilt, and the search for salvation even though one is in the eyes of the world and one's own eyes a total outcast!' She goes on: 'when vampires search for their past trying to figure out who they are, where they come from, if they have a purpose, that's me asking the same questions about human beings' (cit. Zanger 23). Critics concur: 'Rice's other vampires too experience very intensely the tortures of the human soul. They feel love, despair, misery, suffering, and loneliness at a pitch so intense it precludes any suggestion that they might be totally inhuman' (King 78). Not only are their physical abilities superior, vampires appear overhuman in their display of fine emotional qualities.

Without reflection, vampires provide an idealised mirror of human states. In the blanks of Rice's vampiric mirror humans are supposed to see themselves, not in repugnant form, but dressed and made up to look more romantic and exotic, more human, but a humanity masquerading, or 'passing', as its simulated self. At the same time, the vampire marks a twist in a process of cultural analysis: it is because the vampire is a liminal being that it retains so much projective value as modernity's twice inverted mirror, a simulation redoubling the process of simulation which evacuates in order to fill the space of projection. For Jameson, gothic 'depends absolutely on its construction of evil'; it hollows out a space for the projection and ejection of otherness. It provides the 'emptiest form of sheer Otherness (into which any type of social content can be poured at will)' (1991: 290). In times of shifting and dissolving of boundaries and hierarchies, however, the place of otherness becomes uncertain. The projective space can be filled with any image or association. At the end of the nineteenth-century, concerns about femininity, economy and sexuality were given vampiric form: 'by 1900 the vampire had come to represent woman as the personification of everything

negative that linked sex, ownership, and money' (Djikstra 351). For twentieth-century audiences, according to Twitchell's examination of the myth
in terms of Freudian theories of sexual development, 'the vampire is the
most complete condensation of the problem and resolutions of pre-adoles-
cence' (115). In the context of 1970s liberalism and sexual liberation, Rice's
vampires trace the tension between dieting, anorexia and consumption, in
terms of the relation between body image and sexual difference (Tomc).
'New' vampires, like Rice's, embody varieties of American ethnicity to the
point that the 'new, demystified vampire might well be our next door
neighbor' (Zanger 19). Any form of otherness, any liminal state or stage, it
seems, can be found reflected in the figure of the vampire – to the point that
difference elides into sameness: 'we look into the mirror it provides and we
see a version of ourselves. Or more accurately, keeping in mind the ortho-
doxy that vampires cast no mirror reflections, we look into the mirror and
see nothing *but* ourselves' (Hollinger 1997: 201).

In its multiple simple reflections, the screen of modernity is rendered
more flat and more plural, more homogenous and more fragmented at the
same time. Curiously timeless, the vampire's historical dislocation allows it
to view the passing of time in much the same way as its inhumanity establishes its 'passing' relation to humans. Able to cross and define epochs,
however, the vampire is romantically of and outside history. Indeed, in *The
Vampire Lestat*, much is made of the vampire's epochally liminal relationship
to (human) history, a position, or rather repeated and successive positions,
more abject than sovereign (hence, the humanity of it), in which the
increasing decline of grand myths is calibrated against the redundancy of
evil, romance and vampirism itself. It is an equation that Lestat, in *The
Vampire Lestat* and *Queen of the Damned*, sets out to reverse by resurrecting
grand and violent mythological struggles. The temporal crossings are thus
incorporated into the other crossings, between life and death, home and
abroad, self and other (in sexual and racial senses), that constituted so much
of the vampire's frisson, once in horror and now in sympathy. In Rice, the
crossing itself is distinguished as the feature that establishes the basis of the
vampire's positively projective liminality. And crossing, which highlights
between-states, also blurs distinctions, as it does when defining a spirit of the
age as the spiritlessness of any age. Crossing thus erases differences as much
as brings them to the fore. Rice's multiple reflections of vampirism, operating both prospectively and retrospectively at once, delivers an atempo-
rality that is also a vampiric nontime: epochs and identities are conflated in
the loop of a recycled and endlessly consumable history of the present.
Foucault's practice of examining both the 'difference that keeps us at a
remove from a way of thinking in which we recognize the origin of our own,
and the proximity that remains in spite of that distance which we never

cease to explore' is rendered less critical and more consumable (1987: 7). Distance and difference, in the transhistorical figures of the vampire, are almost elided by the return of what is all-too familiar yet not quite the same.

The modern vampire subject thus remains at odds with time and others, an oddness that guarantees his uncertain and ever-unfulfilled identity between periods and selves. The anachronism is reinforced by the defining characteristic that makes him the spirit of any age: his 'broken heart', the heart of a conventionally heartless creature, bespeaks a pallid and incongruous sentimentality. Beyond the risibly vapid pathos of Armand's final comment on Louis, the statement returns on both the romanticism that is celebrated and the post-modernity that is occluded by the vampire's romanticised position. A reflection on an age's broken heart, of course, calls up the spectre of Romantic feeling and the intensities of romance longing that both define and displace Louis humanised vampirism. But it also signals the exhaustion of affect and the an-aestheticisation of feeling that post-modern aesthetics take as their starting point. The appeal to a lost romance, moreover, demonstrates the nostalgia that, in postmodernism, is linked to the loss of grand narratives. Romance will, it seems, restore the meaning, faith and credibility lost to the contemporary world, a 'transfiguring force' which engages 'complete Desire' and an 'extreme exigency' for purity and unity (de Rougemont 16; 61) a 'wish-fulfilment or utopian fantasy' which 'aims at the transfiguration of the world of everyday reality, whether in an effort to restore it to the conditions of some lost Eden or to inaugurate and usher in some new and ultimate realm from which the older mortality and imperfections have been effaced' (Jameson 1975: 138). The desire for romantic fulfilment, moreover, requires the restoration of archaic and grand contraries: it, as Jameson notes, involves a 'struggle between the higher and lower realms, between heaven and hell, or the angelic and the demonic or diabolic'. Such a reading of romance certainly informs Lestat's project after his reincarnation in the second volume. A romantic passion, a passion for the absent all-absorbing structure of romance, is precisely what fuels the escalation of narrative ambition in the vampire chronicles: having diagnosed the meaningless and futility of an age without death and god, Lestat proposes to reinvigorate the intensities of romantic struggle and thereby restore belief, desire and significance to displaced vampirism in a dislocated world. At the same time, as is the case with Louis, the unfulfillable intensities of romantic questing evacuate romance of all but a desire for death – the end (in both senses) of desiring. Even as the broken heart offers a romantic understanding of the loss of romance, it fails to escape the atemporal and repetitive circuit that has constituted the vampire in the first place. Louis' definitive broken heart is an effect of romantic illusion and disillusionment: without death, his unlife remains repetitive to the point of futility, meaninglessness and boredom. This, moreover, is the condition he passes on: the boy interviewer refuses to accept the end of his story, with its conclusion in despair. His disappointment, nonetheless, does not diminish his wish to be a vampire with 'the power to see and feel and live forever' (364). Acknowledging his failure, Louis concedes, and bites the boy. It is a marvellously empty gesture, seemingly without satisfaction on either part, a final comment on the vain romanticism with which the novel tiresomely tours two hundred years of modernity. The romance, exhausted by centuries of repetition, becomes banal. Indeed, with Hollywood replaying romances in accordance with the sanctities of marriage, the genre manifests the 'lost transcendence' of the world which consumes them as its mundane daily diet (de Rougemont 292).

Romance, between males, between vampires and humans, between life and death, is evacuated and reappears in a rhythmic pulse throughout the tale of blood. Spent, used up, rendered banal, the currency of romance is repeatedly returned to by desperate vampires in search of meaning and desire. Romance, its intensities, imagined fullness, its passion, entwines desire and lack: it is sustained in the quest, and dies with satiation; its locus is absence not fulfilment; it is propelled by identification and fantastic projection rather than realisation. In contemporary consumer culture, with its fast everything and instantaneous networks, the rapid gratification of desire is connected to a devaluation of its objects (Žižek 1996: 190). The broken heart of post-modernity, then, signifies the extent of meaningless gratification and the devaluation of romance: affectless, feeling is anaesthetised by an excess of images and commodities, their dizzying glitter stimulating and satisfying desire to the point of its consumption. Romantic love entails a form of consumption itself, conjoining its fantastic and fatal features: it is supposed to realise the 'illusion of living life to the full', sustaining the idea that something 'will alter my life and enrich it with the unexpected, with thrilling chances, and with enjoyment ever more violent and gratifying' (de Rougemont 282). Vampiric consumption, with its impulse to violent gratification, thus mirrors romantic passion; at the same time, the coupling discloses the escalating circuit of an interior excess.

## . . . *Flâneur* . . .

With consumption, the nineteenth-century setting of *Interview*, and its association of vampire and *flâneur*, is significant. At that time, Paris was 'the dazzling manifestation of the new consumer culture' (Jervis 71). The *flâneur*, moreover, alone in the crowd, is witness to the experience of commodity culture. For Benjamin, the *flâneur*'s wandering among the urban mass places him in the 'situation of the commodity' although he is 'not aware of this special situation' (1983: 55). The intoxication with the crowd betrays intoxication with the commodity. Crowded places – the streets, arcades and department stores – are thus, for Benjamin, key loci where the inner experience of modernity is evinced, places where the interchange of people and goods occurs. The context for the interchange is a form of capitalism governed by exchange rather than use value: 'Empathy with the commodity is fundamentally empathy with exchange-value itself. The *flâneur* is the virtuoso of this empathy. He takes the concept of marketability itself for a stroll. Just as his final ambit is the department store, his last incarnation is the sandwich-man' (Benjamin 1999: 448). A human relationship has been replaced by a relation between commodities. The dazzle and distractions of arcades and stores, and the world exhibitions of the period, mark a new mode of mediation transforming human experience:

> World exhibitions glorify the exchange value of the commodity. They create a framework in which use value recedes into the background. They open a phantasmagoria which a person enters in order to be distracted. The entertainment industry makes this easier by elevating the person to the level of the commodity. He surrenders to its manipulations while enjoying his alienation from himself and others.
>
> (Benjamin 1999: 7)

If the *flâneur* is drawn into this phantasmagoria, so, too, is the vampire. The latter's position, moreover, is ambiguous, situated through fictions and images as part of the realm of unreality and sensation as well as figuring, in Rice, as an alienated creature possessed of a curious empathy. The metaphor of the phantasmagoria, drawn from the late eighteenth-century public displays of *camera obscura* in which technological image production transforms the perception of reality and subjectivity, introduces the realm of spectres and the supernatural into the world of thought, uncannily crossing the boundaries of outside and inside (Castle). Unreal, the vampire is sustained through a consuming relation, a metaphor of inhuman feeding that feeds off a captivated humanity. Like the *flâneur*, the vampire is more than an 'observer of the marketplace', he is absorbed in its operations as 'a spy for the capitalists, on assignment in the realm of consumers' (Benjamin 1999: 427). For humans, the effective unreality of the vampire signals the disorientating, uncanny and consuming transformation of subjectivity provoked by the mechanisms of capital, while the curiously empathetic vampire looks back on the realm of humanity from the position of the commodity.

Mortality again emerges to define this relationship. If things have a bearing on the human understanding of life and death, as Bataille suggests, then the system of exchange value and commodities also has effects on self-perception. Bataille discusses the emergence of tool use and the way in which a nascent technological relation brings humanity into being: in using tools to make things, humans encounter a fundamental difference – things are durable, manifesting a permanence lacking in humans. A tacit recognition occurs: things can last, but humans die (Bataille 1955). The vampire, of course, has passed beyond that condition but, problematically in Rice's version, retains consciousness, a consciousness divorced from death. Hence, in Armand's diagnosis of the spirit of whatever age, it is vampires who bemoan change and corruption, caught in the interstices of humanity and exchange, desire and consumption, empathy and feeding.

Death and commodities accompany the *flâneur*. The distractions and dislocations of exchange value open, through bourgeois false consciousness, onto a hall of mirrors in which novelty is homogenised and art is de-sacralised:

> The *flâneur*'s last journey: death. Its goal: novelty. 'To the depths of the unknown to find something new'. ('*Au fond de l'Inconnu pour trouver du nouveau!*') Novelty is a quality which does not depend on the use-value of the commodity. It is the source of the illusion which belongs inalienably to the images which the collective unconscious engenders. It is the quintessence of false consciousness, of which fashion is the tireless agent. This illusion of novelty is reflected, like one mirror in another, in the illusion of infinite sameness. The product of this reflection is the phantasmagoria of 'cultural history' in which the bourgeoisie enjoyed its false consciousness to the full. Art, which begins to have doubts about its function, and ceases to be '*inseparable de l'inutilité*' (Baudelaire), is forced to make novelty its highest value. Its *arbiter novarum rerum* becomes the snob. He is for art what the dandy is for fashion.
>
> (Benjamin 1983: 172)

Death cedes to novelty, its final consumption deferred in the alluring surfaces of new commodities, caught up in a system of exchange which reduces the heterogeneous and human value of art to just another good in a world of goods, subject to the mechanisms of exchange and the fluctuations of consumer desire and fashion. For Benjamin, fashion conjoins the extremes of 'frivolity and death' (Benjamin 1999: 70). Undead, Rice's vampires are tormented by the new that constantly passes them by as much as they are absorbed in the fashions, artifice and theatricality of nineteenth-century Paris.

Lestat, with his penchant for luxury and ornamentation in interior decor and dress, stands at the furthest extreme from Louis. But the latter's position remains defined by the relation of frivolity and death. Indeed, his distaste for the vampire community is spelt out in terms of its frivolity and absorption in fashion: for him, 'they had made of immortality a club of fads and cheap conformity' (274). The dullness of their existence comes of the substitution of novelty for death: beyond death, theirs is a permanent condition of desiring without end, tireless desiring, of course, wearing down the possibility of novelty and interest and flattening it into the infinite mirror of sameness. Without end or final consummation un-life is rendered dull, condemned to the repetitive cycles of fashion and sameness, of novelty that is no longer novel enough. At the same time, unable to die, they feed on others, on the teeming urban hordes lined up for the immediate gratification, permanently in proximity to deaths that are never their own. Agents of death, they remain shadowed by the spectre of death and the return of the wish to die. Rice's vampires, the novels reiterate, too often find immortality unbearable and fall into madness or simply decide to give up the ghost. At least death relieves the boredom and repetitiveness of eternal un-life and terminates the cycles of consumption without consumption. But, like vampire fiction itself, un-life goes on and on, 'its deathlessness *as* narrative, a story that never seems to come to an end, that never quite drops out of circulation' (Glover 1993: 127).

Romance depends on prohibition; it thrives 'where love is fatal, frowned upon and doomed by life itself' (de Rougemont 15). Beyond death, vampires find themselves in a void while still labouring under the illusions of romantic possibility. Their position in this respect again mirrors the situation of the consumer and, as in the positing of a spirit of the age, returns to the question of the subject of history at a time when history has been disneyfied or simulated to death. The identification of a spirit of the age, despite its romantic and Hegelian overtones, does not deliver a resolved dialectic in which self-consciousness and history are fully recognised in human terms. Nor is there an end of history in the sense proposed by Francis Fukuyama, with all human subjects finding recognition in the globally victorious structures of liberal political democracy. Fukuyama's vision includes some disturbing reflections on the relationship between recognition and democracy in which questions of consumption, and romance, loom large:

> While we do not, for now, have to share Nietzsche's hatred of liberal democracy, we can make use of his insights concerning the uneasy relationship between democracy and the desire for recognition. That is, to the extent that liberal democracy is successful at purging *megalothymia* from life and substituting for it rational consumption, we will become last men. But human beings will rebel at this thought. That is, they will rebel at the idea of being undifferentiated numbers of a universal and homogeneous state, each the same as the other no matter where on the

globe one goes. They will want to be citizens rather than *bourgeois*, finding the life of masterless slavery – the life of rational consumption – in the end, *boring*. They will want to have ideals by which to live and die, even if the largest ideals have been substantively realized here on earth, and they will risk their lives even if the international state system has succeeded in abolishing the possibility of war.

(Fukuyama 1992: 314)

Rice's vampire-consumers occupy the position of 'last men', bored beyond death by the consuming that is their wont, yet still wanting grander ideals by which to live. Romance, a romance of risk, war and death returns in the gap opened up by rational consumption: Lestat's ideals, his appeal to myth and romance, attempt to fill the dull void and restore the lost, transcendent dimension of heroic struggle. Despite, or because of, democratic recognition and rational consumption, something is missing: the idealised human individual, dissatisfied, is driven to rebellion, driven by something in desire that refuses to submit to the patterns of rational consumption. With romance, it seems, consumption discloses something excessive, irr-ational.

Immortal, crossing centuries, the vampire is left in the curious position of the last man. The historical dialectic, moreover, is left open to a negativity that refuses full recognition, satisfaction or dialectical resolution. Indeed, the Hegelian language of desire, recognition, risk and the struggle between mastery and slavery, when combined with the impulses of romance, discloses a subject split apart rather than unified in consciousness of itself and the world of spirit. For Kojève, in his extensive reading of Hegel, human identity is forged through the negation of the world of things and the entry into a realm of desiring. Consciousness overcomes nature through desire. Where an 'animal-I' simply negates things through acts of consumption or destruction, desire hollows out being to disclose 'an emptiness which receives a real positive content only by the negating action that signifies Desire in destroying, transforming and "assimilating" the desired non-I' (Kojève 4). Humanity is distinguished by the desire of other desires, that is, a desire for recognition in excess of the world of objects. To be human is to risk one's life in the struggle for recognition. This is how Kojève reads Hegel's master–slave dialectic: in the fight for recognition, the one who is not prepared to sacrifice his life becomes the slave; the other, the victor, attains the position of master. The latter is served by the former, consuming the efforts of his labour. But victory is not satisfying: the master is recognised, not by an equal, but by a slave and thus doomed to a dissatisfying life of consumption.

Rice's consuming vampires, for all their mastery of nature, time and other beings, remain dissatisfied with their position. Their desire is at once animal in its destructiveness and empty in its lack of appropriate recognition. They ought to be sovereign rather than servile, but sovereignty, as Bataille develops Hegel's argument, depends on a relationship to and consciousness of death: while human desire negates nature, because humans remain animals, they, unlike vampires, cannot live outside its limits (1997: 283). It is only the sovereign who is free, momentarily, from the anguish that defines the human relation to death. Sovereignty offers a position outside the world of reasons, morals, utility or need in a life of consumption and enjoyment. Sovereign existence, 'in which the limit of death is done away with', is playful and resolutely opposed to servility (Bataille 1997: 319). While, in Bataille's terms, the sovereign is far from a romantic position, its proximity to negativity rendering idealisations impossible and making death a fundamentally inhuman event, romance is evident in the sovereign's escape from the constraints of servile daily existence to live life in the intensity of the moment. Romance, it seems, idealises the darkness which the sovereign inhabits: 'the idealized eroticism that pervades our culture and upbringing and the pictures that fill the background to our lives; our desire for "escape" which a mechanical boredom exacerbates' are the conditions, for de Rougemont, defining romance (16). Passion, it seems, assumes a sovereign impulse needing 'no law and no custom', it 'obliterates the antithesis of good and evil' taking lovers 'beyond the source of moral values, beyond pleasure and pain' (de Rougemont 39). Indeed, in German Romanticism the elevation of passion sets out to 'achieve the ideal transgression of all limitations and the negation of the world through extreme desire' (224). Having transgressed all social, natural and moral boundaries, Rice's vampires ought to be sovereign, beyond contraries and utterly heterogeneous to the slavery of everyday existence. They have lost the consciousness of death and find intimacy only in acts of killing: it leaves them in a limbo of desiring and consuming without the intensity of death to provide consciousness with self or desire with direction or consumption with finality. Sovereignty, as a permanent condition, is found wanting. In a curious twist, the mechanical, homogeneous existence from which romance offers escape returns when consuming itself becomes a banal, repetitive activity. Vampiric post-mortality, an unlife spent consuming to excess, returns to the void of desiring and turns on an excess all the more strange due to its disconnection from any possible limits, death in particular.

Beyond death, Rice's vampires find themselves beyond meaning, despite the prohibitions on vampire-making and vampiricide that are instituted to give them some sense of community and symbolic value. The girl, Claudia, of course, provides the most extreme example of the transgression sustaining vampire law: a vampire made too young who attempts to destroy another of her kind. The consumption that never comes, the deathlessness that leaves consuming incomplete and its satisfaction ultimately unsatisfactory, situates vampires in the realm of commodities as defining figures of the modern consumer. Life is constantly used up but never subject to a final consumption. Located outside a natural order and use value, subject to the undeath of the commodity, beyond nature, beyond a humanity defined in the face of death, vampires enjoy only a banal sovereignty over life and death: theirs are the cheap thrills of fashion, the little frisson of murder and blood, a quick 'taste' of others' death. While death is eroticised, the act of killing replacing the act of copulation, it remains a thrill whose pleasures steadily pass into banality. Even the sexualised feeding on life, the passionate intensities involved in the moment life slips like blood through the lips of death, lose their charm. That Other, death, eroticised beyond being, is not within their gift. The 'homo-' which defines much of the eroticism of vampire relationships is as much about a sameness of experience than any excitement attendant on passing, be it the passing of and for human life. Having lost the absolute Other that is death, vampires, themselves once emblems of an intimate, in-human otherness, only circulate among sameness. Decked out in the dark trappings of death, another example of a taste defined by fashion and commodities, vampires mock death with their graveyard affinities and coffin couches. What remains, as it does for Louis, is a fascination with human life (and death), a fascination that emanates from an alienated distance, of an enjoyment sacrificed to allures of immortality. Pity the vampire-consumer-ourselves, is perhaps the tacit message of Rice's chronicles. Where vampires once filled the void in human life with the excesses of horror and enjoined the violent, disgusted expenditures that closed the gap, they have now assumed the burden of loss and wear it like an open wound of consumption.

## . . . **Consumer** . . .

In their romantic post-mortality, however, Rice's vampires only masquerade as *flâneurs*. They occupy an era of consuming in which desire is pushed towards any limits but, in finding none, is condemned to recycling styles to the point, if not of death, then of boredom. *Interview* stages its vampire-*flâneurs* as nostalgic creatures and projections of a lost nostalgia, their artifice, decadence and ennui, while exuding all the aesthetics of dark modernity, display the loss defining the postmodern: 'most people have lost their nostalgia for the lost narrative'(Lyotard 1984: 41). Their nostalgia for mortality, for a lost loss, is dressed up as nostalgia for the time when death's intensity and meaning could masquerade in exotic cloaks with a wasted charm and enjoy the frisson of fatal proximity to otherness. Vampires, dressed up as *flâneurs*, thus stand as simulations generated for a contemporary system of consumption which glosses and recycles the past through its own filters to construct figures whose images screen out the past. The association of fashion, novelty and death that brings Benjamin's *flâneur* to the very brink of an order in which art and the commodity system collide is, nearly one hundred years later, totally reconfigured. Baudrillard's comments, while recalling Benjamin, highlight the new relationship. Fashion, 'always *retro*' requires a 'spectral death and resurrection of forms' to the extent that death, rendered banal, becomes absorbed in fashion's circulation: 'the desire for death is itself recycled within fashion, emptying it of every subversive phantasm and involving it, along with everything else, in fashion's innocuous revolutions' (Baudrillard 1993a: 85; 88). No final consumption occurs in this process of simulation and consumer recycling: all images are generated in a meaningless and non-fatal circuit. Vampirism, in Rice, is turned 'into something akin to a posture or style, a *simulation* of the real' (Gelder 110). Fatal desires, it seems, become the norm of a system of simulating-consuming without end. Integral to this desiring-circulation, the banality of system is also displaced from a heterogeneous, subversive, transgressive or sacred status to become a mode of systemic functionality: 'voided precisely of any imaginary substance, it passes into the most banal reality', 'death is when everything functions and serves something else, it is the absolute, signing, cybernetic functionality of the urban environment'. 'In a word', Baudrillard continues,

> *death is confused with law of value* – and strangely with the structural law of value by which everything is arrested as a coded difference in a universal nexus of relations. This is the true face of ultra-modern death, made up of the faultless, objective, ultra-rapid connections of all the terms in a system'.

Hence, computer banks and corporate foyers that are distinguished as the new necropolises of postmodern culture (Baudrillard 1993a: 185). The vampire-*flâneur*, then, is a simulation retrojected by this system of cybernetic-corporate death, a darkly exotic throwback that sustains the comforting illusion that mortality is a peculiarly human thing at a point when it has already been by-passed by screens and simulations in which all human life (and death) finds itself captivated. Within a system of simulations and recycling, *Interview* performs its retrospections on vampire consumption, capturing the difference of the past according to the sameness of the present.

The *flâneur* was a fleeting historical figure, defining a relation between industrial capitalism and incipient commodification that does not last long. Indeed, it stands out as a challenge to bourgeois morality and industrial order that is to be eradicated by the manufacturing processes that reshape mass society. Benjamin quotes Georges Friedmann, writing in the 1930s: 'Taylor's obsession, and that of his collaborators and successors, is the "war on *flânerie*"' (Benjamin 1999: 436). The short-lived pleasures of the *flâneur* are noted in Benjamin's discussion of Baudelaire's increasingly disillusioned experience of crowd:

> The luster of the crowd with a motion and a soul of its own, the glitter that bedazzled the *flâneur*, had dimmed for him. To impress the crowd's meanness upon himself, he envisaged the day when even the lost women, the outcasts, would be ready to advocate a well-ordered life, condemn libertinism, and reject everything except money.
>
> (Benjamin 1973: 195).

The otherness and appeal of the crowd becomes absorbed by the sameness of Taylorist production and bourgeois order. Its agglomeration of differences is sucked into the orbit of commodity exchange. The *flâneur* becomes a figure of nostalgia, a residue of an excess that finds itself incorporated to garnish the scene of consumption with a faint hint of another aesthetic.

Rice's vampiric reincarnation of the *flâneur* while moving backwards to imagine the late twentieth consumer in a more exotically romanticised light, is, nevertheless, pressed forwards, its simulated nostalgia defined by its present. Romancing the past, it returns to the evacuation of romance in the present, where desire, in the manner of fashion, continues to be exhausted by sameness, even as it craves novelty. But the craving never extends beyond simulation or the scene of consumption, instead becoming increasingly entangled in its networks. The second novel of the series, *The Vampire Lestat*, replays and reflects on the consuming desires of its vampires. It extends the tension of the first, pulling in two directions with its romantic nostalgia in dynamic entanglement with the evacuation and exhaustion of simulated desire. Beginning again in the present, this time the 1980s, it moves back to begin again with the pre-revolutionary period of Lestat's childhood to wander across Europe and the East and recount tales of vampirism stretching back to prehistory and myth before returning on a present it never actually left. This, moreover, is a 'global present which includes extremes of deprivation and poverty on the one hand and a paradise of consumer pleasures on the other' (Belsey 88).

More than *Interview*, *The Vampire Lestat* is caught in an abysmal play of simulations, a play not only of fictional allusion and revision, nor merely of cultural historical projection and nostalgia: it incorporates its predecessor and itself within its own pages. *Interview with the Vampire* is not only the name of a novel written by Anne Rice, it is a story by Louis (presumably written up from the anonymous boy's tape recordings) that has become a bestseller in the world in which Lestat awakes. So much so that it prefigures Lestat with his fictional (though for Louis biographical) image: when he introduces himself to a group of musicians they recognise the name and assume him to be 'pretending to be the vampire Lestat', that is, emulating a fictional character (Rice 1995: 20). Fiction slides into simulation, a hall of simulations in which reality and representation become indistinguishable. After reading *Interview with the Vampire*, and offering some critical commentary on Louis' perspective, Lestat decides that the bright lights of celebrity, rather than an anonymous place in the shadows, is a more attractive career path. He forms a rock band called 'The Vampire Lestat' (22) and writes an 'autobiography' with the title, of course, *The Vampire Lestat* (565). And all of this unravels in a novel called *The Vampire Lestat*. In the novel, the superficial density of self-reference (both to the name of the text and to its hero) does not function in the manner of postmodern forms of literary reflexivity in which the frames of reading and writing are opened to critical scrutiny and indeterminacy, but situates itself within a hall of simulations absorbing all productions. Technology is again important to the vampiric circulation of and consumption by images: Lestat is not only the band's singer and songwriter; he is its svengali manager, designer of its look, as well as investing heavily in the production of lavish music videos. Indeed, the name, the sound and, most significant, the visual impact of the group precipitate its success long before they indulge in the traditional rock and roll pleasures of a live performance. Lestat, called out of the grave by the unearthly sounds of a practising band called 'Satan's Night Out', has quickly discerned the differences defining the period: the 1980s is thoroughly hyperreal and everything is filtered through screens of simulation: 'In the art and entertainment worlds', Lestat observes in his enthnocultural analysis of his new time, 'all prior centuries were being "recycled"' (15). Simulation, crossing time and culture, destroys and preserves difference on the singular plane of the undead image. No wonder that Lestat feels at home, 'in love', it seems, with the late twentieth century (18).

The novel tells the story, not only of a vampire, but of 'what America calls a Rock Superstar' (9), a vampire so comfortable with the trappings of the period that he is soon fully in command of its clichés and happily 'roaring around New Orleans on a big black Harley-Davidson motorcycle' (13). Perhaps a vampire rock star is not so preposterous an idea, given the setting in Reagan's America. In terms of popular music, the attractiveness of darkness, decadence and evil had been bombastically staged in the heavy rock of the 1970s, to carry on into the following decade and supported, of course, by the paranoid projections of the moral majority (Badley 1996: 2). Levels of camp darkness and decadent masquerade increased in the imbrications of new romantic and goth styles, liberally adopting fashions in dress and sound from any era imagined to exude a leathery or lacy romanticism. Myths, fictions, aesthetics are exhumed and assimilated by a decade in which style became substance and difference was marked by the cut and colour of one's cloth. Vamps and popular music entwine in the same circuit of faux transgression and camp fashion. The vampire Lestat is no more than a further twist in the loop: a myth, a fiction, a vampire becomes a rock star by masquerading as a vampire like so many rock stars drawing image and inspiration from fictions and myths before him. With Lestat, the circle closes in on itself.

Lestat's story, however, extends beyond the music scene to offer an account, a cultural history even, of his new present that encompasses economic as well as moral shifts: 'the dark and dreary industrial world that I'd gone to sleep in had burnt itself out finally, and the old bourgeois prudery and conformity had lost their hold on the American mind' (14). The economic rationalism of the nineteenth century, with its Taylorist modes of manufacturing, along with its accompanying morality, has been replaced with a post-industrial consumer society and a new set of social freedoms and sexual mores. People were 'adventurous and erotic again' and 'the old aristocratic sensuality now belonged to everyone'. By opposing extravagant aristocratic characteristics to constraining bourgeois values, Lestat shows that his reading of the present is framed with nineteenth-century assumptions in which the bourgeois predominance of reason, utility and morality is established through the negation of luxurious and wasteful expenditures attributed to the aristocracy. The democratisation of sensuality, rather than its repression, suggests that the distinction has been levelled and surpassed by a new socio-economic configuration in which excessive spending, useless and irrational consumption and sexual liberation come to the fore as the norms of everyday existence. So much so that they are a 'right' rather an extravagance: 'all people had a right to love and luxury and to graceful things' (Rice 1995: 14). Lestat notes, with a degree of wonder, the extent to which the consumption of luxuries like cars, swimming pools and expensive clothes permeate every layer of society, the visible wealth overcoming him like a 'hallucination' and the goods on display in shop windows arresting his 'stupefied' gaze (15). There is still much of the *flâneur* informing the vampire's perceptions of the dazzling array of commodities on sale: 'Department stores had become places of Oriental loveliness – merchandise displayed amid soft tinted carpeting, eerie music, amber light. In the all-night drugstores, bottles of violet and green shampoo gleamed like gems on the sparkling glass shelves' (14). The colours and comparisons, the reference to 'department stores' and 'orientalism', throw a nineteenth-century exoticism over the malls and 24/7s that are the daily temples and mundane shrines of contemporary consumption. The nostalgia that presented the contemporary consumer in the more interesting guise of *flâneur* is replayed, but the world that captivates Lestat has fulfilled the destiny of the *flâneur*, to become just another shopper.

Although drawn back to the nineteenth century with the naivety of a nostalgic gaze, everything that Lestat sees signals a proliferation of differences in excess of the antithesis of productive Taylorism and commodified *flânerie* by which industrial and moral order are defined and sustained in terms of exchange and market. Though sign value appears in the guise of exchange value, the entire context for the consumption of commodities is now mediated through simulation: it determines his trajectory towards stardom, the romance of celebrity, and his appeal to a mythic romantic project. Rice's fiction is defined by its consumption of self. For Doane and Hodges, the novels replay what they represent, 'exciting an appetite to consume them that is mirrored and elicited by her vampires, themselves in love with consumption as a way of achieving a radical self-sufficiency, an end of otherness, promised in the infantile relation with the mother' (436). This maternal figure is pre-oedipal, linked to the oral gratifications of child development and the 'consuming Mom' of 1950s TV commercials, and manifests a thoroughgoing refusal of the traditional morality and order imposed by a paternal oedipal relation. Significantly, the disavowal of paternal authority defines consumer culture so that a fixated, consuming vampirism is extended through fiction and simulation to become the norm of consumption. The allure of consuming spreads from vampire narrator to listener, from singer to audience, from viewer to spectator, and novel to reader.

Glossing the present with a nineteenth-century gaze, Lestat acknowledges the wider implications of the shift in economic existence elsewhere in his account of cultural development: his position, like other vampires, serves to mark shifts in values and symbolic structures as much as in material historical and economic practices. In discussions with the ancient vampire, Marius, the pseudo-historiographical role of vampires appears in their ability to chart epochal shifts:

> You have come into being at the end of an era, at a time when the world faces changes undreamed of. And it was the same with me. I was born and grew to manhood in a time when the ancient world, as we call it now, was coming to a close. Old faiths were worn out.
>
> (415)

Marius marks the transition from pagan to classical eras, while Lestat, born before the French Revolution to a minor aristocratic family, straddles the emergence of European modernity. For Marius, modernity eclipses religion,

giving a new humanist gloss to value and enlightening social progress
through science and philosophy. His speculations are not entirely optimistic,
however: 'Maybe a new religion will rise now. Maybe without it, man will
crumble in cynicism and selfishness because he really needs his gods' (506).
These observations clearly inform Lestat's analysis of the late twentieth
century: not only does he echo Marius' acknowledgment that vampires are
unnecessary, without purpose and have no place but notes that the world
which has effaced Christianity has failed to replace it with any new
mythology or religion. All he finds is a 'sinless secular morality' (16).
Although enamoured with its material wonders, Lestat's evaluation of the
sinlessness of the value system, like the astonishingly hygienic cleanliness of
the environment, is somewhat vapid. Lacking sin, the symbolic system of
free flowing exchanges of commodities, signs, images and bodies lacks
substance and, without anchor, no longer needs distinctions of good and
evil. The 'new' vampire emerges in this move from 'a monotheistic, moral-
istic structure to a pagan hegemony of power and pleasure' (Zanger 21). The
liberation of Lestat's contemporary America is a liberation beyond transgression and prohibition and hence a liberation that no longer has any
boundaries or taboos. It exceeds and renders redundant the capacity of any
symbolic system to establish the rules, pre- and proscribe the behaviours,
define the meanings or direct the desires that constitute any sense of culture
or community at all. In the wake of postmodern liberation there trails a
vacuum in which good and evil, presence and absence are neither opposed
to nor a guarantee of the other (Hollinger 1997: 202–3). Another form of
evil emerges, associated with transparency and transaesthetics and a 'viral'
crossing of boundaries. It is boundless, unconstrained by structure or location, diabolically intent on reversal, subversion, multiplication. Its principal
agent is 'the evil demon of images' wherein message and meaning disappear
'on the horizon of the medium' (Baudrillard 1987: 23). Duplicitous, ironic,
resistant to all legislation, the media screen delivers a 'totally new uncertainty', one that results, not from lack of information, but from its excess
(Baudrillard 1990a: 90).

The evacuation, liberation and proliferation of evil disclose the absence
of any symbolic constraints, in the form of religion, bourgeois morality or
sexual taboo: it leaves the imperatives of consumption free to clamour for
more. As evil, as objects of symbolic anxiety and expulsion, vampires once
occupied a (negative) place ensuring the value of propriety and goodness. In
a world without evil, vampires are utterly redundant: 'Pure evil has no real
place . . . I have no real place' (17). They are cast further into the shadows of
history and fiction, 'Old World monsters' who should return to the grave.
Their place lies 'in the art that repudiates evil' ('the vampire comics, the
horror novels, the old gothic tales'), that is, buried in books consigned to

dusty shelves or shrinkwrapped in cellophane on the plastic racks of collectors' stands at fairs and markets. As evil has been dispensed with, there seems nowhere else for vampires to go. Lestat, however, refuses to be buried. The absence of any evil defining symbolic boundaries is not a space of loss, a site of mourning or of self-pity: it presents an opportunity on which he can capitalise. At the end of the spectrum of kitsch gothic aesthetics in which art negotiates evil lies rock stardom. For him, vampires have a place 'in the roaring chants of the rock stars who dramatize the battles against evil that each mortal fights within himself' (17). Any dramatisation of mortal psychomachia, of course, requires it to be simulated. Similarly, the absence of evil requires that it be simulated in image, song and music video. Lestat's choice of rock stardom over burial is not an escape from the procession of simulated objects of evil but demands a reinvention and re-romanticisation that takes him further into abysmal play of its immaterial surfaces.

A void at the heart of symbolic structures, an absence of meaning and purpose, is not, for Lestat, a locus of horror. Rather, it offers opportunities, a site of symbolic death integral to reinvention in the undeath of simulations. If there are no gods, no faith, no religious or mythic framework, then these (paternal) signifiers can be simulated. Gods are replaced by (rock star) celebrities; religion by romance; faith by identification. Lestat romances the absence of myth, reinvigorating it in the banal trappings of rock stardom: 'What are we but leeches now–loathsome, secretive, without justification. The old romance is gone. So let us take on a new meaning' (578). Without the old romance to gloss the vampire with a fascinating and sovereign image, it is perceived for what it is, a creature of abjection, disgust, revulsion. A new romance, however, re-pulsing the vile vampiric image of the past, will return the vampire to its (self) imagined ascendancy over mortals. Lestat's nostalgia for romance pulls him back to throw him forward, in a momentum that returns him and the world to meaning. Here romance works like a metanarrative, assuming a function that invests individuals with a place, direction and significance in the order of things, and reinvesting those relations with the binding intensity of general identification, in the form of the adulation thrust upon a rock star, the new celebrity god and centre of a vapid, sometimes ridiculous, mythology. The return to romance is never a return: it is a thoroughly mediated affair in which rock divinity can only be staged, artificial, constructed, and dependent on the technologies circulating and sustaining celebrity.

To fill the void in meaning and romance, the gaping hole at the centre of symbolic systems must become a site of projection and simulation, a screen on which a multiplicity of images may flicker and a million gazes may linger. The passion of romance is reformulated as an enamoration with the screen. Lestat, of course, chooses this trajectory for his return. The novel climaxes with his appearance on stage before an ecstatic and screaming crowd. As he struts and swaggers, he addresses his fans:

> 'COME ON, LET ME HEAR YOU! YOU LOVE ME!' . . .
> Everywhere people were stomping. . . .
> 'HOW MANY OF YOU WOULD BE VAMPIRES?'
> The roar became a thunder.
>
> (584)

The storm of assent indicates the extent of absorption in the vampire image. Everyone wants to be a vampire, identification captivated by vampiric simulation, sacrificing all self to the lure of the image in the undeviating gaze of the 'wannabe'. A vampire called Lestat in a novel called *The Vampire Lestat* which has been marketed as his own bestselling life story recounts his performance as 'The Vampire Lestat' in a rock group of the same name to an adoring audience who have no doubt read his book and seen his videos, all of which unfolds in a fiction called *The Vampire Lestat*. There are neither the elevating terrors of sublimity nor the paralysing horrors of the void to these reflections, however. The abyss of the simulated *mise en abyme* yawns. The hollow surfaces of simulation flicker to infinity, the emptiness and the image co-dependent in their virtual self-effacements and self-productions. To fill the void one must assume the emptiness of the image as Lestat's new romance turns the redundant vampire into new celebrity figure. Identity is defined in the rock devotion of Lestat's fans, laid out on the mock altar of celebrity. As wannabe vampires, the captivated consumers of the image desire only the same evacuation and simulation of celebrity:

> 'Dear Lestat, my friend Sheryl and I love you, and we can't get tickets for the San Francisco concert even though we stood in line for six hours. Please send us two tickets. We will be your victims. You can drink our blood.'
>
> (568)

Caught up in the simulated romance, their wish is only to give their blood to an image, a sacrifice of self for the undeath of the image. Neither life nor death has any significance in comparison with the attraction of undead simulations. The symbolic structure defined by Oedipus, with its law, prohibition and desire, has ceded to the romance of the image. Narcissus, in love with the reflection more than life itself, replaces the difference of triangular identifications with the dual sameness of the reflective screen and its undeath: it is a 'surface which absorbs and seduces him, which he can never pass beyond' (Baudrillard 1990b: 67). There is no beyond, only the image which flickers on. Otherness disappears. For the vampires, rock fans and readers of *The Vampire Lestat* this all-consuming destiny remains inescapable. Like all the other anorexic starlets intent on wasting their bodies, on reducing mass to almost skeletal proportions, emaciation is determined by the shiny image: the aim is to be as thin as the screen of celebrity itself where death, and perhaps humanity, has become irrelevant. Rice's fiction, displacing humanity onto vampire screens, leaves humanity behind: 'the role of human beings as victims becomes increasingly trivialized and marginal'. The relations between humanised vampires absorb all interest and identification, downgrading humans, in the process, into objects of indiscriminate consumption: 'the victims are as indistinguishable from each other as McDonald's hamburgers – and serve much the same function' (Zanger 21).

Undead, the vampire looks down on humanity from his artificially elevated stage; undead, the vampire looks back on humanity from the screen that consumes both. If death has been relocated to the data banks and corporate foyers of the hypermodern world, then simulation renders humanity already dead, and already subject to ghostly returns in the image: spirit never proceeds beyond spectrality and liberation remains haunted by the ghost of a transgression without end, the lack of limits unfolding precisely in the liminal (virtual) realm of un-death. It remains in limbo, unable to herald post-humanity: as Belsey notes, the third volume returns with a 'moral mission' to save the human race (90). Roles of human and vampire remain reversible, suspended in their difference from the other. There is little romance left, despite the vampire-simulation's attempt to infuse its emptiness with the grandeur of new myth: for all its escalations – back to prehistory and forward to a queen of the damned, exhumed to evil by the throbbing of rock music – it wears out quickly, subject to the urgencies of speed and the exhaustion of desire recycled from repetition to boredom and back again.

## Girly-girly romance

Mark Twain forcefully casts the blame for the backwardness of Southern character and culture on romance. One writer is singled out: the responsibility for the pernicious and corrupting influence of romance lies with Sir Walter Scott. He is to blame for Baton Rouge's Capitol building, 'for it is not conceivable that this little sham castle would ever have been built if he had not run the people mad, a couple of generations ago with his medieval romances' (Twain 195). The South has not recovered from this 'debilitating influence': 'romantic juvenilities' and 'its inflated language and other windy humbuggeries' persist amid cotton factories and steam locomotives. New

Orleans, in Twain's journey through the South and Southern character, remains redolent of Scott's romanticism rather than religious or cultural heritage. Mardi Gras is a prime example, 'with knights and nobles and so on, clothed in silken and golden Paris-made gorgeousness, planned and bought for that single night's use; and in their train all manner of giants, dwarfs and monstrosities, and other diverting grotesquerie – a startling and wonderful sort of show' (218). Though 'a relic' of French and Spanish 'occupation', Twain considers that all religious features of the festivity have been 'pretty well knocked out of it now'. 'Sir Walter Scott', he goes on,

> has got the advantage of the gentlemen of the cowl and rosary, and he will stay. His medieval business, supplemented by the monsters and oddities, and the pleasant creatures from fairy land, is finer to look at than the poor fantastic inventions and performances of the revelling rabble of the priest's day.
>
> (Twain 218)

Romance supplements, supplants even, religion, assuming a definitive cultural role in the South. Much like representations of Catholic southern Europe in eighteenth-century gothic fiction, or the Orient in the nineteenth-century romance, Twain's South serves as the location of otherness, projected in opposition to northern, Protestant, rational, moral and utilitarian values. Significantly, though opposed to the mercantile and commercial dominance of the period, it is as a 'medieval business' that it circulates, conjoining features from different epochs that for Twain's strictly rational argument should be incompatible and remain opposed. The festival, Twain comments, though taken up in other Southern cities, will not spread further afield, either to the 'practical North' or to London. It is too heavily imbricated in the self-romancing of Southern culture:

> For the soul of it is the romantic, not the funny and the grotesque. Take away the romantic mysteries, the kings and knights, and the big-sounding titles, and Mardi-Gras would die, down there in the South. The very feature that keeps it alive in the South – girly-girly romance – would kill it in the North or London.
>
> (218–19)

The agents that would ensure the death of girly-girly romance would be the satirical magazines of urbane rationality and wit; expiration would result from the 'merciless fun' poked at it. But romance persists in the South, despite the 'great and permanent services to liberty, humanity and progress' contributed by the French Revolution and Bonaparte (219). Rational and democratic progress, much to Twain's indignation, then encounter Scott's 'enchantments': he 'sets the world in love with dreams and phantoms', 'with the sillinesses and emptiness, sham grandeurs, sham gauds, sham chivalries of a brainless and worthless long-vanished society', a 'jejune romanticism of an absurd past that is dead' (219). Dead it may be, but romantically resurrected it continues to have devastating effects: 'Sir Walter Scott disease' is what prevents the South becoming wholly modern.

It is no accident, then, that Rice's vampires and her new vampire mythology are reawoken in New Orleans. With the 'Scott disease' as a romantic precursor and the gothic parade of grotesque and carnival monsters dressed-up in their Parisian finery, the South provides fertile ground for the spread of new dark flowers of romance: the chivalric, mannered gentleman turns into the affected, aristocratic vampire; the absurd and dead past of medieval enchantment revived in the fantastic mythology of the undead; girly-girly romance with an over-stylised, if not effeminised, heroic evil from beyond the grave. Like the pseudo-chivalric Southern character debilitated and arrested in development through the influence of romance, Rice's vampires do not manage the ironic or parodic edge associated with camp, mimicry or masquerade, their 'passing' for humans merely passing the latter by, absorbed on a plane of pastiche and simulation. Sillinesses, emptiness and sham grandeurs thus remain their principal romantic characteristics. Romance nonetheless continues its dressing up, mocking seriousness with its all-too serious aspirations to passion, meaning, mythology. Silly, empty and sham-ful, it repeatedly inflates itself with the same 'windy humbuggeries' and, too full of itself, exhales, exhausted. Exaggeration and exhaustion chart the predictable trajectory of romance. Rice's second novel compounds the romantic excesses as it comments upon and extends the trajectory of the first to pursue more and more preposterous mythologisations (a destructive Egyptian vampire Queen awoken from ancient torpor by the sensory assaults of loud rock videos to wreak havoc on the world of mortals and the undead . . . ). In the void of silliness and emptiness left by simulations romance spins ever more hyperbolically.

There is, however, no practical North or mocking London magazines to restrain the flights of vampire romance. The advent of simulations leave reason (and ridicule) behind: distinctions between practical nineteenth-century progress and the shams of (postmodern) simulated romance are more difficult to maintain when hype, passions and desires become staples of the new economic circulation of images. Already realised in the circuits of consumption and simulation, romantic flights unite the celebrity vampire figure and the banal consumer on the same plane of identification and emotional expenditure. Both are absorbed by the excessive yet banal imperatives of consumption and simulation in which all boundaries are subject to incessant crossings and all attempts at differentiation collapse: normal and deviant, real and illusory, living and dead, same and other are flattened on the screen of projective liminality. Every form of otherness, every site of anxiety or line of transition, is absorbed by the vampire screens: adolescence, varieties of sexual identification, modes of transgressive, troubled or outcast individuality, cyborg and technologised being, any form of want-to-be, find themselves incorporated and relayed across cultural screens. Differences are, in the process, rendered recognisable, familiar and banal; otherness, endlessly sought out, is turned into sameness; the indifference of simulations severs difference from meaning and lets images circulate within a hell of the same. Identity, multiplied and rendered plural and readily accessible, is sucked from any centre in the self and relayed across so many self-reflexive screens. Even death, the last locus of one's own hidden uniqueness, in an age of simulations, lifestyles and near-death experiences, is dressed up and displaced among a host of ghostly images.

Simulated to death, the old romance is truly gone. Simulated again, it returns undead, calling up a string of identifications. Rice's vampire romances leave reason and the sickly sham of chivalry behind to simulate vampirism anew in a context of consumption. Their mock romanticism, however, is not quite beyond mockery. There are Northern intonations in the graphic novel, accents and idioms that target the pretentiousness of decadent vampirism, that seem to offer a Twain-like condemnation of Southern romance. An edition of *Preacherman (Cassidy: Blood and Whiskey)* tells the story of a lone and unglamorous vampire, Cassidy, on the road across the USA. Drawn to New Orleans, he encounters another, more familiar, creature of his kind, a vampire called 'Eccarius', dressed in dark velvet breeches, voluminous white shirt open to the waist and long boots and shoulder-length hair. In his library with its chandeliers, leather chairs and grand piano, a crystal glass of blood in his hand, he speaks: 'No my friend, you are not alone in the darkness. You are like me, a lord of nightfalls, piercing veins and drinking crimson, walking the shadows of the mortal world' (Ennis and Dillon 13). The scruffy, unshaven, jeans-wearing Cassidy is not impressed, with the blood, the attire, nor the speech: 'Yeh're a wanker, aren't yeh?' The other, nonplussed, replies: '"Wanker" . . . is that one of the more western-European translations . . . mm. Of vampyre' (14). As the comedy of cultural misrecognition continues, the 'translation' seems to be correct.

Refusing to sleep in a coffin ('it's fuckin' unnatural, that's why') the new arrival accepts the hospitality of Eccarius. The following nightfall they visit a cellar full of want-to-be vampires, appropriately dressed in black leather and lace as they lounge around reciting gloomy poetry and indulging in exhibitionistic bouts of self-cutting. These are 'Les Enfants du Sang' or, 'translated', 'a pack of poncy Gothic rich-kid wannabes' (25). Decidedly unimpressed, Cassidy returns to his preferred haunt, a local bar. There he debunks the superstitions of Eccarius, discounting all the trappings of vampire lore from fear of churches and crosses to the effects of garlic, holy water and stakes through the heart. Soon, Eccarius gets into the spirit of the demystification session: 'I tried the bat thing once . . . broke both my fucking legs' (35). They laugh as the latter admits he has drawn most of his ideas from fiction. Cassidy counters with a sensible point: 'Suppose yeh're an ordinary fella, not like us, an yeh're in a plane crash in the fuckin' jungle . . . By some miracle, yeh stumble across a copy of *Tarzan of the Apes*. . . . Do yeh go an live in the treetops and talk to monkeys?'. He likes the fiction, however, but not as a conduct book or lifestyle manual: 'Don't get me wrong, I fuckin' love *Dracula*. Read it loads of times. But every time I get to the end I think – what an arsehole!' (36) Bringing Eccarius back down to earth requires an extended visit to a bar. After that, heavily intoxicated they revisit the cellar to show their backsides to the aspiring vampires and run off, laughing. But the growing bond between them is severed when Cassidy catches Eccarius feeding on a human victim and the latter admits to an insatiable bloodlust. The last frames of the story show Eccarius pinned out before dawn, awaiting the rising sun that will consume him in an explosively pyrotechnical end. 'Yeh're a self-obsessed, pasty-faced, death-fixated dickhead got up in a poncey shirt.' 'Yeh were too much of a wanker to live.' Cassidy heads for a bar, meets a woman . . .

In brutally debunking the pretensions and self-indulgence of romanticised vampirism, the graphic story seems to return to the norms of a pragmatic and rational world. It is easy to forget that its hero is a vampire himself: he does not dress, act or speak like a vampire from nineteenth-century fiction and resolutely refuses to follow traditional models of vampirism. His killing of the self-romanticised vampire stems from a curious mix of moral disapproval at unnecessary feeding on human lives and aesthetic distaste at the over-ornamented lifestyle and inflated ideas of the New Orleans vampire. The very ordinary example of undeath, in contrast, enjoys the simple pleasures of heteronormal mortal nocturnal existence: bars, beers and exposed women's breasts. His vampirism is no more than that of an everyday carnivore, an appetite satisfied by the blood that comes from a lamb chop rather than another human. Stripped of any aesthetic or decadent pretensions, moreover, his philosophy is no different from that of the average American consumer: 'we've the whole wide world out there waitin' for us, an' we've forever to make the most've of it. And that's the thing, mate: enjoyin' life' (36). Enjoying life no longer means consuming it to the point of death but, beyond death, making the most of life in an infinite expansion towards the fullness of consuming. There is no romance to this enjoyment, just more beers, more bars, more breasts, the world over. The normalised vampire manifests the sameness of the norms of consumer culture, repeating the norms of consumption as it harnesses expressive individualism to the point of evacuation: the consumer finding and filling itself, without end, in the most banal fashion, with more and more beer. Forever

# 3   *Poor Things As They Are*

Political romance from Gray
to Godwin

## Postjustabouteverything

There are few texts which make as extensive reference to the gothic canon
as *Poor Things*. Alasdair Gray's prize winning novel radiates gothic allusions
and citations, making mention of, quoting or paying homage to almost the
entire European pantheon. In name, in literary-geographical location and
in theme, the novel is not only a 'complete tissue of facts' as the fictional
editor suggests in his playfully ironic introduction but a total tissue of texts, a
web of fictions entwining stories of fantastic reanimation, scientific experimentation and monstrous education: an unborn child's brain brought to life
in a drowned woman's body grows up on the edges of the nineteenth-
century Glasgow medical establishment and travels Europe and the Near
East transgressing social and sexual mores with diabolical innocence.
*Frankenstein, Jekyll and Hyde*, the dark Victorian architecture and urban gloom
of industrialised Scotland, the entangled doublings and fictional returns
characterising the density of *Poor Things'* gothic intertextuality seem to
announce the novel's indisputable place in a most persistent genre. But
things are not so certain. The overmarked presence of the novel's gothic
precedents is countermanded by an absence of gothic atmosphere, mystery
or effects: its ghosts are all-too visible as no more than the fictional forebears
it wears for all to see; its immersion in a Scottish gothic tradition, while
acknowledging a thoroughgoing cultural 'gothicisation', eschews the lamentation, gloom and haunting central to its mood (Punter 1999); its one
moment of devastating horror stands opposed to any masquerade of superstitious fantasy or unconscious demonism. Paying its gothic dues in full with
one hand, *Poor Things* disclaims membership with the other. An academic
and political interest in things gothic is juxtaposed with a critical distance
that refuses to take the genre seriously on its own terms, a juxtaposition of
gothic and anti-gothic that shadows the genre from the start.

George Melly observes in the critical notes to *1982 Janine* that, 'if Alasdair

Gray were a pornographer he would be a rather good one. He is not a pornographer, however. His power to titillate is betrayed by humour and pathos, the worst enemies of true porn' (cit. Boyd 111). The same can be said of *Poor Things*, gothic romance. Any relish for dark fantasies, indulgent gloom or numinous mystery is undercut by comic subversions, poor puns, playful reversals and textual games. Fictional self-consciousness begins before the story: a fake potted biography of a fake author is followed by a few humorously self-deprecating lines on Alasdair Gray, the editor, 'a fat, balding, asthmatic, married pedestrian who lives by writing and designing things'. A page of actual and fabricated reviews is followed by title page and editorial introduction, the latter being an account of the discovery of the single copy of the main story, with a debate on the provenance, veracity and value of the book placing the editor at odds with the local historian who found it. Then, the story itself begins: the title page, dedication and contents of 'Episodes from the Early Life of a Scottish Public Health Officer', by Archibald McCandless MD, opens onto an assemblage of stories, letters, caricatures, etchings and illustrations from Gray's *Anatomy*. This section, focusing on the writer's relationship to the heroine of the tale, a woman who becomes his wife, is supplemented by a long letter in which she discredits the 'Episodes' as flights of a sad man's fancy. The novel is not yet finished, however. The final section, by the editor, the 'Notes Critical and Historical', takes the form of a scholarly pastiche entwining biography, history and fiction, its actual and invented sources of textual reference interspersed with maps, architectural drawing and nineteenth-century etchings.

Although Gray has disavowed postmodern intent, complaining of his failure to find an adequate definition of postmodernism, *Poor Things* parades a knowing technical self-consciousness in its clever narrative collage and textual frames, its authorial inclusion and disavowal, its games of fact and fiction, its ironic reversals and tortuously extended intertextuality. The reflexivity of the novel draws attention to itself, to the artifice of its writing and to the generic and interpretative expectations of readers and critics. But it is a reflexivity taken to excess in the jumble of texts and intertexts that make up the narrative – with letters, facsimiles, etchings, styles all stressing the work of fabrication and simulation. Indeed, the artifice of 'making' is foregrounded in the chapter titles of McCandless story. Emphasising the artifice of the text in the fabrication of details, images, references, *Poor Things* presents an over-self-consciousness that refuses distinctions of mere pastiche and more critical parody and exaggerates a playfulness that is already inces- sant in its blurring of boundaries and disturbance of categories. It is this hyper-reflexivity that broaches the question of 'post-postmodernism'. In respect of Gray's work, the term is introduced to account for the manner in which, in *Lanark* and *Something Leather*, the use of critical notes and an 'index of plagiarisms' address themselves to literary scholars, incorporating and defusing criticism within the text itself and thereby doubling the effect of textual self-consciousness. Randall Stevenson explains the function as a 'deflection of criticism', going on to argue that

> it also shows Gray highly self-conscious about using self-conscious forms of fiction: postmodernism, once largely directed by the urge to parody and subvert conventional forms of writing, becomes in its turn a recognised, accepted form to be parodied and played with itself. Perhaps this makes Gray a post-postmodernist, though that might really be a term to puzzle him.
>
> (Stevenson 1991: 56)

Post-postmodernism seems to declare both an irritation with, and ennui towards, the dominant, if ill-defined, style of recent literary transgressions. In doubling the prefix, adding another 'after' to the mode which defines itself negatively as that which comes 'after' modernity, thereby doubling the negation in order to define itself, post-postmodernism implies that what it replaces is merely another style or fashion that may be easily superseded. But the dismissive attitude itself makes a gesture that relies on fashion: in reducing postmodernism to mere fashionable indulgence that can be replaced with the next big thing, it relies on the very linearity and teleology that postmodernism, in theory and practice puts in question. Denouncing the fashionability of postmodernism, the second post of post-postmodernism fashionably moves on. In calling up the sequence rendered suspect by the collapse of modernity's grand narratives and under the imperative of fashion's demand for novelty, the implications of post-postmodernism not only replay a technoscientific consumer economy's imperative to innovate and engender profitable differences but repeat the dynamic of exhaustion and replenishment that inaugurates literary postmodernism. The interplay of excitement and ennui, of renewal and boredom, it seems, becomes a definitively open-ended feature of both postmodernism and reactions to it, incorporated into its aesthetic movement and identifiable in the broader context of postmodernity.

Stevenson's 'perhaps' already hints that post-postmodernism may not be a particularly felicitous term to apply to the doubled self-consciousness of Gray's fiction, since that doubling, while acknowledging a degree of dissatisfaction in the way that innovative subversion of aesthetic conventions becomes predictable norm, does not turn away from playful fictional games, but increases their scope and intensity. Where post-postmodernism indicates a movement away from or beyond subversive or parodic conventions deemed, through repetition and familiarity, to be both tired and tiresome, the textual play of *Poor Things* manifests an excessive immersion in reflexive techniques. Such a strategy, however, does not simply display heightened literary self-consciousness as an end in itself, but engages with cultural and political questions often occluded from the practice of reflexivity. Nor does it replay the dynamic that leads from innovation to ennui, from excitement to irritation, and back again, but engages with questions of a more disturbing dis-illusionment, one that recognises the defusing and diffusion of parody and subversion: in a culture of loose boundaries and distended limits, the effectiveness, the possibility, even, of parody and subversion, is severely challenged.

Questions of (post)postmodernism, moreover, have a significant bearing on the role of gothic citations and motifs in *Poor Things*. Declared to be a 'boring and exhausted paradigm' by Fred Jameson, the gothic genre should have played itself out over two hundred years before (in the first decade of the nineteenth century) when the formulaic and repetitious patterns first became objects of overfamiliarlity, satiric comment and ridicule. As if the genre at that time, imploding on itself, needed any external criticism, titles of novels, like *The Monk of Udolpho*, signal an overplaying of formulas without any outside prompting. The features inspiring easy criticism, however, may well form the basis of the genre's resilience and adaptability, the predictable formats and recognisable devices providing ready-made screens for the projection of familiar fantasies. In returning self-consciously to well-worn gothic paths, and in placing them in relation to postmodernism, *Poor Things* stages an unexpectedly subtle and complex interaction. It is not simply a matter of assimilation, with either postmodernism being gothicised – the comic turns resist that – or gothicism being postmodernised and rendered post-gothic (or post-post-gothic): there is no nostalgia for a sublime law and a purging, righteous terror characteristic of reactionary fantasy (though fantasy is one of the novel's main concerns); nor is it a matter of opposition, with the lightness of postmodern play set against gothic gloom on the assumption that it remains a genre worth parodying or subverting. All the same, a strong smell of anti-gothic sentiment permeates the text. Instead, the critical interplay of gothic and postmodern styles engenders an interrogation of a modernity that was always-already gothicised, unavoidably informed by fantasy and inescapably articulated by desires, a modernity, indeed, whose ostensible otherness was of its own making. Here, things get post-modern in a Foucaultian sense with an investigation into the doubleness of modernity – inventing both the liberties and the disciplines; at the same time, there remains a Lyotardian trajectory which notes, in a paradoxically historicist and ahistorical manner, that postmodernity emerges, sublimely, not only at the end of modernity, but in its nascent state.

*Poor Things*, with its games of history and fiction, fantasy and materialism, requires a critical interrelation of past and present in order to establish the significance of its interplay of gothic romance and postmodern textuality. Its gothic citations invite a line of inquiry that moves in a different direction to the critical feminist retellings of *Frankenstein* and male science with the focus on a female monster (a revision already performed by Liz Lochead). Mary Shelley's name, nonetheless, continues to be important, but it is her full name – Mary Wollstonecraft Godwin Shelley – that opens up an intertextual reading of *Poor Things*: in Gray's novel, the doctor-scientist who creates life from death is called Godwin Bysshe Baxter. The name combines references to a Scottish family visited by Mary in 1812, to her husband and to her father, William Godwin. In the context of considering the politics of romance, the latter, radical philosopher and romantic novelist, does not function as an idle, intertextual aside. Godwin's writing, his novel *Caleb Williams* in particular, offers a crucial examination of the complex entanglements of romance, reality and political change. Its narrative frames and effects, moreover, provide critical reflections on the work of fiction which can inform an understanding of how *Poor Things* engages with late twentieth-century fantasies, both gothic and political.

## True romance

Originally entitled *Things as They Are*, but changed to avert potential anti-jacobin hostilities in the reactionary 1790s, Godwin's *Caleb Williams* was written after, and in the spirit of, *Political Justice*, his monumental proto-anarchist treatise that outlined the corruptions of all systems of government and their injurious effects on the inevitable rational development of human freedom, co-operation and happiness. *Political Justice* not only specifies the corruptions and injustices attendant on the feudal ruling hierarchies of the time, but maintains a vision of a rational order to come. It is, then, a text that documents things as they are – and identifies the causes of contemporary injustice; it also outlines things as they ought to be. *Caleb Williams*, too, powerfully illustrates the injustices of an aristocratic class system supported by a corrupt legislature and a cruel penal regime. Local squires, in the novel, can get away with murder, while persecuting anyone who brings charges against them. That, indeed, is the story Caleb vividly relates, a young innocent whose naiveté is shattered by his confrontation with the everyday sufferings of a tyrannical order based on property and privilege. Though it engages with things as they are, the novel offers no hint of things as they ought to be: instead its project tends only to analyse and further demonstrate how things come to be – and, horrifying thought, remain – as they are. Its two endings, moreover, present particularly gloomy outlooks, in which neither reason nor justice is seen to prevail.

*Political Justice* grounds its argument on an unwavering faith in reason, the gradual spread of its light irresistibly and transparently heralding in a new order of rational, just and humane political relationships. Godwin's insistence on the progress and eventual potency of reason, however, seems to lose much in the translation from one form of writing to another: while a work of political philosophy may assume a rational method of argumentation, a work of fiction, a romantic novel at that, operates according to antithetical principles. It is curious, then, that Godwin should extend his rational political enquiry by means of a romance, a genre notorious for its indulgence of the emotions, given that, throughout *Political Justice*, passion is identified as one of the main impediments to the progress of reason and justice. For radicals in the 1790s, the gothic romance had a strong, negative political significance, connoting, not only the current aesthetic criticisms of the genre – its superstition, immorality and barbarism – but also a singular resistance to reason and persistent adherence to a feudal framework of power. Edmund Burke, with his reactionary appeals to chivalry, gallantry, monarchy and church, was the chief offender in the eyes of radicals and reformers. Mary Wollstonecraft, who became Godwin's wife and was Mary Shelley's mother, was among the most indignant of the radical respondents to Burke's *Reflections on the Revolution in France*. Her passionate invective against Burke's irrational and inhuman position, his 'mortal antipathy to reason', employed gothic images to damn him: in her *A Vindication of the Rights of Man*, she exclaimed 'man preys on man; and you mourn for the idle tapestry that decorated a gothic pile, and the dronish bell that summoned the fat priest to prayer' (58). Burke's nostalgia blinds him to the cruelty of existing social relations and perpetuates a conservatism that refuses the possibility of change. Why 'repair an ancient castle, built in barbarous ages of Gothic materials?' Why, argues Wollstonecraft, have legislators 'rake among heterogeneous ruins', implying that the current form of government is too old to be worth salvaging, its labyrinth of law become incommodious and rotten. In an argument littered with monstrous examples of feudal corruption, Wollstonecraft uses the gothic image of an ivy-covered ruin to describe the parasitical nature of the ruling class (41). Gothic stinks of all things aristocratic, tyrannical, irrational and useless, its romanticism archaic, barbaric and resistant to change.

Godwin, too, is thoroughly versed in anti-romantic rhetoric. His account of the 'evils of marriage' highlights the deceiving and insidious role played by romance ideas: 'the method is for a thoughtless and romantic youth of each sex to come together, to see each other, for a few times and under circumstances full of delusion, and vow eternal attachment' (Godwin 1985: 762). Unlike Wollstonecraft, Godwin is less ready to denounce all manifestations of gothic or romantic sentiment as merely remnants of a long gone and outmoded regime. Referring to Burke's famous lamentation for the Queen of France, he observes (against both Burke and Wollstonecraft) that "'the age of chivalry is" not "gone"! The feudal spirit still survives that reduced the great mass of mankind to the ranks of slaves and cattle for the service of a few' (1985: 726). The persistence of romance is strangely, in a rational treatise, a matter of concern. In romance, the feudal spirit continues to have powerful effects, its deceptive gothic decorations so antithetical to rational judgement manifesting a capacity to subjugate using surface appearances alone. In a discussion of government by courts and ministers, Godwin offers a rich image of how the process works:

> The feudal system was a ferocious monster, devouring, wherever it came, all that the friend of humanity regards with attachment and love. The system of titles appears under a different form. The monster is at length destroyed, and they who followed in his train, and fattened upon the carcases of those he slew, have stuffed his skin, and, by exhibiting it, hope still to terrify mankind into patience and pusillanimity.
>
> (1985: 472)

For the strict rationalist, the image is one of perplexity and anathema: there is no reason, given that the ferocious monster of the feudal system has been relegated to the past, that feudal values, titles and customs should have any sway over the populace. Without substance or economic and material basis, feudalism is dead, and superstition, barbarism and tyranny ought to be interred with the monster's corpse.

Godwin's stuffed monster is echoed, over fifty years later, by Marx's contention that 'the tradition of all the dead generations weighs like a nightmare on the brains of the living' (1943: 315). The past which determines the circumstances in which 'men make their own history' in conditions not of their choosing allows a process of revolutionising to occur in an ambivalent manner, looking back but also moving forward, 'they anxiously conjure up the spirit of the past to their service and borrow from them name, battle slogans and costumes in order to present the new scene of world history in this time-honoured guise and this borrowed language' (Marx 1943: 315). For Marx, 'the awakening of the dead' enables the glorification of new struggles. For Godwin, in contrast, the persistence of dead political forms holds out no such promise: the stuffed monster serves to check any forward momentum and thwart even the imagination of a different future. Dead, the monster continues to exert its power over credulous and cowardly minds. Against all reason, the stuffed monster perpetuates its old terrors; to the consternation of a position that advocates the transparency of enlightened rationality, this political terrorism is baseless, delusional, exerting its effects by virtue of the imagination alone. The stuffed monster functions as a 'real phantom' that preserves feudal and chivalric powers (Damrosch 223). The progress of reason encounters the obstacle of human passions, confronting, moreover, a resistance that is subjective and imaginary rather than material, though no less powerful for that. The imaginary, even ideological, dimensions of romance, ensuring the persistence of feudal values and attitudes in an economic context that has moved beyond them, offers a challenge to both rational philosophy and to the possibility of radical political change.

Recognising the power of romance in sustaining a feudal spirit long beyond its sell-by date, Godwin, the rationalist, makes some effort to incorporate it into his political analysis. 'Perhaps', he writes, 'government is not merely in some cases the defender, and in others the treacherous foe of the domestic virtues. Perhaps it insinuates itself into our personal dispositions, and insensibly communicates its own spirit to our private transactions' (1985: 81). The boundaries between public and private, between internal states and external conditions are permeable in this line of thinking. Human character, for Godwin, develops in relation to external circumstances. Thus, social and political conditions give shape to subjective existence, minds forged by the manacles of government. Romance, it would seem, forms part of the process whereby feudal attitudes are imprinted on the minds of late eighteenth-century not-so rational subjects. Yet Godwin, in his account of 'History and Romance', also suggests that romance can be an instructive form of writing, adding an idea of flesh, feeling and authenticity to the abstractions of historical writing.

The extent of the insinuations of romance in the formation and development of human character constitutes a major part of the project of *Caleb Williams*. The focus on individual character – underlined by the use of first-person narrative – emphasises the subjective dimensions of 'things as they are'. Notions of character are problematic, and are tied to narrative forms to the extent that Godwin's novel 'refuses to distinguish between an existence and the narrative of an existence'. The lack of distinction, moreover, means that the novel's contrast is not 'between roles and selves, but between true roles and false ones', especially in the manner that it highlights concerns with 'counterfeit' character (Edwards 2000: 541; 544). The recurrence of romantic figures and rhetoric tied to Godwin's analysis of character is shown to shape the understanding and attitudes of protagonists and direct the movement of the narratives. Romance, while enabling a greater appreciation of character and individual passion, is inextricably bound up with the various modes of persecution and tyranny documented in the fiction. *Caleb*, as Godwin notes in his preface, continues the project of *Political Justice* by telling a story of how 'the spirit and character of the government intrudes itself into every rank of society' and offering 'a general review of the modes of domestic and unrecorded despotism by which man becomes the destroyer of man' (1988: 3). Government, it seems, can be both the destroyer as well as defender of 'domestic virtues', its insinuations into 'personal dispositions' and 'private transactions' as inevitable as they are extensive. Romance, then, with its capacity to both idealise and ruin character, is deployed not only as a theme – perhaps appealing to a broader, and more profitable, readership – but as an integral part of the novel's political analysis, an attempt to show the imbrication of internal and external worlds.

Early in Caleb's story, as he begins to discover the truth about his employer and finds his condition of servitude to be less rosy than expected, he makes an important comparison between internal and external forms of tyranny: 'the vigilance of a public and systematical despotism is poor, compared with a vigilance which is thus goaded by the most anxious passions of the soul. Against this species of persecution I knew not how to invent a refuge' (144). Though Caleb will encounter many forms of physical ordeal, from imprisonment to pursuit and persecution, the mental suffering that is centred on his relationship with his master, the novel's villain, Falkland, proves to be more acute and devastating to his well-being. Falkland, a local squire who takes the young Caleb into his service, initially appears in the most charming and beneficent light. His virtues are contrasted to the brutish and violent character of his rival, another local squire called Tyrell. But the flattering comparison does not last long, not only because Tyrell is murdered, but because Caleb discovers Falkland to be the murderer: the squires emerge as opposite sides of the same corrupt class system that maltreats tenants and relatives. With Tyrell gone, moreover, the duplicity of Falkland's character comes to the fore. He is represented as both romantic hero and gothic villain, a conjunction which the novel insists is identical. Indeed, the honour, chivalry, noble reputation and character which impress everyone, especially Caleb, at the beginning of the novel is revealed to be the cause of the malevolent darkness that increasingly defines Falkland. The latter has also been described as haunting Tyrell (Graham 110). After Caleb discovers the guilty secret of Falkland's past, the latter discloses his gothic character in violent displays of demonic anger, his face showing 'supernatural barbarity', his threats exorbitant in their assumptions of power (1988: 118; 159–60). His brother notes that he holds to the language 'of romance, and not of reason' (182). Adherence to that language and the code it inscribes determines Falkland's actions to the extent that he is willing to live out the split between private vice and public virtue: 'though I be the blackest of villains', he declares to Caleb, 'I will leave behind me a spotless and illustrious name' (142). Honour and reputation – central to ideals of chivalry and romance – are to be preserved at any cost, as Caleb discovers. Indeed, these ideals and their dark implications lie at the root of

Falkland's character, the secret hidden in his past. His early romantic life in Italy, of which he never speaks and which gives him an air of mystery, is assumed to have involved a duel and a death. Chivalry is underpinned by violence, the novel makes plain; its codes of honour and virtue mask cruelty and tyranny. At the end of the novel, the point is again reinforced: 'Falkland! thou enteredst upon thy career with the purest and most laudable intentions. But thou imbibedst the poison of chivalry with thy earliest youth . . . ' (336–37). Fine hopes are blasted as he lives only with a 'phantom of departed honour'; benevolence gives way to jealousy, honour to imposture, good intentions to madness. Romance, so the novel maintains, is not only spectral but poisonous. Chivalric ideals, the novel demonstrates, are outmoded fantasies which lead to violence and ruin. But the novel also demonstrates their insidious persistence as it sets out to perform the dangerous and inescapable coupling of romantic ideal and gothic violence.

Falkland, though demonstrating the extremes of romance, is not the only character to imbibe its poisons. Caleb is far from immune to its idealised image. If Falkland stands out as the novel's gothic villain, then Caleb, from the start, is positioned as its gothic heroine, caught between terror and romance, curiosity and persecution. From the opening pages, Caleb speaks of his interest in romance: his inquisitive interest in natural philosophy was coupled with 'an invincible attachment to books of narrative and romance' (6). He even presents his life as such: an orphan who is taken into the service of Falkland, he states that he does not view his situation 'with terror', but 'formed golden visions of the station I was to occupy' (7).

Though acquainted with Falkland's gloomy side early on, Caleb's romantic visions lead him to conclude his account of Falkland's travels in Italy with a comment on how he had 'acquitted himself in the most brilliant manner as a man of gallantry and virtue' (18). The initial idealisation of Falkland forms a crucial point of identification for Caleb, one that shapes his destiny, causes his sharpest mental anguish and, of course, defines his character. His overidentification with the romantic figure of Falkland leads him to his first transgression: prying into the secrets of the locked chest. His imagination, excited to the levels of curiosity characteristic of one of Radcliffe's heroines, leads him into an inescapable and destructive bond with Falkland. The latter is forced to suppress wider knowledge of his secrets and persecute Caleb by legal and surreptitious means. For all the suffering he is forced to endure, Caleb is reluctant to expose his former master. The extent of Caleb's identification, however, means that his attempts to prove his innocence, which would also mean publicising Falkland's guilt, are half-hearted. He, too, is split between justice and romance, double bound to two codes and split between them. At one point he observes, 'I determined never to prove an instrument of destruction to Mr Falkland; but I was not less resolute to obtain justice for myself' (167). To achieve one end, however, he must sacrifice the other. His dilemma is reflected in the double and reversible relationship between master and servant, each bound to the other in a relationship of pursuer and pursued, flight and return, fear and desire for recognition, persecutor and victim (317). Because the relationship depends on a shared secret, the bonds of identification and romance are impossible to sever. The drama of character de-formation, mental subjection, of internalised conflict takes precedence over the more obvious methods of persecution and oppression. As a result, the novel defers, and finally fails to deliver, any satisfactory romantic resolution: the first, unpublished, ending leaves Caleb bemoaning the injustice he has suffered, languishing in jail where his misery and isolation causes the steady erosion of his mental faculties. This version of the novel ends in broken phrasing: 'Nobody can complain of me – all day long I do nothing – am a stone – a GRAVE-STONE! – an obelisk to tell you, HERE LIES WHAT WAS ONCE A MAN!' (346). The inhumanity of the condition to which Caleb is reduced by the class system and its legal superstructure leaves no doubt about the novel's position with regard to 'things as they are'.

While the first version is more total in its image of living death, of human life marked out as a tombstone, of identity dissolved to nothing, the second, published, version presents a dissolution of identity that retains the pessimism of the story but accentuates the destructive romantic bond between the protagonists. In the latter, Caleb and Falkland finally meet before a magistrate. Neither, however, receives any satisfaction from this belated legal encounter. Caleb is shocked by the other's appearance: from having the 'haggard, ghost-like and wild energy' of the Gothic villain, he now had 'the appearance of a corpse', weak, wasted, colourless and limp (329). Disarmed, Caleb nearly withdraws his case. In an agony of indecision, Caleb comments on the 'cruelty' of his own action, on the reverence, love, 'ardent admiration' he held for his master. Though accusing him of Tyrell's murder, Caleb is more concerned to point out the defects and praise good qualities of Falkland's character, along with his own mistakes. In response, Falkland offers none of the gothic bombast and demonic rebuttals previously shown to Caleb. Instead, the latter is also praised in course of a confession full in its indulgence in self-blame and self-execration. Exonerated, Caleb feels no exhilaration. Rather, he is made to feel guiltier by Falkland's praises: they 'aggravate the baseness of my cruelty' (336). Publicly cleared but privately considering himself the criminal, Caleb's position, the inverted image of Falkland's, leaves him 'truly miserable'. He closes with a devastating realisation: 'I began these memoirs with the idea of vindicating my character. I have now no character that I wish to vindicate' (337). His character, so long dependent on his romantic relation to Falkland, is destroyed as surely as it is in the first ending of the novel. Falkland's desire to maintain his reputation at all costs has left him with only the 'simulacrum of character' while Caleb 'ends up with neither': there is no 'true' character in the story which 'ends with nothing but a hole where a man used to be' (Damrosch 236). His legal victory, in every sense, is 'hollow' (Everest and Edwards 141). Neither law, nor narrative, nor truth, is able to fill the gap. Reduced to nothing, Caleb is left with no one with whom he is able to identify, no imaginary, romantic figure on which to secure some sense of identity.

The conclusion of the novel, with its stress on the negative effects of romance in the dissolution of character, draws attention to the feudal code and its persistence in fiction and, further, attempts to demonstrate its dangerous social effects. While romance constitutes ideals of character, internalising models of self and behaviour, its poison also leads to ruin. In focusing on the relationship between Caleb and Falkland – representatives of different social classes – the novel also foregrounds the pervasive power of romantic ideas in maintaining irrational political divisions and antagonisms in an interdependence of positions that eventually consumes both parties. One, it seems, cannot survive without the other and thus both remain condemned to destruction. In moving from romantic idealisation and aspiration to ruin and devastation, in tracing the romantic extremes of honour and disgrace, nobility and cruelty, benevolence and violence, the novel demonstrates that these antitheses function reciprocally within the same system. The system, moreover, pervades internal as well as external space, as the focus on Caleb's psychological bondage to figures of romance shows.

*Caleb Williams* thus manifests its own doubled form as both a romance and an anti-romance. In its characters and narrative, the novel sets out a fully romantic stall, only to undermine any subjective investment in illusions of personality, plot or mystery. The anti-romantic trajectory of Godwin's romantic novel, moreover, is evident in its attention to its own textuality and narrative composition as much as in its tale of the constitution and dissolution of romanticised character. Self is very much a textual effect (Hogle 1979. Truth, too, becomes entwined in textuality: working through various types of truth, the novel manifests its place in an 'abysmal' structure to suggest that 'truth constructs itself like a fiction, in a fiction' (Lecercle 79). Composed of numerous different but intertwined narratives – from the positions of Caleb, Falkland, Tyrell, Emily Melville, Collins Hawkins – the novel's frames display not only the interdependency of stories and selves, but 'frame' characters in a criminal sense, promoting false ideas that, nonetheless, are acted upon as though true. In Caleb's case, this is most evident when he hears stories of the notorious robber 'Kit Williams': at first he fails to recognise himself as the infamous criminal, and when he does so he realises that these tales are part of his persecution at the hands of Falkland's agent. Later on, pursued and in hiding, he is forced to circulate concocted narratives about his own disguised identity. Towards the end, Caleb, having assumed so many fake identities, describes himself as having a 'counterfeit character' (265). Another figure observes that reality has been 'palavered over' (183). Character, reality and truth emerge in the light of fiction and in the guise of narration. 'Things as they are' are utterly penetrated and entangled with fictions.

In charting the complementary extremes of romance – as both feudal code and fictional form – the novel draws attention to the role of narrative in the imaginary constitution of political life. Tracing the extremes of romantic identification, from Caleb's early golden visions to his final dissolution, it plays romance against romance in an attempt to exhaust all romantic affects and lay bare all the deceptive illusions of fiction. It is an effort at demystification, at dis-illusion. Hence, the significant absence of resolution or reconciliation at the end: to offer a glimpse of justice would provide too much reassurance in times in which, as Godwin notes, 'terror was the order of the day'. To return to character, its innocence and reputation re-established, would also contradict the aim of exhausting the romantic paradigm. Rather than dis-illusioning the reader, in the manner that Caleb, romance reader, has his illusions shattered in the course of the novel, a vindication of character would reinscribe the pact of readerly identification which the novel is at pains to undermine. Structurally, the different narratives refuse any reconciliation, even of a single subjective position that would serve as a point of closure and secure identification. As a 'badly written novel', the text evinces anachronistic 'avant-garde' effects, exposing its own narrative construction and inconsistencies, and thereby 'laying bare the device' (Everest and Edwards 141). In bringing truth into textual relations and in evacuating character, the novel refuses to close gaps and unify positions, drawing a sense of absence to the fore: truth is disclosed as a 'structural absence', a 'lack' around which the subject is constituted in a 'chain of repetitions' that is only arrested in death (Lecercle 92). Without truth or single character, the position left for the reader has no substance or consistency: he or she is left to consider the construction and effects of fiction.

Fiction, romance in particular, is not a rational form, as the novel constantly insists: to reinstitute romance at the end, then, would be at the expense of reason. Instead, romance is expended in order to open the way for reason: the refusal of resolution, romance, identification, or readerly satisfaction, eschews the predictable closure of generic fiction and requires the dis-illusioned reader to adopt a rational response, a response, however, that, because fiction is the object of criticism, cannot be presented in fictional terms. Fiction, however, as the novel also makes clear, pervades inner as well as external worlds; it is one of the modes by which government, politics, social circumstances, insinuate themselves in personal disposition, character and mental life. Reason, then, never gets beyond, nor fully separates itself from romance, despite the latter's exhaustion. The interrogation of fictional effects and mechanisms, however, does offer an analysis of the ideological implications of romance, which acknowledges its imbrications in and perpetuations of political power. Indeed, in the interrelation of fiction and political reality, imaginary, or ideological, questions are brought to the fore.

## Gothic anti-gothic

Ideology is 'the imaginary relation of individuals to their real conditions of existence' constituting subjects in structures of ideas and meanings that are lived as though they were natural facts (Althusser 39). For Godwin, with his stuffed monsters and romantically overidentified characters, romance – with all its feudal connotations – fulfils an ideological function in the interpellation and constitution of political subjectivity: the deference, obedience and fear engendered by class division and aristocratic hierarchy appear to be unchanging natural facts, occluding the contradictions that would engender questioning. Having been something of a literary counterfeiter himself, Godwin was well aware how genres of writing serve in the maintenance of political divisions. Earlier in his career, he had played with various types of composition and critical institutions, writing numerous fake texts (reviews of nonexistent books with made-up excerpts, for instance) that raised questions of truth, fictional form and the cultural establishment (Klancher 23–25). The strategy of using romance against romance is one which acknowledges, rather than simply denouncing as fiction or as illusion, the extensive real and imaginary effects of ideological codes in naturalising a set of class relationships. In doing so, the aim is to exhaust romance's uncritical hold on the expectations and identifications of readers and prompt, beyond the text perhaps, a more interrogative, if more dis-illusioned, stance in regard to social conditions. 'Things as they are', then, involves imaginary as much as real materials, with the former embracing subjective, narrative and textual formations.

If *Caleb Williams* uses romance against itself in an effort of narrative expenditure, then *Poor Things* sets gothic against itself in order to interrogate the fantasmatic and political implications of the genre's persistence in modernity (a modernity, at least one of the figures in the novel contends, that should know better). Drawing the reader into a highly recognisable web of fictional allusions, rewritings and canonical names, while all the time drawing attention to itself as a tissue of other fictions, a playful panoply of comfortable readerly enjoyment, *Poor Things* spits the gothicised reader out by its change of tack towards the end, shifting narrative mode and address with a down-to-earth debunking of the main story and the addition of crit- ical notes comprising actual, fake and fictitious histories, biographies and supporting textual evidence. The effect is one of narrative dis-illusionment. With *Lanark*, so Stevenson argues, a similar strategy is employed:

> The real achievement of *Lanark* is not in seducing readers with illusion, but in allowing them to escape from it; in forcing them to consider conjuring and to examine and experience imagination as a process rather than securely finished product.
>
> (1991: 61)

*Lanark* ends without offering redemption, but suggests it as a political possi- bility beyond the text. *Poor Things* ends with two conflicting stories, and crit- ical notes that muddy the waters between them by mingling history and fabrications, thereby forcing the reader to decide, to take a position that cannot but be political. It is not simply a choice of two stories or versions of events – Archie's or Bella's: the metacritical position, a postmodern relation to the political or its inextricable immersion in the relativity of clever-clever textual games, is also at stake.

To dis-illusion, of course, first requires an exercise in creating illusions and making fantasies. The novel turns on a notion familiar to heterosexual adolescent males: what could be more perfect than having the body of a beautiful woman encasing the brain of a suggestible little girl? That, crudely put, forms the main plot device of *Poor Things* in a story in which the female monster of Frankenstein is relocated to the grave-robbing anatomy depart- ments of Scottish medical science. A pregnant, drowned woman is fished from the Clyde, her body saved and her brain replaced with that of her unborn child. Her 'creator', the gifted but physically-impaired surgeon, Godwin Bysshe Baxter ('God' for short) assumes responsibility for her education in every respect other than sexual. Here his failings are unleashed with innocent excess on the rest of mankind. Frankenstein's female monster – here called Bella Baxter – is finally loosed to create unpredictable and devastating effects. She is not the demon that Frankenstein imagined, and she does not spawn a race of devils. Her artlessness, education and un- manacled experience of the world, however, do offer monstrous interroga- tions of human systems of prejudice and morality; her diabolical innocence, indeed, does cause serious problems with a number of men.

Though Bella is able to tell part of her own story and some of her letters are included in the text, she, like Frankenstein's creation, is framed by the narratives and letters of others, mostly men. Godwin's disciple, a medical student called Archie McCandless, relates the events by means of a brico-lage of textual, mostly epistolary, sources, including the letters of the liber-tine lawyer with whom Bella elopes. A figment formed of fragments of Gothic fictions, Bella is fabricated by medical expertise and male fantasy. Though the scale of Archie's fantastical attributions are only contested later, the presentation of a woman who is corporeally fully-formed but mentally neonate circulating freely in the world of suitably uptight nineteenth-century professional men, doctors and lawyers in particular, embraces a range of fictional and social stereotypes, proper and improper alike. With a Wollstonecraftian freedom of mind and body, Bella pursues knowledge and experience on a tour of different cultures. The world in which she moves is, of course, defined in male terms. 'God' is the father and protector of a child-woman; Archie the suitor of a domestic and sexual object; Wedderburn, the libertine lawyer, with whom she flees. The latter considers her a romantic plaything and an object of passionate excess. But, from being 'a beautiful young woman' for him to ravish (77), Bella turns into 'a lemur, vampire, succubus and thing unclean' (89). In addition, she forms the object and prize in the intellectual contests between cynics, refugees and political philoso-phers that take place on her voyage. Latterly, she works in a Parisian brothel, and finally becomes the stake in a legal battle over her own identity: the husband of her body, a belligerent, jingoistic Victorian war-hero MP aristocrat claims her as Lady Blessington, his wife.

Bella, then, is a poor thing, a creation of male fantasy, an object of exchange and rivalry between men, defined in their terms and dependent on their munificence. But Bella is much more than an object, exceeding the fantasmatic projections that make her and the limits imposed on her. Possessed of a diabolical innocence she asks and her existence performs the most devastating questioning of social and political morality, a humane monster of boundless empathy untainted by the corruptions of wealth or prejudice. Bella's exceeding of male fantasy is exemplified in her relation-ship with the libertine lawyer, Wedderburn. He is soon disabused of his fantasy of eloping with a beautiful and pliable young woman, an ever-ready source of sexual satisfaction. Bella is too ready. Unashamed of her sexuality, she is perfectly happy to spend nights copulating and days touring the sights of Europe. Wedderburn struggles to maintain the pace. He attempts to contain her by making her his wife, but she refuses; he tries to exhaust her but ends up utterly exhausted himself, worn out by an appetite and level of activity he is unable to sustain. Bella breezes through it all. Wedderburn ends up physically, mentally and financially wrecked. He recoils from her, recognising he is no longer in control but reduced to 'a man of straw and her helpless plaything'. The tables are turned, he having become the sexual object: 'you are only good for one thing, Wedder,' comments Bella, 'but you are very good at it indeed, a true grandee monarch magnifico excellency emperor lord-high-paramount president provost bobby-dazzler and boss at it' (87). And grateful tears stream down his face. The compliment underlines the reversal of their roles and the decomposition of his fantasy image of her. Exhausted, wretched, miserable, Wedderburn turns to the Catholic church. A new image of Bella emerges, as Eve, Delilah, Helen, Cleopatra, Salome. She is presented as another incarnation of the demonic female sexuality that threatens male self-mastery. His letter to Godwin, accusing the latter of mephistophelean and satanic deception, demonstrates, through religious ravings, his slide into madness.

Bella, then, has exceeded his fantasy construction of her. The polarised images of woman drawn from fiction and myth which chart the range of feminine roles, innocent, lover, wife and sexual demon, do not touch or capture her. Indeed, in taking on and exceeding the extremes by which women are represented, she succeeds in hollowing them out, just as she has done to Wedderburn himself. The reversal enacted in her relationship with him manifests an overturning of the assumptions and value systems supported by his fantasmatic projections: the male gaze is turned back on itself to reveal its own limitations and lack of foundations. In transgressing the roles and boundaries within which she is supposed to live, in much the same way as she innocently and unashamedly oversteps lines of sexual taboo and moral and class prejudice, she exposes the groundless, ideological basis of fantasy. Identity is a construction, a projection which, as in the case of feminine representations, requires antithetical poles to delimit the proper and improper range of social roles. In assuming and exceeding both, as beauty and beast, Bella's excess exposes the void underlying these limits. Her excess constitutes fantasy then causes it to collapse: it provides a screen for projection but then shows too much, disclosing the process of and necessity for projection itself, just as transgression allows limits and prohibitions to be defined even as it dispels any assumption of naturalness or fixity, allowing the artifice and fabrication of all cultural values to come to the fore. Lines of prohibition are crossed; they must, however, be re-established: Bella exceeds the limitations of beauty and compliance, so she must be turned into a monster. In disclosing the phantasmatic process of making monsters, however, she enables the monstrosity of the system to be displayed in much the same way that the creature's interrogations in *Frankenstein*, disclose the monstrosity of the systems that made him.

The exhaustion of Wedderburn is one instance of the effects of excess. One of the longest chapters of the novel concerns the attempt of General Blessington, the husband of Bella's body, to reclaim her. Interrupting the marriage of Archie and Bella, Blessington, accompanied by lawyer, doctor, detective and her father, demands his rights. The ensuing wrangle over her identity becomes a power struggle between discourses of law, psychiatry and medicine in which two fathers, a husband and a fiancé, vie for prominence. Despite the various statutes and diagnoses that are invoked, the case is impossible to settle. Bella – or Victoria Blessington – escapes definition and confounds distinctions. She has two fathers, Godwin and Hattersly, both giving her life in different senses. Her body may be Victoria's, but her mind is that of her child's, so that, legally at least, Blessington may be both husband and father. Property and person, woman and child, mind and body remain split but indivisible: all the efforts to reconcile her curious doubling of identity fail: she has exceeded the constraints of legal, medical and psychiatric discourse, along with the projections of male fantasy. In terms of historical and cultural contexts, Bella embodies the inherent divisions in the fantasy-formation of a Scottish national identity (Kaczvinsky).

The question of fantasy continues as the novel moves from the conclusion of Archie's tale to Bella/Victoria's rebuttal. A letter is appended as a corrective to the tale, signed by Victoria McCandless MD and addressed to her descendants. It offers a much more probable version of events than that related by Archie, a more banal, but no less heroic account, of a nineteenth-century woman's journey through poverty, wealth, and bad marriage to become a caring doctor and a participant in the development of socialist politics. Most of Archie's garish elaborations are dismissed as the flights of a foolish man's fancy: the work of an 'idle, dreamy fantastical' man is countered by that of a 'practical busy-in-the-world' woman (252). Archie's are not isolated as the fantasies of an individual, however. Victoria's letter identifies their provenance:

> My second husband's story positively stinks of all that was morbid in that most morbid of centuries, the nineteenth. He has made a sufficiently strange story stranger still by stirring into it episodes and phrases to be found in Hogg's Suicide's Grave with additional ghouleries from the works of Mary Shelley and Edgar Allan Poe. What morbid Victorian fantasy has he NOT filched from? I find traces of The Coming Race, Dr. Jekyll and Mr. Hyde, Dracula, Trilby, Rider Haggard's She, The Case-Book of Sherlock Holmes and, alas, Alice Through the Looking-Glass; a gloomier book than the sunlit Alice in Wonderland. He has even plagiarized work by two very dear friends: G. B. Shaw's Pygmalion and the scientific romances of Herbert George Wells.

(272–73)

For a practical and worldly nineteenth-century woman, Victoria is well versed in the tradition of Gothic romance. After posing and answering (it is a case of envy) the question of Archie's motivation for writing, she goes on to locate gothic literary fantasy in a broader cultural and political field:

*As I said before, to my nostrils the book stinks of Victorianism. It is as sham-gothic as the Scott Monument, Glasgow University, St. Pancras Station and the Houses of Parliament. I hate such structures. Their useless over-ornamentation was paid for out of needlessly high profits: profits squeezed from the stunted lives of children, women and men working more than twelve hours a day, six days a week in NEEDLESSLY filthy factories; for by the nineteenth century we had the knowledge to make things cleanly. We did not use it. The huge profits of the owning classes were too sacred to be questioned. To me this book stinks as the interior of a poor woman's crinoline must have stunk after a cheap weekend railway excursion to the Crystal Palace.*

(275)

Gothic fictions, like sham-gothic architecture, participate in the fantasy that occludes filthy material conditions with indulgently over-decorated structures. Fantasy, moreover, becomes entwined with capital's excesses and the production and maintenance of those conditions. Though Victoria's criticism of Archie's fantasy and gothic romance more generally invokes the opposing principles of realism – probability, factuality, common sense – the link made between fantasy and the ideological reproduction of attitudes and beliefs demonstrates the inextricability of actual life and fantasy, demonstrating how worlds of materiality, production, profit and poverty are rife with phantasmatic elaborations and supports. Purporting merely to correct the lies, delusion and fictions of Archie's fantasy with a return to realism, practicality and common sense, Victoria's rendering of a modern world suffused with gothic images does not deliver a state in which fantasy and reality are opposed: rather, they are entwined in their ideological function, morbid, dark, exciting fantasies bound up with, at the same time as they screen, the filth and misery of capitalist modes of production.

The novel does not traverse histories of fantasy and romance to return to an uncomplicated and straightforward (fictional) presentation of reality. That is, for all its sympathies for Victoria's socialist leanings, it refuses to offer an unqualified endorsement of her position. Her political position, its underlying morality, and her common sense, are also underpinned by fantasy, a fantasy that the notes go on to dis-illusion. Victoria's letter is dated August 1914, but she lives on until 1946. The notes fill in some of the blanks, with various fictitious writings, biographical, political and epistolary. Domestically Victoria's is disappointed: her three sons do not grow up into the caring adults she hoped for. Her theories of child development, elaborated in her politically-inspired handbook called *A Loving Economy*, do not, it seems, yield practical benefits. Worse still, her children become patriots and serve (and two die) in a capitalist war she believed the workers of world would not allow to break out. Though she lives to see the birth of the Welfare State, her struggles depend on a fantasy of human dignity, benevolence and proletarian power as its reality. As her account so often demonstrates, goodness, cleanliness and social sympathy are all-too often overwhelmed by poverty, degradation and suffering. Curiously, in this respect at least, versions of Victoria accord with Archie's representation of Bella. Both retain their faith in humanity, their sympathy and concern to help others.

The one overpowering moment of horror in the novel comes, not from the realm of gothic romance, but from an encounter with human suffering. On her travels and as part of her education, Bella is offered a lesson by a missionary, Hooker. He believes it will show 'the innate depravity of the unredeemed human animal'. Bella is then taken to the 'seamy side of Alexandria' (142–43). Her response to what she sees is recorded on six ripped and tear-stained pages of barely legible scrawl. Unspeakable or writable in any cogent form (at least for twenty pages of the novel), the horror causes Bella to break down and lose her senses. It involves extreme human suffering and poverty. She also witnesses the sight of wealthy western tourists enjoying that condition and experiences the powerlessness of not being able to do any good. Gothic fictional technique in the representation of horror, in the manner of *Udolpho's* rendering of the unspeakable, sense-dissolving encounter that remains unmentioned for four hundred pages, or *Romance of the Forest's* shredded manuscript of murder, is set against a most un-gothic horror. The horror is doubled: belief in humanitarian impulses are shattered in the blind face of suffering and their own powerlessness to ameliorate it; at the same time, the spectacle of others enjoying the scene presents a glimpse of intolerable inhumanity, the latter horror more suggestive of 'the innate depravity of the human animal' than the former. Gothic and un-gothic, the conjunction of horrors polarises a humanist fantasy and a morbid Victorian fantasy in which money and degradation combine in gothic enjoyment, opening on to the horrifying Thing around which the novel circulates.

*Poor Things*, in which almost every character is described by the phrase, frames a range of figures, human, imaginative, emotional and political, in terms of poverty and materiality. In disclosing the unpresentable, formless Thing, neither object nor subject, neither actual nor imaginary, neither material nor immaterial, at the centre of human symbolic systems and fantasy formations, it offers a broader interrogation of gothic fiction and modernity. What the novel discloses is the doubleness of modernity, a period of light, progress, reason, materialism and production sustained in relation to darker fantasies, desires, regressions and repressions. One, however, defines and penetrates the other in a reproductive circuit of mirror images and imagined reversals. Modernity not only produces things – the goods and commodities of a materialistic culture – it also makes values, persons, meanings. Chapter titles like 'Making Me', 'Making Bella Baxter', 'Making a Maniac', 'Making a Conscience' emphasise the production of more immaterial things, such as identities and psychological states. Fantasy and (ideological) reality thoroughly interpenetrate each other in this era of production, exchanges of signs and images as crucial as exchanges of goods. Wedderburn comments on the doubleness constituting 'Modern Man': 'a noble soul fully instructed in what is wise and lawful, yet also a fiend who loves beauty only to drag it down and degrade it' (77). This self-image, too, is deluded, fantastical. He declares himself a fool for crediting such a comforting duality. The horror, the Thing that Bella's excess discloses to him, is more disturbing: his fantasies collapse, identity dissolves in madness.

Just as *Caleb Williams* dissolves character in order to traverse the romance that sustains political power in the 1790s, *Poor Things* traverses the gothic fantasies that in-form and are in-formed by Victorian modernity. Caleb's romantic overidentification with Falkland and his futile pursuit of justice empties out character, narrative, truth and law to expose class antagonisms, and reveal both the absence underlying symbolic fictions and the fantasy constructions that screen it. Beyond fantasy, divested of all illusions at the end, he cannot preserve the distance between self, Thing (absence) and Other (a liveable social structure) that staves off subjective collapse. Traversing the fantasy does not mean that one gets to an imagined 'other side', an uncontaminated reality beyond its influence, as Victoria implies in her criticism of Archie's fantastical tale. On the contrary, fantasy is taken to its unbearable limit, exposing, through excess, the absence underlying its workings and disclosing its effects in supporting the structures of desire and identification within which reality is lived. *Poor Things*, in textual games that are neither consistent nor reach a conclusion that redefines boundaries of truth and fiction, discloses a similar absence and excess: Bella – child, woman, monster, innocent and fantasy-Thing – multiplies, condenses and unravels the class, gender, and political antagonisms and constructions of her cultural context.

Rather than restoring the limits that enable a safe distance to be maintained between subject and Thing, thereby allowing identification and desire to pursue appropriately structured paths, the traversal of fantasy engenders a breakdown or decomposition. For Lacan, it raises the question of how a subject 'who has traversed the radical phantasy' can experience the death drive at the centre of imaginary and symbolic articulations of language and desire (1977b: 273). Lying beyond the structured circulation of desires, meanings, identifications associated with the pleasure principle, the death drive, as it comes to the fore, ruptures all frameworks, leaves the subject without the protection of a fantasy screen and manifests a destructive (and, perhaps, creative) 'will for an Other-thing' (1992: 212). The role of fantasy and its traversal is explained by Žižek:

> The paradoxical point is, rather, that fantasy intervenes (serves as support) precisely when we draw the line of distinction between what is merely our imagination and what 'really exists out there'. 'Traversing the fantasy', on the contrary, involves our *over-identification* with the domain of imagination: in it, through it, we break the constraints of the fantasy and the terrifying, violent domain of the pre-synthetic imagination, the domain in which *disjecta membra* float around, not yet unified and 'domesticated' by the intervention of homogenizing fantasmatic frame.
>
> (1999: 122)

In the radical identification with the work of imagination, in all its inconsistency, the role of fantasy in framing 'our access to reality' (Žižek 1993: 51) comes to the fore. Fantasy 'just masks, fills out a certain void, lack, empty place in the Other' (Žižek 1989: 74), it co-ordinates desiring and works as a screen 'concealing the gap, the abyss of the desire of the Other' (1989: 118). As such, it serves as 'a means for an ideology to take its own failure into account in advance'. To traverse the fantasy, in contrast, means, rather than a return to prescribed reality, to 'experience how there is nothing "behind" it, and how fantasy masks precisely this "nothing"' (Žižek 1989: 126). *Caleb Williams*, traversing the boundary between fiction and reality, discloses the frames that give shape to reality and identity, and breaks them: 'Godwin sees that if experience is fictive and if consensus breaks down, then fiction is *nothing but* fiction' (Damrosch 227). When reality is, in Godwin's phrase, 'palavered over' and the identifications of romance and character are taken to their limits, to dissolve to nothing, readers are left with nothing but a world composed of the broken frames of texts. Pushing fantasy against an assemblage shown to be a web or tissue of fictions, *Poor Things* discloses the emptiness, the unsynthesised, inconsistent and heterogeneous fragments of an unformed world: the texts, letters, images and allusions do not add up to an organised whole, but form partial screens dotted with holes.

With its layers of textual allusion, its attention to the fabrications of fiction and its repeated presentation of the fantasies of its characters and modern culture, the novel over-identifies with imaginative construction at the expense of narrative resolution. Identification and fantasy are over-played and played out to the point of exhaustion. Refusing resolution, moreover, leaves the reader confronting a void, at a remove from fantasy and its screens. The position is neither coherent nor unitary, neither contained within nor safely outside the frames of the novel. In respect of eschewing a final, authorised narrative, the strategy of *Poor Things* resembles *Lanark*. Towards the end of the latter, Lanark, the main protagonist, has an audience with the author of his fictional world. They discuss fictional form and the stealing of ideas and sentences from other writers (483). The author, described as a 'conjuror', even defines the basic constitution of the world he has created: 'some worlds are made of atoms but yours is made of tiny marks marching in neat lines, like armies of insects, across pages and pages and pages of white paper' (485). He goes on to discount the metaphor, because the tiny marks do not move: they are fixed and lifeless. A nameless annotator, in a footnote, also has qualms about the distinction between atoms and words, since, words, too, have atomic structure. The continuing discussion is instructive, nonetheless: 'how do *they* [printed marks] reproduce [. . .] movement and noises . . . ,' asks the author? 'By being read', Lanark replies: 'Exactly. Your survival as a character and mine as an author depend on us seducing a living soul into our printed world and trapping it here long enough for us to steal the imaginative energy which gives us life' (485). A reader's identification is paramount, it seems, in making the meaning of the text, as further discussion makes plain. Lanark, despondent that he is not getting the ending he wants, complains of the author's power: 'that *ought* to be the case', the latter replies, 'but unluckily the readers identify with your feelings, not with mine, and if you resent my end too much I am likely to be blamed rather than revered, as I should be. Hence this interview' (495). The reader appears sovereign. However, Lanark does not get his way, the happy ending of which he approves, being summarily dismissed as a lowly effort akin to the work of 'ten thousand other cheap illusionists' (492). Other endings are suggested, but no resolution is achieved and the main protagonist departs, unsatisfied, leaving a less than omniscient author mumbling to himself. The novel continues, without, so it seems, any direction, to its own uncertain end. It will require further reading. As in *Lanark*, *Poor Things'* narrative structure and self-consciousness underlines that there is no meaning or message safely framed within the text. Rather, the reader is left to read in a process of reading divested of securities of genre and convention. With the narratives of various less than reliable characters to choose from, moreover, the reader is left without a single figure or position with which to identify, suspended, critically perhaps, between gothic romance, idealistic realism and the indeterminate awareness of textual constructions and literary games.

*Poor Things*, then, leaves the reader with a horror beyond the conventional terrors and thrills prescribed by gothic romance. In glimpsing the void at the core of modernity, the novel offers its own reading of the tradition it so liberally uses and abuses. In this context, gothic fiction is understood to fulfil a different role to the one that is often ascribed to it: its presentation of monsters, illicit desires, dark wishes and threatening figures, constitutes a production, a fabrication and an apprehension of an otherness all-too close to home. In giving to form to anxieties, gothic figures allow them to be apprehended, giving that which was objectless and inchoate an image with which to arrest and direct fear and desire. Gothic thus provides a fantasy screen to mask the void of modernity, offering up figures of fear and desire that occlude some Thing more horrifying, thereby allowing modernity to take its own ideological 'failure into account in advance' (Žižek 1989: 118). Progress, reason, civilization, for all modernity's imperial inclusiveness, depend on exclusions: surplus resources and wasteful energies must be expended and by-products homogenised. Its own heterogeneous elements, that would consume it in internal turmoil, must be directed to an often imagined outside (hence the alien, the foreigner, etc.). The others it produces give vent to these energies and provide the antitheses that establish limits and define boundaries. Gothic, then, is one form of the fantasmatic frame that deals with the doubleness of modernity.

Published in 1992, *Poor Things* offers more than a critical history of gothic modernity. It offers a history of the present which engages with the politics of the post-modern as well. Dis-illusioning gothic credulity, its traversal of romance breaks open the fantasmatic frames of narrative. Its sublime is one of dissolution without thrilling recuperation; it refuses the nostalgia for romance and terror, for a fantastic seizing of reality and instead 'bears witness to the unpresentable', not to fill the void of modernity with so many new and commoditised presentations but to leave the space open as one of radical possibility rather than popular prescriptions (Lyotard 1984: 81–82). Its strategy stands opposed to other gothic romances of the period. Theirs advocates a return to terror and fantasy, a nostalgia for the whole and the one. Anne Rice's vampire romances in particular nostalgically reinvigorate a form of terror according to the prevailing political and economic context. In *The Vampire Lestat*, the hero regularly complains of the redundancy of vampires, the absence of romance and the consequent loss of sacred meaning in the modern world. His efforts to reinvent the struggle between good and evil on a grand and unifying scale stem from a terrifying and traditional romantic fantasy. His means, however, are very much of their time: rock video and stardom, media and simulation. The context in which the ancient creature is re-awoken drips with the easy wealth, consumer pleasures and sexual freedoms of Reagan's and Thatcher's 1980s. Lestat, unsurprisingly, finds himself very much at home.

*Poor Things* was published just after Thatcher was ousted, but in a period still reeling from the effects of Thatcherism. Its concerns with suffering, socialism and the filth of Victorian modernity relate to its present: the dismantling of the Welfare State, the collapse of the Labour Party and, of course, the invocation of Victorian values as the ideological gloss of monetarist conservatism. Individualistic ambition and opportunity, prudence, private enterprise, self-reliance and family, rather than State organisation and social responsibility provided the political rhetoric. *Poor Things'* critique of Victorian fantasy pertains as much to the persistence of Victorian values in the late twentieth century: Gray, in his *Glasgow Diary*, sets out to puncture the 'romantic notion nowadays that most Victorians pursued private gain through the channels of public spirit and moral rectitude' (cit. Bernstein 116–17). 'Maggie', the homely diminutive who ran the economy like a household, privileging individual over society and family over state, was the alter-ego of the 'Iron Lady', an unbending ideologue whose only freedoms were those of market and enterprise. A warrior-queen of the new economic values or a psychotic matron from a dystopian nightmare, Thatcher's rule was no less rife with romance and fantasy, its dream, in the main, being money, and its actuality a rising mass of workers cast out from the industrial sector and into the consuming economy of goods and services. Poor things.

# 4  Monsters of the imagination
## Science, fiction, romance

### Dark romance

Science fiction *and* gothic? When two generic monsters combine, their coupling delivers monstrosities of hitherto unprecedented dimensions. Both genres, from the start, are hybrids, combinations of various of literary and mythical forms exploring strange ideas, locations and events and imagining unnatural or more than natural creatures and creations from beyond the limits of the known world. In the multiple crossings between the genres, the zones of intersection tend to be dark and disturbing, obscure regions, populated by terrors and horrors that knowledge has failed to penetrate or control. Stranger still, despite the evidence of so many science fiction gothic mutations, is that the paths of both genres should cross at all. Gothic fiction conventionally deals in supernatural occurrences and figures, its demons and hauntings looking back, as do its architectural and cultural settings, to a past of superstition and barbarism, a feudal, 'dark' age precisely without the rational and civilised enlightenment, without the scientific techniques, so important as the platform for science fiction to look forward. Prospective, speculative, science fiction launches into the future with the aid of natural properties and technological powers, the imaginative expansion of human consciousness materialised in the wonders of other times, peoples and planets. Gothic fiction, for all its wanderings in desolate landscapes and invocations of diabolical forces, never strays far from home: it plays upon human fears and anxieties, its hauntings emanating as much from within as without. In their overlap, however, a long and interwoven association in the realms of modern popular literature and culture, both genres give form to a sense of otherness, a strangeness that is difficult to locate: monstrosity appears in the future and the past, in the mind and in culture at large, taking form in individual, social and textual bodies. As long as it is not 'predictable', 'calculable', or 'programmable', 'the future is necessarily monstrous' (Derrida 1992: 386).

Gothic fiction begins as a hybrid, a 'new species' of writing combining, so its founder Horace Walpole notes, ancient and modern romance (9). A 'strange monster', the genre was not received enthusiastically in the eighteenth century (Williams 1970: 151). Critics considered its plots improbable, its narratives ill-formed and unrealistic, and its morality dubious: in exciting readers with impossible adventures, fanciful ideas and tales of love, fiction leads away from the paths of virtue and towards licentious, vicious and thoroughly improper behaviour. 'Monsters of the imagination' – the flood of tales, romances, and novels threatening familial and social mores – propagated only depravity (Williams 1970: 162). Negative critical judgements followed later productions: M. G. Lewis' *The Monk* was described as a 'monster'; *Frankenstein* a 'monstrous literary abortion' (Anon. 1796: 677; 1826: 56). Hybrid, disturbing, monstrous, gothic fiction developed in the shadow of acceptability. Science fiction, too, emerges in illegitimate, monstrous forms. According to Brian Aldiss, the genre relishes 'its vitalising bastardy, its immoral interdisciplinary habits, as it feathers its nest with scraps of knowledge seized from the limit of the expanding world' (1973: 41). The disrespectful attitude to disciplines reflects science fiction's diverse generic emergence from fantasy, fairy tale, myth and romance (Aldiss 1973: 8–19). The 'genological jungle' of critical taxonomies is more dense, however (Suvin 19). Patrick Parrinder identifies the influence of fable and epic (39). Northrop Frye is more specific in describing the genre as 'a mode of romance with a strong inherent tendency to myth' (1976: 49). Among the many genres with which science fiction is associated, romance comes to the fore: H. G. Wells described his tales as 'scientific romances'; Hugo Gernsback (introducing the popular *Amazing Stories* magazine in April 1926) defined 'scientifiction' as 'a charming romance intermingled with scientific fact and prophetic vision' (Ketterer 50).

Romance, in its modern, eighteenth-century form at least, provided the matrix in which gothic and science fiction gestated. Monstrous in form, romance bred monstrosities: on the one hand, idealised figures drawn from chivalric or fairy tales were so impossibly unrealistic as to be 'monsters of perfection'; on the other hand, grotesque and deformed, were characters 'out of nature', alien to the familiar models of social virtue and reality. The creations of romance, moreover, work monstrously to 'transport the reader unprofitably into the clouds, where he is sure to find no solid footing, or into those worlds of fancy, which go forever out of the way of human paths' (Williams 1970: 162). Romances idealise and deform, just as science fiction creates 'as many hells as heavens' (Nicholls 1976: 181). That romance reading is unprofitable signifies the literary values of moral instruction and didacticism it lacked, placing the genre in the category of low, worthless fiction, a 'paraliterature', to use a term applied to popular science fiction

(Broderick vii). In eschewing firm ground in favour of flights of fancy, romances establish the trajectory of science fiction's unbounded imaginative explorations of change, outsiders, escape, its 'freedom of imagery' and freedom from realist conventions. In this respect, science fiction liberally exploits the possibilities of metaphor: it is 'the great modern literature of metaphor' (Nicholls 1976: 179–82). Metaphor, etymologically, is a form of 'transport', substituting terms, moving readers to new locations, creating new associations and combinations.

Science fiction, in exploring metaphor, defines itself against the bounds of realism. Raymond Williams, discussing the differences between utopian and science fictional treatments of paradise and hell, altered worlds and willed or technological transformations notes that 'the presentation of *otherness* appears to link them, as modes of desire or of warning in which a crucial emphasis is attained by the element of discontinuity from ordinary "realism"' (Williams 1979: 54). The metaphor of the monster, a 'presentation of otherness', an unnatural and unrealistic figure, repeatedly, in the eighteenth century, served in cautionary accounts of improper behaviour, a demonstration of and warning against immorality: 'Vice is a monster of so frightful a mien / As, to be hated, needs but to be seen' (Alexander Pope, *Essay on Man* II, 217–18). Discontinuities in and disturbances of reality and morality are registered and, depicted as monsters, held at bay. Realism and social reality recoils from strangeness and monstrosity. In contrast, science fiction embraces the possibilities opened up by metaphor's monstrous capacity to 'defamiliarise the familiar, and make familiar the new and the strange' (LeFanu 21). As a 'literature of cognitive estrangement', a mode of fiction in which a 'strange newness, a *novum*' is presented (Suvin 4), science fiction enables the wondrous and monstrous imagining of diverse metaphorical creations: the 'novum' is simultaneously a 'monstrum'; the difference is only a matter of position and perspective turning on the (im)propriety of metaphorical movements. Strangeness, indeed, applies to the uncanny as much as science fictional metaphor invention, an experience of the disruption of boundaries between reality and fantasy caused by the return of repressed psychic forces or uncertainties surrounding technical and textual simulations of human beings (Freud 1955; Jentsch; Cixous). In making the familiar strange, the new can be seen as threat (monstrum) or promise (novum): conventions, norms and realities are challenged, upheld, restored, destroyed or transcended, depending on whether the new is viewed as horrifying or exciting, imaginatively delineating a limit or transgressing conventional borders. Suvin, however, is careful in his terminology: 'estrangement' marks the distinction from realism (while maintaining a close relationship to rational, empirical and scientific realism), 'cognition' is differentiated from myth, fantasy and fairy tale. As a result, science fiction is firmly located at a distance from any gothic associations: 'even less congenial to SF is the *fantasy* (ghost, horror, Gothic, weird) tale, a genre committed to the interposition of anti-cognitive laws into the empirical environment' (Suvin 8). The novum-monstrum imagines difference and otherness in terms of desire or fear, a projection that reflects back on the society from which it emanates and a crucial node articulating gothic and science fiction, particularly when the latter's success, as Aldiss notes, stems from having 'diversified the Gothic tale of terror in such a way as to encompass those fears generated by change and technological advances which are the chief agents of change' (1973: 53).

## Hideous progenies

In the 1831 introduction to *Frankenstein* Mary Shelley allows her 'hideous progeny' to slide from authorial control and 'go forth and prosper' (1969: 9). The monster in the text and the monster that is the text (a novel composed of diverse generic fragments, multiple literary and cultural allusions and different epistolary narratives) complies. While Frankenstein refuses the monster's demand for a mate, fearing they will spawn a 'race of devils', the culture that receives the novel has no such qualms: in a proliferating host of dramatic adaptations, literary reworkings, cinematic productions and popular citations, Frankenstein and monster are repeatedly invoked as synonyms for acts of ungodly presumption or uncontrollable technological invention (Forry; Baldick 1987; Easlea; Turney). The novel, 'a new and hybrid fictional species' (Spark 128), begins in a ghost-story competition but takes its bearings from the contemporary scientific endeavours of Erasmus Darwin, Humphrey Davy, Giovanni Volta and Luigi Galvani. It looks back and lurches forward, like its monstrous protagonist, moving between the work of alchemists seeking the magical *elixir vitae* and the empiricism of new scientific ideas and techniques for understanding and transforming the physical world. Generically, too, the novel is difficult to categorise: emerging from a context of Romantic companions, aesthetics and experiments, it abandons the supernatural events and superstitions of gothic fiction. Geographically located in Northern, rational, Protestant and bourgeois countries and set in the present, its letters dated '17__', rather than feudal past, there is little evidence of the castles, abbeys and ruins so central to gothic formulas. Wild, desolate scenery remains, but in a manner redolent of Romantic investments in the sublimity of Nature. The desolation and wildness of natural spaces in the novel offer darker reflections on the solitary figures, Frankenstein and creature, that inhabit them, opening Romanticism to the return of gothic horror as the 'progressive internalization and recognition of fears as generated by the self' (Jackson 24). Self is divided, the novel becomes a psychodrama. At the same time, monstrosity is also located in external formations and institutions: in class antagonisms, revolutionary mobs, social and familial exclusion (Vlasopolos).

Indistinctly gothic, until later revisions and interpretations firm up the association, *Frankenstein* is also problematically related to science fiction. One editor states its protagonist to be indulging in 'switched-on magic' and 'souped-up alchemy': he is a 'criminal magician who employs up-to-date tools', while in the novel 'the technological plausibility that is essential to science fiction is not even pretended at'. It 'skips the science' (Shelley 1974: xxvii). In the novel no mention of scientific theory or innovation informs Frankenstein's laborious suturing and reanimating of dead body parts, though it is made clear that the 'secret of life' is taken from nature. Only belatedly, in the 1831 introduction's discussion of electricity and its passing reference to 'some powerful engine', is there a hint of any imaginative extrapolation of current scientific discoveries (Shelley 1969: 9). The mention of electricity and engines is enough, however, to inspire the cavernous laboratories filled with glowing generators, lightning conductors, tubes, wires, dials, so prominent in subsequent films. The fact of scientific creation, too, is enough for the novel to be declared 'the origin of the species' (Aldiss 1973: 7). *Frankenstein* is 'the first literary work which was indisputably a science-fiction novel, in the modern sense' (Priest 189). It is the 'first, definitive, unmistakable, science-fiction novel' (Russ 126). As the inaugural work of science fiction, Shelley's novel sets the patterns for others to follow: 'combining social criticism with new scientific ideas, while conveying a picture of her day, Mary Shelley anticipates the methods of H. G. Wells when writing his scientific romances' (Aldiss 1973: 23). It sows the 'seeds of all diseased creation myths', leading to the monstrous experiments of Dr Moreau and the threatening robots of Carel Capek's automated and dehumanised industrial society in *R U R* (Aldiss 1973: 33). *Frankenstein*'s influence is extensive, pervasive even:

> Every robot, every android, every sentient computer (whether benevolent or malevolent), every non-biological person, down to the miniscule, artificially created society in Stanislaw Lem's *Cyberiad* ('The Seventh Sally' – it's small enough to fit into a small box) – is a descendant of the 'mighty figure' Shelley dreamed one rainy night in the summer of 1816 and gave to the world two years later.
>
> (Russ 126)

*Frankenstein* casts a gigantic shadow over science fiction: incessantly alluded to, repeatedly cited, regularly adapted and reworked, its presence is everywhere. Writers frequently return to its theme and story for inspiration, to develop or correct its science, to explore further its ramifications or to pay homage playfully to its influence: Arthur C. Clarke's 'Dial "F" for Frankenstein' (1965), Harrison's 'At Last, The True Story of Frankenstein' (1965), Kurt Vonnegut's 'Fortitude' (1968) (see Haining 681–88; 728–34; 697–715). The origins are revisited most spectacularly in Aldiss *Frankenstein Unbound* (1974) in which a modern protagonist returns to the scene of creation to meet Mary Shelley and encounter the monster.

Mary Shelley wrote another novel concerned with questions of humanity and nature, a novel in which utopian ideas of social and political organisation are confronted with a disaster of global proportions. *The Last Man* (1826) is set in the twenty-first century and adopts a visionary tone at the beginning but has few modern innovations in which to dress up its future: balloon travel is used and the political and social structure of its England takes the form of an idealised Republic run by figures modelled on Percy Shelley and Byron. Politically, it remains tied to its time, to Romantic ideas of the Revolution in France. Personally, its representation of its heroes is more poignant, its author mourning the recent losses of her husband and close friend. It is hardly a science fiction novel: for Aldiss, its abandonment of the pretence of futurity and the paucity of its scientific extrapolations renders it 'no more than Gothic' (Aldiss 1973: 33). Although Suvin finds it the 'precursor of the SF biophysics of alienation' (Suvin 136), the enduring impact of *The Last Man* lies in the manner in which it represents global catastrophe. Frankenstein's monster of nature, left in the 'darkness and distance' of the Artic at the end of her first novel returns in feminine and devastating form in *The Last Man* to wipe out humanity and leave its civilisation in ruins. A great plague, a natural rather than supernatural disaster, is the cause, marking a turn from religious apocalypticism that, via Romanticism (Byron's 'Darkness' is a powerful example), poses questions about the limitations of human aspirations.

*Frankenstein* and *The Last Man* inaugurate 'two great myths of the industrial age' (Russ 126). Their engagement with the effects of economic, political and scientific change on individual, familial and social structures informs the speculations and fears that they present (O'Flinn, Baldick 1987). Enmeshed in the uneven development of modernity, in economic shifts to commerce, industrial production and imperial expansion, political calls for reform and democracy, aesthetic notions of the free, imaginative individual, and the pace of scientific innovation which visibly transforms the ideas and practices defining human existence, the novels identify the monstrosity in the new: revolutionary mobs are multicephalic monsters, industrial workers hulking brutes. But the new economic and political structures reducing humanity to slaves or automata, and ravaging familial and natural balances, are also monstrously inhuman, like the legal system that, in *Frankenstein*, executes an innocent servant, or the social values that reject the creature and thereby exacerbate his monstrosity. The gothic parts of Shelley's fictions take their bearings from the same, modern conditions of change that allow the emergence of science fiction, a genre that 'draws its beliefs, its material, its great organizing metaphors, its very attitudes, from a culture that could not exist before the industrial revolution, before science became an autonomous activity and a way of looking at the world' (Russ 10). Gothic and science fiction emerge, in often contradictory and complex fashion, with the emergence of modernity, bound up in the metaphors that are in the process of rewriting the world and instituting (wonderful/fearful) change.

Modernity, in inventing an array of disciplines along with its new economic, individual and political liberties is a curiously doubled formation. It is, like *Frankenstein*, bound up with matters of production and reproduction, concerned with developing the economic, industrial and technological apparatuses of modern society along with the renewal of groupings, ideas, values and procedures that shape and define individuals, making humans and making monsters at the same time. *Frankenstein*'s concern with a split or alienated self is thus highly appropriate to a context in which the human individual is doubled and divided. Suvin, in charting the relationship between the industrial revolution and Romanticism further divides the novel between 'flawed hybrid of horror tale and philosophical SF' (127). Where the Romanticism of Coleridge traces the decomposition of human relationships in the context of an increasingly alienating society and Percy Shelley appears as the 'great poetic forerunner' of 'SF anticipation', Mary's novel participates in a 'widespread recoil from Promethean utopianism' (Suvin 124; 127). Where Victor Frankenstein is located 'in the tradition of the Gothic story' and bound up with effects of horror and disgust, his creature is identified as 'both the compositional core and the real SF novum that lifts *Frankenstein* above the level of a grippingly mindless Gothic thriller' (Suvin 129–30). The division is important, if difficult to sustain, in marking out two very different trajectories for fiction. Science fiction is 'oriented towards humanity's furthest horizons' (Suvin 170) and thus takes its bearings from a distinctly Romantic idealism which transcends reason and science in its imagination of human progress. William Godwin and Percy Shelley are exemplary figures in this line of flight: the former, a radical, rational and humanist philosopher imagined the perfectibility of social relations. New developments in technology, he optimistically speculated, in relieving want and the material hardships of labour, were part of this process, indications of the capacity of mind to overcome matter (Godwin 1985: 770). Similarly idealistic, Percy Shelley allied a fascination with the benevolent and transformative potential of scientific discovery (his interests in electricity as the 'spark of life' are reflected in *Frankenstein*) with his politicised poetic imagination of human freedom.

Romanticism, it seems, extensively informs the intellectual aspirations and aesthetic attitudes of science fiction. H. G. Wells acknowledged his debt, noting, in his *Experiment in Autobiography*, that 'Grant Allen and I were in the tradition of Godwin and Shelley' (1966: 552). Gernsback, too, in speaking of 'charming romance', 'scientific fact' and 'prophetic vision' belongs to the tradition. So, too, Isaac Asimov, as he, in practice and critically, locates the genre in a modern humanist and rationalist framework concerned with scientific advancement, human improvement and understanding (cit. Broderick 4). The triumph of mind over matter appears strongly in Arthur C. Clarke's fiction: scientific progress has the power to save humankind and develop the 'overmind' that emerges in *Childhood's End* (1953). While Clarke is seen to indulge in 'naive romanticism' (Priest 189) and 'transcendental mysticism' (Hollinger 1990: 34), the 'supermind' that takes form in the immense modern network of electrical, telecommunicational and satellite relays in 'Dial "F" for Frankenstein' contains a more malignant aspect. Aesthetic attitudes and critical judgements of science fiction are also outlined in Romantic terms: for Aldiss, opposing the vulgarity and banality of mass consumption, science fiction is related to a 'love of art and science', a 'rebellion against smug bourgeois society', Romantic in its higher cultural enamorations and defiant individuality (cit. Broderick 53). For Ursula Le Guin, it is the imagination that supplements reason on a journey 'leading us towards the freedom that is properly human' (cit. Broderick 76).

Although enabling the distinction that allows science fiction to ascend imaginatively to poetic heights or collapse in monstrous dissolution, *Frankenstein*, its doubles too entangled, makes it difficult to sever Romanticism from its darker romantic counterpart. Both are inextricably bound together, one defining the other in a relationship of difference and reversal akin to that of creator and creature. In the novel, science is associated by one of Victor's mentors with visionary enthusiasm, wondrous discoveries and miraculous knowledge (Shelley 1969: 47–48). The motivation for reanimation is framed in aesthetic as much as empirical terms: poet and experimenter, Frankenstein, in part modelled on Percy Shelley, engages in what might be called 'Romantic science'. The project has benevolent and humane aims, ideally imagining the end of disease and death. Although oversized, a prototype of science fiction's enhanced, invulnerable superhuman bodies, the creature is designed to be beautiful: it will be the first of a 'new species' happily blessing its creator as father (Shelley 1969: 54). Borne on the wings of fantasy the project encounters its limit in horror. Creation takes Victor through charnel houses and graveyards, places of death and horror; it requires the theft of the 'secret of life' from feminised nature, a usurpation implying the unnaturalness, the monstrosity underlying Frankenstein's project. The moment of success, the animation of the dead body parts, is also perceived as absolute failure: the creator is appalled by his handiwork rather than elated by his technical achievement. The only grounds for his horror, it seems, are aesthetic: the creature is ugly. Frankenstein's world is overturned at this point, beauty collapsing in horror, heaven becoming hell. His rejection of the creature sets the patterns for the mental, social and corporeal dissolution that turn the rest of the novel into a nightmare of desolation and exclusion: rejected, outcast, the novel's main definition of a monster, both by Frankenstein and the idealised Romantic family that unwittingly educates him, the creature accepts his monstrous role to destroy his creator's family and haunt him in his isolation.

Idealisations, the novel suggests in its engagement with Romantic aesthetics and politics, readily engender monsters, the latter manifesting the corporeal, social and sexual relationships excluded by the imaginative aspirations of the former. The two poles of existence cannot be separated: though Victor imagines a form of life that overcomes the ravages of death, his theft of the vital spark only invigorates the latter's work. The painful education of the monster allows him to make some astute observations on an irreparably divided modern humanity: 'was man, indeed, so powerful, so virtuous, and magnificent, yet so vicious and base?' (Shelley 1969: 119). Humans are doubled beings, the novel suggests, minds and bodies, individualistic and social, noble and base. The novel's appreciation of doubleness, its attention to ideas and materiality, to aesthetics and knowledge, to bodies and institutions resonates with the formation of modernity in which the body is located as a crucial object of power: a site of knowledge, discipline, normalisation, individuation, the body is constituted and structured by a network of discursive and material practices from schooling to legal and medical procedures. The body, moreover, is crucial in establishing an imaginary sense of individual wholeness, its mirror image serving in the process of motor and psychological co-ordination. In *Frankenstein*, poised between the idealisations projecting a new, free, humanist individual and the material consequences of industrial and bourgeois revolutions, modernity has yet to co-ordinate fully an integrated sense of itself as individual, social or political body. Monstrosity remains. *Frankenstein* does not resolve its antitheses: modernity remains human and monstrous at the same time. Historically divided, the novel is generically split: neither gothic nor science fiction, both gothic and science fiction, it is productively, if indeterminately, placed with regard to the progress and/or regression of humankind.

## Dark science

Science, its theories, tools and effects, is often given a horrifying, gothic aspect and atmosphere when incorporated in tales of terror, ghostly possession and vampiric assault. While science forms a part of the fiction, its introduction remains a device subordinated to gothic ends, the occasion for the unleashing of demonic energies or the broaching of sacred and super-natural mysteries. In the tales of Edgar Allan Poe mental spaces are rendered gothic, places where empirical rationality flees in the face of extreme psychological disturbances: pathological and guilty hallucinations, the nightmares of a diseased imagination are consumed by a sense of strangeness, acutely aware of the indeterminacy of borders separating reality and fantasy. Poe often engaged with scientific ideas and his tales show the 'markedly "scientific" or science-fictional nature of his visionary reality' (Ketterer 55). In 'The Facts in the Case of M. Valdemar' (1845) the new technique of mesmerism enables a dying man to be placed in suspended animation. The procedure becomes stranger still when a voice declares 'I am dead': does consciousness or the body itself speak from beyond the grave. In the very act of speaking, moreover, the attribute of living beings is transferred from the side of life to that of death thereby inducing a ghostly disturbance of the boundaries of reality. The effect, of course, is uncanny.

Mary Braddon's short story, 'Good Lady Ducayne' (1896), sets up a curious gothic encounter with science. A young companion to an elderly lady is seen to be growing visibly weaker, paler and more drawn. She has a mysterious 'bite' on her body. Gothic expectations of a vampire lurking in the household, the 'good lady' herself perhaps, are excited until the cause is revealed: in an effort to extend her life the old lady has ordered her doctor to siphon blood from her young companion. Equating blood transfusion and vampirism, a parallel that also occurs in *Dracula* (1897), the story punctures its air of mystery and apprehension with the disclosure that, instead of super-natural powers and diabolical agents, the root of evil is no more than an old woman's vanity and the unethical employment of a scientific technique. A gothic aura, however, still hangs over science, giving forms to fears about its capacity to penetrate and affect living bodies. In *The Strange Case of Dr Jekyll and Mr Hyde* (1886) science has a more evident role, the notion of a 'case' itself identifying a modern professional world of legal arrangements and scientific studies. Dr Jekyll, however, is a scientist in the Frankensteinian mode, professing 'transcendental' ideas against the 'narrow and material' outlook of a colleague (80). His experiments, though conducted using scien-tific instruments and chemical processes, are orientated in more philosoph-ical and moral directions: the impure chemical compound which enables Jekyll's transformation to brutal and beastly Hyde is merely a device that allows an inherent, in-human, evil to be materialised. In a cultural context obsessed by fears of decadence and degeneration, human corruption and depravity, the regression to savage or bestial states, is a matter of abhor-rence. In a similar manner, science gives way to bodily instincts and decay in a manner that brings out the occult: Arthur Machen's *The Great God Pan* (1894) begins with an experiment in brain surgery (conducted by a doctor of 'transcendental medicine') and ends with the patient confronting the pagan divinity; in Machen's 'The Novel of the White Powder' (1895) a compound purchased innocently from a chemist's shop turns out to have spectacularly horrible effects: an accident of time and variations in temperature produced a witches' potion. In *Dracula*, too, modern science (theories of hypnotism, degeneration, criminality and unconscious cerebration) and modern technologies (phonographs, typewriters, transfusions and telegrams) provide a contemporary setting allowing the return of barbaric forces and primitive energies. At the same time, scientific knowledge gives credence to the mysterious and occult powers embodied by the vampire: the novel's priest-scientist, Van Helsing, speculates that Dracula's castle is located in a spot where geological, chemical, electrical and magnetic forces combine to produce natural anomalies, occult powers presently beyond the reach of scientific understanding. Gothic fiction in the *fin de siècle* aspires to a realm of mystery beyond the scientific and commercial materialism debilitating Victorian culture.

In December 1897, so Judith Wilt emphatically declares, Victorian gothic turns into Victorian science fiction with the publication of H. G. Wells' *The War of the Worlds*. To emphasise the shift she contrasts two scenes: the first, from *Dracula*, breathlessly details the vampire's bloodsucking embrace, a first-person account oozing with horror and eroticism; the second from Wells' novel is a dispassionate description of how the invading Martians feed by injecting the living blood of their victims into their own veins (Wilt 618–19). In the case of Wells, the difference lies in the tone: 'the image is of carnal appropriation, not metaphysics but physics, and biology; the morality is scientific tolerance' (Wilt 619). The distinction is important, and one that has been employed by Sontag to distinguish horror and science fiction films: the latter subordinates shocks and horrors to encourage a 'technological view' of proceedings (428). The alien invasion depicted in *The War of the Worlds* emphasises rationality and necessity: running out of food on their own planet, it is a matter of survival, as is the consumption of humans. Technologically sophisticated and possessing a cool, callous and refined intelligence, the aliens are nonsexual (they bud rather than breed) and tireless. Since humans are so much lower on the evolutionary ladder, the Martians have no qualms about subjugating and consuming them. Invasion is experienced from the position of the colonised, the greatest imperial nation on Earth at the time finding itself on the receiving end of superior forces of rationality and science: 'we must remember what ruthless and utter destruction our own species has wrought, not only upon animals, such as the vanished bison and the dodo, but upon its own inferior races' (Wells 12).

The near future of the story reflects back on the present: progress and civilisation encounter their barbaric mirror image.

Beneath the cold scientific tones, and because of their callous, objective indifference, a glimmer of horror appears to acknowledge recognisable complementarity between British and Martian imperialism, and to register the possibility of the former's demise. Not only is imperialism threatened: the story evinces a 'fear of the end of the empire of man' (Wilt 627). Anxieties and fears about human existence disclose another generic residue: Wells' romances remain 'dark with the threat of the Gothic, but plotted to the remorseless logic of scientific progress' (Wilt 620). The destruction of bodies and the encounter with otherness disturbs the idealised self-image of Victorian culture. For Wells, discussing *The Time Machine* (1895) in his account of scientific romances, the effect is an 'assault on human self-satisfaction' (cit. Philmus ix). Science, as much as horror, launches such an assault. In *The Island of Dr Moreau* (1896) the combination is brought to the fore: 'the study of Nature makes a man at last as remorseless as Nature' (73). The result is science, red in suture and scalpel. The coldness of scientific rationality is nowhere more chilling than in the figure of Dr Moreau, a 'notorious vivisector' who turned an isolated island into a laboratory for cutting up and stitching together animals into new, malformed hybrid mockeries of human shapes (33). The novel has him detail the various techniques (vaccination, inoculation, transfusion, surgery), the failed experiments and, of course, the intense physical suffering that contribute to his plan to 'burn out all the animal', to 'make a rational creature of my own' (76). For all his successes in creating 'humanised animals', bitterly ironic 'triumphs of vivisection', these are just, the narrator exclaims, 'monsters manufactured!'(68–69). Worse, for Moreau, is that his creatures 'revert'. Amid the horrifying confusion of corporeal and species boundaries, the hideous creations of accelerated, technological Darwinism are much less monstrous than their maker. In speeding up evolution to demonstrate the superiority of reason and science over nature, it is not animality that is finally overcome by civilised humanity. The reverse occurs: the humanised animals, automatically chanting the nursery rhyme 'sing-song' of 'Law' ('not to go on all-Fours' etc.) mock the values of human culture and civilisation as little more than fragile, superficial masks. The taint of horror, at first contained by the island's isolation, spreads to the heart of the empire. The narrator, on escaping, returns to England, but finds in London 'the horror was well-nigh insupportable', populated by 'prowling', mewing women, 'furtive craving men', 'gibing' children, gibbering preachers (128–29). Urban culture is itself rife with evolutionary chaos, humans rendered as mirrors of the 'Beast People' on Moreau's island.

Fears of degeneration, of Darwinian evolution progressing into reverse as culture loosens itself from nature and descends into its own luxurious, decadent corruption while the latter continues its course, are vividly presented in *The Time Machine*. A traveller relates his journey into the future. Amid the ruins of great palaces, awesome machines and an abundant natural landscape, a race of soft, delicate, graceful, but physically and intellectually weak beings, the 'Eloi', live gentle, idle lives. It seems, to the traveller, to be the culmination of scientific and agricultural progress towards a balanced and harmonious 'subjugation of Nature' (32). He is soon disabused by the appearance of another species, the loathsome Morlocks, nocturnal underground creatures who feed on the Eloi. Soon, the 'truth dawned':

> that man had not remained one species, but had differentiated into two distinct animals: that my graceful children of the Upper-world were not the sole descendants of our generation, but that this bleached, obscene, nocturnal Thing, which had flashed before me, was also heir to all the ages.
>
> (45)

A parodic legacy of class hierarchies remains in this process of evolution: the upper classes, indolent, decorative, feeble, have become food for their brutish, subterranean, industrial servants. As the traveller heads further into the future, he witnesses not only the extinction of humanity, but the end of the solar system. Enveloped in the desolation and thickening darkness of a dying world, the sky turning black, evolution is seen to run its course: 'a horror of this great darkness came on me' (78). The entropic certainty and circularity of the universe descends on humanity in horror. It is an encounter, Wells notes in his essay 'On Extinction', in which the traveller is swept 'into the darkness from which his universe arose' (Philmus 16).

*Frankenstein* ends, not with the glorious, self-immolating conflagration promised by the monster, but with the figure disappearing into 'darkness and distance'. The fires which consume the great cities of civilisation, at the end of *The Last Man*, light up a desolate world devoid of humanity. Wells' scientific romances, for all their careful plotting of contemporary theories and techniques, disclose a darker visionary mode in which differences of civilisation and savagery, humanity and monstrosity, mind and body, collapse. The rosy illusions of humanist aspiration, underpinned by commercial and technological expansion, see their assuring self-image crumble in the face of monstrous doubles and the darkness of ultimate planetary dissolution. The horror! Looking back and forward, a gesture which the progressive-regressive narratives of Wells frequently conjoin, the influence of Shelley's fiction is apparent, as is the influence on subsequent writing. *Brave New World* (1932), for instance, opposes the strict rationality of interwar modernisation with the excesses of human corporeality, art and religion. The bureaucratic mechanisms of State, furnished with immense technical expertise, assure control through rigorous social classification, medical surveillance and chemical pacification. Pervasive sterility, however, engenders a fascination with more natural, bodily pleasures considered primitive and savage. The excluded, anti-modern world seeps into its homogenised counterpart. The novel ends with a descent into the 'savagery' centred on corporeal violence and the 'horror of pain', to close with the body of the Savage dangling on a rope (Huxley 201).

Gothic and science fiction share a common fascination with the ruination of the idealised image of the species and in specific yet repeated encounters with the monstrous dissolution of the imaginary integrity of the human body. Wells' Martians have a distinctly indistinct shape: a 'greyish rounded bulk', quivering lips dripping saliva, 'Gorgon groups of tentacles', 'fungoid' skin, and immense eyes' that were 'inhuman, crippled and monstrous' (23). Dr Moreau confounds human and animal with his 'half-bestial', 'animalised', 'humanised' creatures, his Hyena-Swine, Leopard Man, Wolf-Bear, Horse-Rhinoceros and the utterly indeterminate 'Hairy Grey Thing'. The future, too, is populated by 'ghosts', 'dim, spectral', 'white ape-like' beings (43). The last creature on Earth, in *The Time Machine*, is a 'monstrous crab-like creature'. Corrugated, scaly, with long tentacles, 'its evil eyes were wriggling on their stalks, its mouth was all alive with appetite, and its vast ungainly claws, smeared with an algal slime, were descending on me' (76). Disgust, abhorrence, revulsion, nausea. Horror is supposed to engender rapid recoil from extreme images of otherness, but a lingering fascination testifies to its proximity: caressing the face, like Wells' crab-Thing, or crawling over the skin, it serves a role in crossing and delimiting sanctioned norms and boundaries while showing the beast within. Hyde, 'troglodytic', 'ape-like', is another figure of degeneration (Stevenson 1979: 140–42). Dracula, transmuting into bat, wolf, mist, manifests the return of archaic and primitive characteristics, a hunter in the midst of urban modernity. There is a term for these figures that uncannily disturb and horrifyingly dissolve the image of modern humanity into in-human shapes. William Hope Hodgson, another writer of scientific-supernatural tales, calls it the 'abhuman' in *The Night Land* (1912) (Hurley 3–4). Formless, vile, shapes of revulsion and recognition, abhumanity defines the outer limits of monstrosity, corporeal 'Things' from supernatural and scientific dimensions that include vampires, chimeras, hybrids and zombies. In E. F. Benson's ghost story, 'Negotium Perambulans', the 'Thing' is without head or hair, a 'slug-like' slimy shape with 'an orifice of punctured skin which opened and shut and slavered at the edges' (238). The horror that revolts the human is also its destiny. The chemical potion imbibed in Machen's

'The Novel of the White Powder' leads to a horrifying dissolution of the human body:

> a dark and putrid mass, seething with corruption and hideous rotten-ness, neither liquid nor solid, but melting and changing before our eyes, and bubbling with unctuous oily bubbles like boiling pitch. And out of the midst of it shone two burning points like eyes, and I saw a writhing and stirring of limbs, and something moved and lifted what might have been an arm.

(233)

Neither solid nor liquid, human and abhuman, the few remaining identifi-able features present a nauseating image of a body consumed at the threshold of life at its most vigorous and lethal. Death is neither neat nor humanised, but natural and supernatural at the same time, a writhing caul-dron of decay and physical corruption.

Horror and science precipitate the extremes of life beyond the securities of modern knowledge and culture. Bodies are repeatedly invaded, pene-trated, dissected, slashed, possessed, snatched, manipulated and controlled in the horrors that link gothic and science fictions. As the image precariously preserving a sense of human values, assaults on the body also testify to other forces at work. Philip K. Dick's 'The Father-Thing' (1954) depicts an insect of unknown origin assuming the shape of the father of a family: growing in the garage from a 'mound of filth', it forms into 'a pulpy mass', 'a mouldy cocoon' with 'an indistinct half-shaped head' (Seed 152). This Thing threatens domestic security. Other Things come from outer space to occupy bodies, as in John W. Campbell's story 'Who Goes There?' (1938), subse-quently filmed as *The Thing*. In *The Blob* (1959) another American institution, small-town life, finds its comfortable conformism threatened with oozy, seething destruction from outer space (Jancovich 63), while Inoshiro Honda's *The H-Man* (1959) presents a blobby mass that dissolves all fleshy susbstance in its reflection of Cold War nuclear anxieties (Sontag 433). Bodysnatchers, in a theme that reaches back to Shelley and Stevenson, also have Cold War resonances in the way that invasion involves the possession and control of human bodies (Seed 154). Robert A. Heinlein's *The Puppet Masters* (1951) makes the political allegory explicit with slug-like aliens grafting themselves to humans (Seed 160). Not all bodysnatching involves revolting images of formless, fleshly creatures: Sontag suggests the zombie-like form of aliens represents a 'vampire fantasy in new dress' (433). Possession is not diabolical or primitive, however. The snatched bodies in *The Creeping Unknown* (1956) are preserved, though the person is transformed into the aliens' 'automatized servant' (Sontag 433). Here, bodysnatching aligns itself with fears of technological modernity, of industrial processes and regimented social norms turning humans into soulless, depersonalised, automated mechanisms: the zombie-like snatched body, efficient, obedient, emotionless, becomes 'the very model of technocratic man' (Sontag 434). Alienation and dehumanisation appear as a pervasive condition. In contrast to these instinctual and automated flesh eaters, the near future consumer of William Gibson's *Idoru* (1994), slumped before a TV screen, remote in hand is 'something the size of a baby hippo, the color of a week-old boiled potato, that lives by itself in the dark, in a double-wide on the outskirts of Topeka. It's covered with eyes and it sweats constantly' (1996: 28–29). The bodysnatcher, working from without and within, comes ever closer to home, charting the extremes of automation or fleshy dissolution between which more palatable versions of humanity are situated. With chemical, biological and genetic technologies the process of dehumanisation and dissolution seems absolute. Rudy Rucker's *Wetware* (1988) describes a drug, 'Merge', that has the capacity to break down bodies at a cellular level. Its allows genetic experiments to deliver a freak show of hybrids, chimeras and monstrosities, creatures composed of claws, mandibles, feelers, snouts and gills (Rucker 1994: 180). When taken to intensify sexual pleasure it causes skeletons to loosen and flesh to drip into puddles on the floor, 'like Jell-O rolled over some bones': 'Splatter a merged person into a bunch of pieces, and the drug wears off – the cells firm up – and there is . . . uh . . . this guy in a whole lot of pieces' (Rucker 1994: 186–87). In the face of total decomposition the restoration of a familiar body-image seems vain, horror revolted at the sight of utter dissolution barely able to recoil far enough under the insistent pressure of technological innovation.

## Future noir

Beyond horror, beyond darkness and dissolution, desire and fantasy thrill to the touch of technology. In the dispassionate tones and dull, automated suburbia of J. G. Ballard's *Crash* (1973), the impact of technology on human bodies promises a new, quasi-religious order: the wounding and mangling of flesh, most spectacularly in the car crash, but also in the photographs and TV screens of late modernity, is charged with ecstatic and erotic intensity. The transformation of human life by technology is devastating and uplifting at the same time. It is a union that produces a new mode of being, post- or transhuman, involving an interdependence of bodies and machines that suggests a cyborg rather than human relationship. It turns into a new genre, the name of which, belatedly, is proposed by James Cameron's *The Terminator* (1984): 'tech noir'. The film's dark littering of urban decay and technological encroachment are suggestive enough, but its images literally and reflexively spell out in disco lights the 'Tech Noir' that visibly informs the aesthetic of much recent SF, but its regressive and circular time-travel plot also narrativizes the genre's symbolic comprehension of the 'end' of modernism, of 'futurism', or the belief in 'progress'.

(Sobchack 249)

Older visions of a future centred on human progress no longer apply, they are as ruined as the modern buildings, the apartments, factories, bars and police precincts smashed up by the terminator. In *Blade Runner* (1981), too, the extent of urban, gloomy decay is emphasised by the 'excess scenography' (Sobchack 1987: 262). The wasteland (all that is left of the paradigmatic postmodern city – Los Angeles) is piled with rubble and the waste-products of consumerism. Consumption signals exhaustion, the wearing out and wasting of things and bodies (Bruno 185). Replicants retain a touch of the gothic, 'monstrous doubles' in a genealogy stretching from *Frankenstein* to *The Invasion of the Bodysnatchers* (Telotte 154). But, unlike E. T. A. Hoffman's uncanny automaton, Olympia, replicants are simulations, copies without originals (Bruno 188). Creatures of digital and genetic programming, they are detached from nature and reproduction. So, too, the terminator, whose vat-grown skin conceals a metallic robot skeleton. Arriving from the future beside a garbage truck, the rippling body presents a 'Star Wars' 'fantasy of invulnerability' (Goldberg 239). The irony of Ronald Reagan's project to defend the USA from nuclear attack with an array of laser-armed space satellites is played up in the film: the interlinked network of military computers and satellites – 'SkyNet' – becomes self-aware and, using the same weaponry, destroys the planet. More rubble, more crushed human bodies. The sexy and rebellious gloss of black leather jacket and shades soon peels away: the decomposing, ripped skin, the sliced eyeball, signify the accelerated obsolescence of humanity and modernity.

Cyberpunk, sharing the aesthetic of Scott's and Cameron's films, also plays among the ruins of modernity, celebrating a very different relationship to science and technology. Istvan Csicsery-Ronay contrasts the genre with the 'expansive mode' of science fiction which reaches forwards and into outer space to 'show that human consciousness can contain the future' (186). From the 1960s, he argues SF begins to go 'into reverse' becoming a 'SF of implosion' and manifesting a 'desire for dissolution': 'Implosive science fiction finds the scene of SF problematics not in imperial adventures among the stars, but in the body-physical/body-social and a drastic ambivalence about the body's traditional – and terrifyingly uncertain – integrity.' Here, it overlaps with features from the literature of horror and 'splash-splatter films' of the 1970s and 1980s (188). A different sense of the physical and social body manifests itself, one in which disintegration and dissolution come to the fore in more rapid and proximate technological environments. William Gibson's image of the urban near-future, 'Night City', highlights the situation: 'a deranged experiment in social Darwinism, designed by a bored researcher who kept one thumb on the fast-forward button' (1984: 14). The casual attitude of the researcher and the accelerated obsolescence implied in the video metaphor discloses an indifferent attitude to the decaying, sprawling cities with their hustling, wretched populations scavenging among the ruins of industry. These are not ruins to be lamented or inhabited; they manifest a disintegration that heralds something else. Ruin, in cyberpunk, is represented as a 'place of possibilities' (Sponsler 261). The implosion of social and physical bodies allows the future to be reassembled, retrofitted, from the shattered fragments of the past.

In the 'manifesto' for cyberpunk, the preface to *Mirrorshades*, Bruce Sterling contrasts the 'careless technophilia' of Gernback's days with the observation that, in the 1980s, 'technology is visceral', it gets under the skin and creeps within skulls, 'pervasive, utterly intimate' (xi). Old themes are enhanced by the proximity of technology and are embraced by cyberpunk, the body invasion of 'prosthetic limbs, implanted circuitry, cosmetic surgery, genetic alteration' and the 'mind invasion' by means of interfaces, AIs and neurochemicals. Given the range of links, interfaces and attachments, the line between human and machine, however, is difficult to draw: cyberpunks are already 'hybrids themselves', hooked up to networks and hardwired with circuitry (ix). Neither science, nor fiction, is out there, in the future, in space, or in fantasy; it is very much part of the everyday environment, as Sterling notes: cyberpunks are the first generation to have grown up 'in a truly science-fictional world'. Having fallen to Earth and landed on the body, technology seems to set its own agenda and direction:

> Technical culture has gotten out of hand. The advances of the sciences are so deeply radical, so disturbing, upsetting, and revolutionary, that they can no longer be contained. They are surging into culture at large; they are invasive; they are everywhere. The traditional power structure, the traditional institutions, have lost control of the pace of change.
>
> (Sterling x)

Traditional structures, including SF itself, are washed away in the tide of technological revolution whose momentum, the 1980s showed, pulls economies and policy along with it. The 'excess scenography' of cyberpunk fiction is visibly informed by the 1980s, with technology in the avant-garde of economic and social transformation: shiny, obscure all-powerful corporate networks preside over a ruined, decaying socius littered with consumer goods and biotechnical innovations and lives are lived in the rapid and shifting virtual realities of digital code.

Romance lingers on in cyberpunk, as the title of William Gibson's first novel declares: *Neuromancer* (1984). Neural pathways and circuits, rather than bodies and future worlds, provide the locus of this new romance. Plugged, or 'jacked', in to the matrix of digital networks, the 'console cowboys' of Gibson's fiction see computer images unfold in their heads: this virtually palpable nowhere opens out in what is described as the 'nonspace' of the mind. A 'consensual hallucination' inhabited every day and for real by millions of users, the zone that is generated in and between minds and machines is called 'cyberspace'(1984: 12). It is the preferred sphere of existence, a realm of awesome datascapes, brilliant images and impossibly rapid movement. Cyberspace generates exhilaration akin to the Romantic experience of sublimity. The matrix engenders terror and delight, like Burke's sublime; a human-made monster like that of Frankenstein, exceeding comprehension, it is 'vast, haunting, and inexplicable' (Olsen 284). The sublime, however, is distinct from a Romantic encounter, amid mountain or moors, with the wonder of Nature: it is thoroughly 'interiorized', the artifice of neural and digital impulses (Voller). Nonetheless, it exceeds bodies and embodiment: to live outside cyberspace's illusive paradise, a realm of 'bodiless exultation', is experienced as 'the Fall' (Gibson 1984: 12). The body is jettisoned, discarded, in the novel's terms, as 'meat', the useless residue of corporeality left over when all valuable information (knowledge, memories, consciousness, genetic code) has been uploaded as data. Wrecked, damaged, cryogenically frozen, cloned bodies populate the novel, burnt out by military, corporate and neurochemical excesses. Bodies can easily be replaced, remade, enhanced; body parts are bought and sold like any other hi-tech commodity. In the novel, the romanticism that virtually transcends corporeality in the human-machine interfaces is secondary, an accidental by-product, or side-effect, of technoscientific innovation: the love affair with new technology turns into a purely technological affair. The principal plot, orchestrating the fates of the novel's human characters, involves a romance between two sophisticated artificial intelligences, a union promising a new being of unimaginable power and proportions: it becomes the entire matrix, everywhere, nowhere. No longer terrestrially-bound, it communicates with intelligences from other planets. The human protagonist remains on Earth, buying some new hardware and a couple of internal organs and goes back to work.

There are gothic inflections in neuromanticism (see Cavallaro 164–203). Death is irrelevant, consciousness, in a curious form of premature burial, can be stored and operate on disks alone. Neuromancer, one of the AIs, describes itself as a 'necromancer': 'I call up the dead' (Gibson 1984: 289).

The dead are neither zombies nor ghosts in the traditional sense, but are computer constructs, digitally remastered memories, replayed in the mind. 'Consensual', mediated hallucinations are simultaneously 'spectral'; the ghosts of cyberspace, banal, virtually-realised hauntings of digitised memory and projection: 'holograms twisted and shuddered to the roaring of the games, ghosts overlapping in the crowded haze of the place' (Gibson 1984: 141). Gothic figures lose their force, pallid spectres of the surpassed past, the shadowy remains of a disappearing family-controlled, residually modern corporate order. In the novel, 'gothic' means 'archaic'. The Villa Straylight, home of the Tessier-Ashpool corporate dynasty and the headquarters to be penetrated in the romantic liberation of the AIs, is described as 'a body grown in upon itself, a Gothic folly' (Gibson 1984: 206). The image applies to the labyrinthine structure of the house and the archaically corrupt corporate body itself, both of which have imploded. Gothic fears are tied to this order, modes of confinement, restraint and discipline. The 'Turing' police, responsible for maintaining corporate interests and locking down the development of AI influence, invoke gothic fears in order to shore up an older law and morality tied to the preservation of humanity. They accuse the human protagonist of something like species treason: 'you have no care for your species. For thousands of years men dreamed of pacts with demons. Only now are such things possible' (Gibson 1984: 193). The demons in question are the AIs – the Turing police are seen to be merely holding the inevitable briefly at bay. Their gothic images dress up unimaginable new anxieties in familiar, reassuring, and irrelevant, form. In cyberpunk, horror cedes to excitement, thrill, promise: the dissolution of older corporate and corporeal orders offers occasion to celebrate new possibilities. Gothic forms, fending off the past and the horrifying monsters of futurity it throws up, also precipitate unthinkably different and in-, post- or transhuman futures, providing the camouflage for an invasion from the future. Cloaked as vampires, monsters, zombies, 'cybergothic' manifests the emergence of an order in which humanity and its supporting institutions are discarded, rendered obsolete by the speed, processing power and multiplicity of utterly machinic networks: 'crazed AIs, replicants, terminators, cyberviruses, grey-goo nano-horrors', 'apocalypse market overdrive' are the deceptive vanguard of 'v(amp)iro finance', 'commercial parthenogenesis', 'webs of haemocommerce' (Land 1998: 79; 81; 86). Any illusions of humanity peel away, like the terminator's rotting skin, in the face of machinic incursions and transformations: the future is not what it used to be, nor is it even vestigially human.

In his first story, 'The Gernsback Continuum' (1981), Gibson writes about the art and design associated with earlier visions of the future and, tacitly, provides a commentary on the development of science fiction and its 'lost future' (Gibson 1986: 41). What remains of that future, however, is compared to the psychological effects of meeting aliens or seeing UFOs. These encounters are neither actual nor fantasised, but effects of 'semiotic ghosts' and 'semiotic phantoms', virtually real experiences bound up with media vision, commoditised images and cultural projections (Gibson 1986: 44). For Tom Shippey these ghosts ask telling questions of genre: 'if science fiction admits that all its futures are dead or stillborn, it removes most of its *raison d'être*. How can the semiotic ghost coexist with the classic science fiction mode?' (Shippey 212). The semiotic ghost, like the spectres proliferating in Sterling's *Islands of the Net*, 'consigns to "ghost" status virtually every cultural piety left to Western readers' (Shippey 214). Left among the ghosts of humanised modernity, science fiction itself becomes a curiously gothicised genre. And cyberpunk, too, with its bricolage, its 'retrofitting' ('looking at things retrospectively and making them fit a new system') conducts a familiar procedure of stitching together diverse bits and pieces: Shippey calls it 'Frankensteining' (214). But semiotic ghosts emanate from the machines of culture, cast-offs of a technological evolution that heads, like the AIs of *Neuromancer*, in different directions. Hans Moravec, author of *Mind Children*, tells another story about this nonhuman trajectory. For him, the 'human soap-opera' has played itself out (Platt 104). The evolution of artificial intelligences, machines developed by machines, will occur in an exponential acceleration that, surpassing humankind, will run everything on Earth and rapidly expand into space, thereby realising the pleasures of machinic science fiction. Curious about their strange corporeal origins, however, the machines will save humanity, save it, that is, in and as an enormous heritage computer simulation of all cultures and civilisations . . .

# 5 Flight of the heroine

## From feminised gothic to postfeminist romance

### The monster's mother

She lies, anaesthetised, on an operating table in a sterile, hi-tech medical research laboratory. Covered in a silver-grey surgical gown, only her face and her lower torso are exposed to the gaze of the scientists manipulating the equipment from behind a protective glass screen. In close-up, the camera follows a laser as it slices easily across the patient's midriff, leaving a dark line on pale skin. Opening an oozing gash, robotic forceps probe inside. A slimy, bloody lump is tugged from the hole to be held up for scrutiny. It squirms between the metal pincers. A membrane peels back and its head thrusts forward baring shiny rows of razor teeth. An aggressive little thing: penis dentatus. But it is not male. She is far more valuable and far deadlier, a queen, a breeder of monsters.

She, however, is not the monster's mother. The 'host' remains on the table, her usefulness at an end, as the parasite, her unwitting progeny, is gently carried away. She could be discarded, like all the others. But she is healthy and orders are given for her to be sewn back up. The next time she appears it is in the blurred form of a shrouded figure seen from above, as if thrown down a well, the heavy boot of a guard in the corner of the shot. She lies at the bottom of a dark metal cell, sewn into a pale gauzy sac. Her body slowly turns and writhes in the filmy cocoon until her head breaks through, her sharp, black nails tearing the fabric. She examines herself, touching the skin of her fully-formed body as if it is new to her. It is, a first time, though the number '8' tattooed on her forearm suggests this is just one more in a series of births.

The opening of the fourth film in the *Alien* series is full of births and rebirths. It is, after all, called *Alien Resurrection*. Prior to the caesarean and her emergence from the sac, a figure is seen, androgynously pre-adolescent and barely recognisable, naked, completely hairless, upright, incubated and illuminated in a long glass container, a giant test-tube baby. As the camera closes in, her features quickly morph into the familiar contours of Ripley, the heroine of the series. Unlike the bloody, meaty birth of the alien queen, this birth is hygienic, sterile, asexual. No other body is involved in the making of this real and yet artificial being: with its unblemished, hairless skin, the form has an otherworldly appearance. Born from tubes, torsos, fabric sacs, the various forms of life that emerge in the opening scenes have little of nature or humanity about them and, only residually perhaps, an aura of horror. The opening births, however, preceded by images of repellent and aborted efforts at procreation, portend numerous hideous pregnancies and monstrous parturitions to come.

Gothic modernity turns on the question of femininity; feminism turns on modern gothic. It is a critical commonplace to note how women in gothic fictions are represented as objects of pursuit, imprisonment, violation (critical reversals of this victim status, of course, shift the identification of monstrosity from sexualised otherness to tyrannical patriarchal systems, just as Wollstonecraft and other radicals did with the figure of the enlightenment monster). At the same time, and in a context in which a critical establishment feminised the genre and its readership, gothic fictions allow a greater space for female authorship, for some degree of female agency and adventurousness in fictions and for flights of fantasy among a growing audience. These are the contours of 'female Gothic' (Fleenor). 'Heroinism', in Moers' discussion of the development of literary feminism, concerns female selfhood and centres on 'the woman who moves, who acts, who copes with vicissitude and adventure'. It allows women to create and enjoy fictional journeys and excitements 'without offending the proprieties' (126). Clery's reappraisal of the Radcliffean heroine, in expanding Moers' notion, sees in heroinism and Radcliffe's use of the supernatural a consciousness of women's subjection and the changing commercial and political context of the times: romances, *The Mysteries of Udolpho* notably, displayed 'the contradictions and dangers which every gentlewoman of the period potentially faced' (1995: 128). Displaced in fiction, contradictions of women at the mercy of patriarchy or the marriage market are not necessarily resolved in gothic romances. Nor do romances – teaching women to suffer like heroines – necessarily offer unequivocally subversive reflections of the situation. But there are other options and enjoyments. Clery later argues that it would be a mistake to read female gothic fictions as solely 'parables of patriarchy', thereby missing other stories of 'wild passions, the sublime, supernatural phenomena, violent conflict, murder and torture, sexual excess and perversion, outlandish settings, strange minglings of history and fantasy' (2000: 2). Women's gothic, it seems, straddles contradiction and challenge, persecution and pleasure.

Lines of interpretation become unclear as lines of flight open up: the feminised monstrosities of gothic fiction rendered various romantic and domestic freedoms imaginable at the same time as they were configured as an imagined threat to familial and social values. In political terms, too, 'gothic' points in contradictory directions, a sign of the continuity of British constitutional liberties and a mark of the despotism of patrilineage and monarchical government. The myth of the warrior tribes grouped under the name of the 'Goths' is also bound to ideals of freedom, chivalry and fierce independence (Kliger). The invention of gothic in the eighteenth century cuts across aesthetic and political lines of demarcation, its emergence complex and ambiguous. Appearing at a time when scientific reason was promoted above religious superstition, when industrial urbanity was prevailing over nature and agriculture, and when democratic revolutions cast feudal monarchs aside, gothic romances simultaneously hark back to and caricature barbarous dark ages. It is not so much nostalgia that governs these inventions: characterising change in gothic terms looked fearfully towards a near future in which the bonds of custom, order and continuity had broken down in the face of a rampant, revolutionary, monstrous commercialism, as Edmund Burke (1969) suggested. As the formations of modernity institute themselves against a 'gothic' past, the genre also condenses knots of fear and apprehension at the perceived imminence of a destructive future.

The prefix 'post' has come to signal a period of uncertainty, crisis and fragmentation, in which the structures of modernity are rendered unstable and suspect. It should not be surprising that the prefix can also be applied to those structures in their nascent state when lines of differentiation are yet ill-formed. The rise of gothic forms and their current cultural persistence function as a curious knot in the formations of modernity, figures of excess, monstrosity and sublimity around which reason, progress and knowledge cohere or collapse. Combine post-modern and gothic with (post) feminism, then, and the pattern becomes even more complex: feminism, taking its bearings from Wollstonecraft's extension of enlightenment precepts to women, contests modernity on its own terms, opening up categories of human progress, equality, rights and reason to challenge patriarchal preju-dice; gothic fictions, disclosing the tyrannical, barbaric and irrational obverse of those structures, seems to offer a regressive movement that coun-ters light with darkness and reason with force. Beyond the oppositions, however, a space of disturbance becomes partially visible in the crossing and reversing of terms, an unknown and ungrounded space linked to the sublime and the unpresentable. In Maurice Merleau-Ponty's phenomenological account of seeing and visibility, the chiasmus that emerges between subject and object, sight and body, discloses an 'abyss' that leads to a fundamental reversal of relations of seeing (136); in Irigaray's reading of this chiasmus, the place of the other is destabilised by the breach between oppositions, causing the reversibility of world and self and disclosing a nocturnal prediscursive site to appear (1993: 151–54). Paradigmatically, and against all paradigms, the space becomes a woman's, 'awoman', that is, woman before signification has fantasmatically fixed her in a symbolic and subaltern place. Such a space, in Deleuze's terms, in his discussion of sense and series, forms an empty place, 'an extremely mobile *empty place*' that is constitutive and destructive, locus for the establishment and dissolution of signifying relationships, against which old chains of signification founder and new connections emerge (1990: 48–49).

While postmodernism and feminism are linked, often problematically, in opposition to a (patriarchal) monolithic modernity as modes of interrogation, play, resistance and liberation, the question of their respective ties to a political project render any firm alliance suspect (Nicholson). Prefixing feminism with a 'post', compounds tensions: it situates the former in the place of an established formation in order to suggest that its project is finished or has been superseded. The move, as a gesture that simultaneously feigns a concession of defeat on the part of conservatism and conceals a dismissive and restorative response, constitutes a 'backlash' or 'misogynistic turn' that testifies to the contrary (Coppock *et al.*; Negra). It does, however, situate feminism amidst a plural and shifting scene of diverse cultural-political engagements in which the appeal of any unified or binary framework fades, as Negra's account of Pojansky implies. Such a position allows a more positive, if less prescriptive, version of postfeminism as 'continuously in process, transforming and challenging itself' (Wright 5). Or, further, it can be considered a challenge to think in innovative and radical terms and engage with questions of time and futurity: rather than be hung up on an outdated idea of political revolution and its now predictable goals, postfeminism might 'generate a new' able to negotiate 'the more disconcerting idea of *un*predictable transformation, upheavals in directions and arenas which cannot be known in advance and whose results are inherently uncertain' (Grosz 215). Such a future would indeed be monstrous (Derrida 1990; 1992).

There are questions raised by the invocation of newness; questions, indeed, thrown up in a period in which innovation and linearity themselves have been thoroughly interrogated: the 'post' of the 'post-modern', indeed, poses an irrevocable challenge to modernity's narrative linearity and teleology; the assimilation of innovation, with the new ceding to novelty, by technoscientific and accelerated market imperatives – as creative or entrepreneurial capitalism – threatens the possibility of imagining the future in any other terms. Indeed, the monstrous figure of an unpredictable future, as Derrida outlined, cedes to the banality of a 'normal monstrosity' that is already recognised, contained, homogenised in various hybrid forms of pre-packaged connection (Derrida 1992). Such monstrosities emanate from the creativity and inventiveness of marketing and sales rather than any radical innovation of modern artistic, philosophical or political revolution (Deleuze and Guattari 1994: 10).

'Post-', for all the illusions of a progressive movement (beyond the limitations of modernity or feminism, say) that its dismissive gesture implies, seems to sanction only a disavowal that liberates a shift to an ateleological circulation of banal monstrosities, commoditised presentations, consumerist desires evacuated and exhausted by the entrepreneurial creation of hybrid novelties. The demons spewing from the hellmouth of contemporary culture are no more than simulations parading the 'hell of the same' (Baudrillard 1993b: 113). The limits of progression, of time and futurity, are, perhaps unsurprisingly, presented in gothic form. Gothic, however, changes its significance in the context of 'postality': the archaic figures it regurgitates are only partially continuous with modernity; they do not serve to occlude or give shape to future terrors, the predictability of which renders them monstrous, but offer solace to a culture confronted by the absence of any future whatsoever, the comfort of familiar figures recycled as history goes into reverse.

In her reading of the witch figure, in the *Blair Witch Project*, Linda Badley (2003) notes how, in becoming an icon of postfeminism in a contemporary culture full of Buffys and Willows, what was once a disturbing image of sexualised heterogeneity turns into a homogenised and domesticated picture of contemporary femininity. Anne Rice's vampire chronicles, according to Doane and Hodges, also bring postfeminism and consumerism into close alignment. The movement of 'posting', thus fails to move forward, despite a rhetoric promoting seriality and innovation: its gothic recourse, moreover, turns it back to excesses associated with consumption and expenditure, a reversion to a consumerist logic of desiring, defined, in Angela Carter's terms, as that of an 'inexhaustible plus' (206). Desire means always wanting more; and wanting more, in postmodern capitalism, is the key to creative entrepreneurship (Goux 1990). 'More', moreover, is also the cry of woman constructed in the fantasy of modernity's Man: her sexuality lies in excess of masculine or phallic jouissance; it guarantees her otherness and his identity as the limit to which he is both attracted and from which he is repelled (Lacan 1982; Wright; Mitchell and Rose). If the relation between post-feminism and post-modernity takes the form of a chiasmus, then gothic productions can be situated at the point of their crossing, their interdiction and excess, knots of formlessness and significance tied over a gap of non-meaning as points where sense can be temporarily re-established.

It is only when transgression has occurred, of course, that a limit or law can be identified (Foucault 1977). The figure of law, the name-of-the-father, as Lacan noted, is thus an imposture, a projection into and over an occluded and feminised space (Lacan 1977a: 310–11). The fantasy of feminine excess and transgression is one, albeit crucial, example. Innovation and the mores of modernity's fantasised femininity inhere in gothic romance from the start: the Radcliffean heroine's 'curiosity', a cipher for the readerly pleasures of the mystery, takes the form of a desire that pushes at the limits of paternal law, family and gender. She is looking for something more. The genre, too, especially in the device of the 'explained supernatural' – which excites, frustrates and ultimately disappoints readerly curiosity – depends on desire: considered appetitive, sensational, indulgent, feminine, the repetitive fictional formulas are designed to stimulate a passive readership, to inflame curiosity and expectation, to sate base passions, and then invent more mysteries and shocks to excite anew. With postmodernism shattering the constraints of cultural tradition, these low exceptions, no longer excluded as gothicised negatives of high romantic Culture, become, like Derrida's monstrosities, the norm. A certain type of transgression – unbound from restraints yet tied to consumption – also prevails in the shape of an imperative to consume beyond limits, to live life, as the fizzy drink ads used to declare, 'to the max'. Terror and sublimity, in modernity, disclose some Thing excessive, something abyssal and unpresentable in cultural and symbolic formations, a site of horror from which subjects, on the verge of seeing all boundaries dissolve, recoil. With postmodernity, in contrast, terror becomes endemic and transgression is both limitless and exhausted, ceaselessly used up in playful circulations of aesthetic games that interrogate less than nothing. The unpresentable is little more than a resource to be capitalised upon: a space to be filled with so many different images, hyperactivating and passifying consumers at the same time as they leave them wanting more: all subjects, perhaps, become woman in the process (Goux 1998). This woman, as the definitive subjective figure of hypercapitalism, however, is only the global instantiation and revision of a modern, bourgeois fantasy of desiring and excess. There may be other modes of becoming, an awomanly space in which unrecognisable, troubling, unpredictable and monstrous forms have yet to appear.

## Becoming-(gothic)-woman

In Deleuze and Guattari (D&G), all becomings turn on becoming woman. This is not 'woman' in the conventional sense of a discrete identity tied to a bodily form and represented according to cultural types and signifying structures: there is no final or fixed subject position in D&G, only composite, multiple points of movement, change, process. D&G's notion of desiring production locates 'woman' as a 'line of flight' and as a crucial nexus among the proximities and relations, the flows and dis-connections, by which (in)dividuals remain in fragments, multiple and changing, thereby slipping from the mortifying grasp of regimes of state and signification. Their analysis critiques the 'molar' level of structure, system, territory and integration in favour of a 'molecular' account of relations, flows, lines of escape and deterritorialisations, focusing on networks or assemblages, on borderline interactions and cutting across lines of demarcation (Deleuze and Guattari 1983: 367). Organisations, as they try to arrest flows and inhibit movement, are criss-crossed by a whole variety of energies and intensities that can neither be contained nor controlled at a systemic or molar level: indeed, the entities that appear and disappear at molecular instants, below the threshold and among the interstices of structure and system, are fundamentally disorganised, self-organising, even. A matter of shifting individuations, and always in process, 'self' occurs between multiplicities, a 'threshold'. 'Lines of flight' connect these becoming-selves to the movements across territories (of signification, social strata, bodies, geographies): a line of flight is a deterritorialisation, not just an escape from a system (Deleuze and Parnet 36). It involves change, opening up possibilities, not 'running away from' but 'causing run offs' since 'there is no social system that does not leak from all directions, even if it makes its segments increasingly rigid in order to seal the lines of flight' (Deleuze and Guattari 1988: 204). Hence, fleeing can be active and 'put a system to flight', or produce 'a sort of delirium', a going 'off the rails' (Deleuze and Parnet 36; 40). Lines of flight, though productive in the links and connections they make possible, are condemned as negative excesses by a signifying regime; organisations remain intent on stopping their movement (Deleuze and Guattari 1988: 117; 204).

Writing, for D&G, is an instance of the deterritorialising effects of lines of flight (Deleuze and Guattari 1988: 276). It presents a conjunction involving the 'transmutation of fluxes through which life escapes from the resentment of persons, societies and reigns' (Deleuze and Parnet: 50). Language, indeed, 'is criss-crossed by lines of flight that carry off its vocabulary and syntax' (Deleuze and Parnet: 116). Gothic forms, too, feature prominently in Deleuze's and D&G's discussions of the deterritorialising movements of desire: vampires and werewolves offer images of the fluxes of becoming, infectious figures that cut across lines of patrilinear and familial reproduction and, as packs or multiplicities, undermine the ideological reproduction of identity; nomads and warriors, very much the 'northern tribes' associated with the Goths, roam the forests and plains, insurgents destabilising the military machine of (Roman) imperial domination. Gothic art and architecture, in the shape of the 'northern line', transforms spaces of formal classical representation with disturbing contours, contrasts and zigzagging lines that allow sublime flights of the imagination.

Woman, writing, gothic: the assemblage, unsurprisingly, emerges in a period of aesthetic, political, economic and social transformations. The move from feudalism, monarchy and religion, to reason, democracy and commerce entails upheavals in the organisation of cultural and familial reproduction. Romance offers a world of love and adventure beyond the constraints of paternal control and domestic responsibility, a fantastic, monstrous, immoral space that takes readers out of human paths. 'Wound up', as one critic of the time noted, by repeated stimulation and mystery, readers, as the metaphor of the clockwork mechanism implies, are little more than desiring machines. The gothic genre itself becomes a contradictory, multiple site of affects and intensities: anti-classical, it undermines rigid Roman (Augustan) forms; anti-Catholic, it dispels religious ignorance and superstition; freedom-loving (like the Goths), it purveys a counter-imperial tendency. At the same time, it reduplicates the tyrannies, prejudices and corruptions of government, as Wollstonecraft and Godwin complained; or, in rejecting them, presents the terrifying image of rampant, monstrous commercialism, a market, beyond the restraints of church, state or morality, that monstrously encourages selfishness, vice and excess (Burke 1969). In gothic fictions of the eighteenth century, women are transformed economically and psychologically, becoming less figures of romance, idealisation and patrilinear power, and more objects in a marriage market, their morality and propriety calibrated to their emerging status as commodities in a system of economic exchange. Woman writers, indeed, stay at home, but earn a living, crossing over, often through necessity, to the world of work and, from there, begin to write beyond the 'proper' bounds of gender and genre (Poovey). No wonder sex became such a political topic, especially during a period of revolutionary ferment with its various, and 'unsexing', libidinal energies and excitements (Matthias). The world gothic fiction engages with is one in the throes of successive and diverse de- and re-territorialisations.

Radcliffe's heroines are always in flight. Her novels move towards and away from disturbing worlds of danger and immorality. *Romance of the Forest* begins with Adeline fleeing from convent imprisonment. She, like so many heroines of the time, is an orphan: without family and protection, she is free to fly towards love, romance, mystery and terror. But she is also escaping from a cruel and tyrannical familial order, a victim of a malevolent and immoral Marquis. Her persecutor and potential violator is a family member, a fratricidal uncle who, she speculates at one point, may be her father. Her flight from the family, then, impeaches its cruelties. Who she is, uncertain of her lineage, is similarly in question: her father, long dead, is a character in a horrifying manuscript, a ghost, a victim. Like many fathers in the genre, his and thus her identity is suspect: the paternal name that holds social and symbolic circuits in place, directing desires along proper channels, is an imposture. As a result, desire wanders, off course. In *Udolpho*, the possibility of paternal scandal drives the mystery: prohibition (not to read the father's letters) becomes an occasion for curiosity, speculation, adventure. The flight of the heroine moves beyond the structures of paternal power and into zones of indiscernibility, 'wild zones' where femininity encounters the possibility of becoming something other: the ruins and forests that are uncharted places of darkness and danger are also loci free from the restraints of law. Indeed, from the start of *Romance*, it is unclear what Adeline's trajectory will be: though possessed of innate goodness, she, as the comparison with La Motte's weaker character suggests, has the capacity to incline towards vice as much as virtue. As her sense and senses are frequently overwhelmed by imagined and real shocks, it is not only physical, but emotional and psychological, security and stability that are thrown to the winds. A kind of delirium possesses her, a loss of reason, morality and self that throws identity off the rails. Like the heroine, the genre depends on such expenditures of emotional energy, its techniques inducing excitement and shocks in the heroine's double, the reader, at the expense of rational and moral discrimination.

Lines of flight are also lines of fright: a rhythm of pulses and re-pulsions subtends gothic narrative with affects and intensities buffeting and traversing the borders of fictional structure. But the deterritorialisations that introduce new fictional, imagined and desiring geographies to eighteenth-century romance readers are accompanied by processes of reterriorialisation: the authorial voice of the narrator tries to maintain a controlled and moral perspective on the fanciful flights of heroine and reader alike. The exploration of a woman's becoming, of desire and imagination wandering off proper paths, is situated as a cautionary tale by the structured interventions of romance didacticism: the heroine (and the reader) are forced to learn the dangers of excessive imagining and the immorality of unconstrained desiring. Lines of flight are arrested; lines of fright turned against themselves: horror, recoil, expulsion of excess. Nightmarish possibilities give way to fairytale cautions. The becomings of woman are directed towards becoming a model of bourgeois and domestic femininity: the endings of both *Romance* and *Udolpho* see the heroine returned to propriety, morality, reason and good sense. Her reward is to find herself secured within structures of law, property and marriage: a paternal order is restored; her line of flight bound within the economy of the son-in-law.

The lines of flight that are ultimately constrained by moral and meaning in Radcliffe's narratives, returning women to the frameworks of home, family, marriage from which they fled and the authority of which they challenged in the course of those narratives. Horror is turned into fairytale – as at the end of *Udolpho*, marking the becoming-bourgeois of femininity, the figure of woman constructed as the object sustaining emerging modern systems of subjection and exchange. Lines of flight are, however, underpinned by other lines of de- and re-territorialisation: lines of fright. The mechanisms, the narrative machinery, of the genre that produces intense affects of horror, terror, thrill and excitement continue to pulse beneath the moral and regulative frameworks of high culture, reconfiguring patterns of identification and affection outside the parameters of spiritual elevation, didacticism, or aesthetic education and enabling new conjunctions and different connections that fly from the grasp of regulatory regimes. In *Frankenstein*, for instance, epistolary techniques and trappings of science combine to engender an enlightenment monster that refuses its subjection to narrow human and bourgeois structures: as a monstrous conjunction of otherness linking mob, woman, nature and writing itself, its uncontrollable monstrosity reflects back on the systems that produced it at the same time as it moves beyond their grasp, an unthinkable breach in the mechanisms of modernity open to the vicissitudes of an entirely other future.

In *Dracula*, however, the breach in modernity is configured from the outside as an unbearable object – a 'Thing' – to be identified and expelled in the restoration of modern boundaries: the spectre of an archaic, in-human hunter (aristocratic, eastern, animal, other) feeding upon a decadent and defenceless bourgeois civilisation presents an uncanny figure that requires a return to vitality and violence, and demands that modern, professional men recover a lost masculinity and vigour to become hunters themselves. The homosociality and eroticism of the novel invokes a warrior romance in which women are the key stakes of a masculine economy: Lucy, lost to sexuality and excess, must, once she becomes a vampire, be sacrificed as 'Thing'; Mina, despite the temptations of new womanhood, retains enough composure and subservience to be saved, a potential mother, for a patriarchal familial ideal. Throughout, and almost as invisible as the vampire initially appears, an ambivalent and inhuman technology signals a different path for modernity: phonographs, typewriters, telegraphs, railways and timetables tap out a different rhythm and new conjunctions of otherness (Wicke; Kittler 1997). Vamp-machine, womachine, figures visible in Lang's *Metropolis*, or Villiers de L'Isle Adam's *Future Eve*, set the pattern for what, in the popular culture of cinematic makes and remakes, will become different lines of fright and identification causing tremors along the borders of modern patriarchy. In the intensities and pulses of so many popular cultural screens, a gothic 'technology of monsters' (Halberstam) emerges to confound the gendered categories of modernity's human figure. In the horror genre, gazes are dis-engendered in prurient overidentifications and violent reactions (Clover); monsters and vampires find themselves connected to technological reconfigurations like the cyborg or the 'replicants' that manifest a technological supercession of patriarchal modernity (Haraway 1990 and 1997; Stone; Plant); or, as vampire celebrities like Lestat, become entwined with romanticisations of postfeminism and consumption (Doane and Hodges). Gothic, indeed, its technological subcurrent raised to visible predominance, finds itself bound up with the delivery of the post, that is, a system of writing and communication that was, always-already, a technological formation. As a genre, it traces lines of flight and fright that move beyond modern and human structures.

## Alien romance

The *Alien* series of films traverses the chiasmatic postings of gothic, modernity, gender and technology, drawing out diverse lines of flight punctuated with lines of fright. Initially, female humans are paired with animal (cat) and opposed to android and alien: the chiasmus is located at the point of female sexuality and maternity (woman, alien, cat, android – in the service of a computer called 'Mother'). At this crossing of birth and death, the series dis- and re-organises various conjunctions of sex-work-war-monstrosity, displacing positions and oppositions, so that women become elided with aliens and androids and are set against military, corporate and male human figures and institutions. Post-feminist professional women, martyr-victims, wannabe mother-men, alien-mother-killing-machines, abject-sovereign-compassionate-heroines, all emerge in the re-pulsive slashes of SF/gothic. Where *Alien* closes with a cat and a woman (a combination resonating – in horror and psychoanalysis – with accounts of narcissistic female sexuality), the fourth in the series closes with cat-suited female-alien grandmother and feminine-identified self-loathing android.

*Alien* paints its future in recognisably dark gothic colours, giving its account of gender and modernity a familiarly re-pulsive dimension: the crepuscular gloom of a windswept, deserted planet and the cavernous spaces of the crashed alien craft sketch a familiar gothic landscape and architecture; the slimy abjection of the alien young and their monstrous and parasitic emergence channel a blood-curdling pulse of body horror along lines of invasion and explosion; the horrifyingly alien creature, its dripping carapace, acid blood, razor teeth offering a monster beyond the darkest reaches of nightmare. The heroine, Ripley, is steadily manoeuvred into the position of gothic heroine: unable, with the crew, to expunge this utterly destructive threat, she is isolated to become the 'final girl' of horror movies, pursued through the labyrinthine corridors of the mining vessel. Her status as persecuted female victim, her sexualised vulnerability fully exposed in the final scenes when she is left in only her underwear, signals a regressive stripping of femininity to a bare object of a persecuting look, her professional status as a skilled crew member reduced by the mechanisms of callous killing machine and prurient narrative from efficient pilot and leader to quivering figure of abjection. However, with a sovereignty born from abjection and desperation, she survives, escaping the ship, the alien and their destruction. A feminised humanity barely saves itself in the face of monstrous, all-consuming horror.

The final destruction of the alien, however, leaves the question of identity open even as it appears to return to strictly opposed differences between human and alien. The ambivalence that characterises the relationship is never fully expunged, to form the basis, precisely, for a variety of permutations in the succeeding episodes of the series. The horror that the first movie presents, indeed, is as much an internal and external threat to human boundaries: bodies are penetrated, seemingly assured identities collapse in the face of the alien threat. The security of human imaginary and modern symbolic structures is shattered by the violent proximity of destructive, abject and uncontrollable energies. These, the film suggests with its images of dark, repulsive womb-like shapes, connote a conventional patriarchal version of dangerous female sexuality and archaic, primal maternal energy (Creed). Such a figure, however, for all the disturbances it engenders remains a construction of patriarchy (Penley 1986): its horrifying emergence, the dissolutions it presents in shocking form, ultimately form the occasion for an expulsion from and a restoration of limits – at the very point of utter, imagined decomposition into an abject and destructive black hole.

The first three films of the series are full of the monstrosity of maternity. The invasion of human bodies, their transformation, still living, into expendable hosts of alien reproduction, is suffused with a horror of corporeal evacuation and dissolution. Humans are preyed upon as the series of films 'takes up the vampire's iconography to depict alien interference with human reproduction' (Roof 149). The slimy egg sacs in the crashed womb-like alien spaceship, the squirming alien young that cover human faces and enter their bodies, growing inside and bursting out, locate birth, the body and maternity in the realm of horror and abjection. The milieu is one in which birth and death and are tied to life's horrifying excess: 'this amoeba-like flattened creature that envelops the subject's face stands for the irrepressible life beyond all the finite forms that merely its representatives, its figures . . . immortal and indestructible' (Žižek 1999: 280–81). The alien forms the fantasmatic Thing, beyond language and the life it structures: libidinal, amorphous, instinctual, it manifests the pulsing excess at the heart of life. It precedes the formation of distinct identity, like the mashed-up, bi-sexual 'hommelette' underlying and interrupting all modes of cultural division and organisation (Lacan 1977b: 197). As the formless basis around which human structures are erected, it marks a locus for the destruction and transfiguration of sacred horror (Bataille 1997: 288). Like the abject, this formless substance, though it never goes away, must be pushed aside in order to live.

In the *Alien* series, the horror which threatens from without and within establishes the point at which a feminised humanity is precariously differentiated from monstrosity. The return of the body in its most horrifying form, composed of slimy oozes and violent energies, manifests the internal excess represented by the deadly female alien. This pole of monstrous femininity is counterpoised by the 'Company' that wishes to control and exploit its power. 'Mother' is the name for the corporate computer and signifies a sanctioned, subservient female position, but one equally inhuman: 'she' is prepared to sacrifice the crew for corporate profit. In between, the single crew member to survive, Ripley, must defy both and be stalked through the dark labyrinths of the mining ship by a barely visible killing machine. 'In space no one can hear you scream', ran the advertising slogan on posters for the first film: as isolated, unprotected, abandoned as any of Radcliffe's heroines, she remains continually under threat, a victim until her desperate combat at the close of the film displays the beginnings of a movement from abject passivity to sovereign activity.

Subsequent films continue to explore the relationship between representations of abject otherness and violent expulsions of its all-consuming formlessness, the proximity between alien and human is traced over the maternal body. As Ripley, in *Aliens*, becomes more like the alien, protective of a young female child and ferocious in her defence, she evinces a calmness and self-reliance that moves away from conventional, hysterical responses to terror: abjection, it seems, becomes less a state to be expelled, and more a condition that allows for a different self-relation, one that leaves behind an autoaffective fragility, an ego-centric insecurity, and assumes a strangely sovereign posture in the face of violently imminent death. Initially opposed to the alien, almost impotent in the face of her murderous strength, she comes to resemble her, becoming a killing machine herself: at the film's climax her skills in the operation of machinery equip her to engage in direct combat with the queen of the alien species, finally, it seems, destroying her monstrous counterpart. The fight with the alien never, however, diminishes the proximity between them. She has not destroyed her enemy, *Alien 3* reveals: she has turned into her opposite, carrying the embryo of a female alien and thus becoming a breeder of all that she most fears, pregnant with a monster whose offspring will threaten humanity with extinction.

Horror crossed with maternity distinguishes the point where meanings assigned to the film are confounded, collapse and become diversely re-established. The doubleness of the monstrous figure – alien killing machine and destructive primal mother, more and less than human, an uncontrollable excess simultaneously from the heart and outer reaches of human imaginings – resonates with an irresolvable ambivalence in interpretations of the film as a feminist, anti-feminist, post-feminist or humanist document. Subsequent doublings and shifting pairings in the course of the film compound diverse lines of interpretation. In destroying an alien associated with dangerously abject feminine sexuality (and returning to a more patriarchally-recognised figure of woman), the humanism that is restored at the end takes a traditionally male form in the subordination of women even as it recognises and refuses a disarmingly female power and excess. The phallic mother is aligned with the phallic monster, the profit-hungry 'Company', in the form of its all-controlling computer, 'Mother'. On the other hand, the film is 'seemingly feminist' in its content (Newton 84). With the final survivor (and champion of humanity) being female, however, the contours of heroism are altered in a reversal of conventionally gendered expectations and conventions: in the heroine's emotional attachment to the cat a recovery of 'ideological humanism' is glimpsed, human and animal feeling paired against the callous rationality of corporate android (Ash) and its murderous alien prize (Kavanagh 79). Further, the female associations and the power of alien display the inadequacy of paternal authority: the connections between alien and android, company and alien displace monstrosity from the destructive creature to the inhumanity of robot and the 'moral monstrosity' of the corporation (Greenberg 100).

Even as boundaries seem to be restored and meanings begin to cohere around the figure of monstrosity, in contrast to a progressive, feminised humanity, there is something 'almost postfeminist' in the setting: women can be equally strong, weak, reasonable and authoritative as members of the crew, while the context is one of a technocratic elite of middle-class professionals without much evidence of internal discrimination (Kavanagh 77; Greenberg 97). The post-feminist trajectory overlaps with post-modern and post-human concerns: 'post-modern Gothic and post-gender sexualities are haunting the imaginary of post-industrial societies' (Braidotti 58). A return of the 'others' excluded by modernity – woman, nature, ethnicity (all conventionally associated with monstrosity) cohere as symptoms of a postmodern anxiety about social identities and symbolic structures (Braidotti 196). Indeed, it is only in terms of a masterful position that otherness is linked in the form of monstrosity: 'only in his gaze are their respective differences flattened out in a generalized category of "difference" whose pejorative status is structural to the establishment of a norm that is inevitably masculine, white, heterosexist and promoting naturalistic and essentialistic beliefs' (Braidotti 197). In horror, the transgression of norms is manifested and, in repulsion, restored. Monstrosity – the knotting together of callous corporate violence, robotic rationality and primal maternal sexuality – displays the excesses of a normative system and allows its return to traditional gendered, human and modern arrangements. It functions doubly: as a point of coherence and dissolution and as a site for the restoration of traditional boundaries and the opening up of different possibilities.

But, simultaneously impeaching the artifice of the construction of those norms and displaying incredulity in regard to their imposition, the chiasmus allows a movement beyond their restriction and systemic borders, revelling in the unravelling occasioned by the monstrous knot of horror. This is the trajectory of post-feminism as it encounters the pulse and repulsion of horror to question the stability of all norms. In this respect, horror becomes post-modern, a cause of both fragmentation and play. Opening up modern horror's knot of otherness, the movement of the *Alien* series complicates and compounds traditional norms and gendered assumptions. From this perspective Sigourney Weaver emerges as a 'post-feminist heroine' (Braidotti 196). In *Aliens*, Ripley returns, a beauty awoken from hypersleep to a world of nightmares, the same figure but different: the film's Vietnam-horror pastiche (*The Green Berets* meets *The Thing*) shows her becoming strategist and warrior and aggressively protective surrogate mother. The pattern (it is a James Cameron film) approximates the flights of *The Terminator's* heroine, from and to a killing machine, away and back from terrifyingly apocalyptic futures. *Aliens* situates Ripley in a variety of traditionally non-complementary roles, to return to previous themes and reverse gendered expectations: a redundant, or so it seems, civilian advisor in the eyes of the military, Ripley, early in the film, impresses with her abilities as a machine operator. Characterised as 'Snow White' by a female marine, Ripley is the one who comes to the fore as a military leader: a fairytale heroine rescues a squad of battle-hardened troops (Constable). At same time as she is depicted as becoming evermore active and resourceful, the film further develops her maternal associations as she cares for the last survivor among the colonists, a girl nicknamed 'Newt'. Her resemblance to the alien queen becomes ever closer: a 'mother' herself, she rescues Newt from the alien nest and torches the offspring of the breeding queen. Mother, worker, warrior, champion: her becomings coalesce at the film's climax as she straps herself into the mechanical exoskeleton of the loader to fight a duel with the vengeful queen: hero/heroine, she again saves humanity.

By *Alien 3*, Ripley is again transformed, becoming the thing she most fears: a mother of monstrous motherhood (she is carrying a queen inside her). The film's progression, in terms of the series, is a regression from the hi-tech futures of earlier episodes: it is set in the ruins of an industrial, penitentiary colony populated only by male inmates. As Ripley changes, moving into ever closer proximity with the alien that she still plans to destroy, the human environment becomes increasingly shabbier and degraded: the post-human logic of the series, in which Ripley's humanity is shown to diminish in terms of convention, identification and species, steadily jettisons positive representations of human beings. Humans appear as the cast-offs and detritus of a different order, one dominated by aliens and the equally strange figures of 'the Company' that appear at the end: led by an android, the soldiers and scientists who arrive to capture Ripley and the alien inside her are dressed in identical white protective suits, their faces concealed by breathing apparatus. Ripley, and the series, it seems, reaches a dead-end: to destroy the alien – and conform to the narrative pattern of the series – she must kill herself. The film culminates in messianic sacrifice: become the bearer of all she most fears, she must kill herself to end the alien line, a bringer of apocalyptic fire and monstrosity overcoming both with a saintly fall into the flames. The religiosity of her final gesture, her body forming the shape of a cross to become as statuesque as a tomb carving as she throws herself backwards into the flames presents closure as transcendence: life, body, materiality must be sacrificed in order that the spirit of humanity live on. However, the jettisoning of human bodies, nature, and materiality also conforms to the logic of post-humanism in which reproduction cedes to replication, in which virtuality and code are extracted from the anchors of corporeal and natural material (Hayles).

The last of the series plays upon the religious images of its precursor: messianic sacrifice seems to be the prelude to a resurrection. Yet transcendence is illusory: rebirth, staged in so many monstrous forms in the movie, occurs on a very material and immanent plane of digital and genetic *manipu*-lations. In a technological medium obsessed by technical innovation, however, the death of the heroine and only link establishing continuity between the films is a small obstacle to be overcome. The device to reanimate the heroine and bring the narrative back from the dead is also incorporated as the film's principal theme and locus of anxiety: genetic experimentation enables the cloning of a new Ripley and a new alien at a stroke. In line with the films' steady erasure of boundaries between heroine and alien, the two are now one, retroactive genetic mutations having knotted both together at a cellular level. Fortunately, on a visual level, both are left with the capacity to develop their familiarly distinct appearances. In *Alien Resurrection*, the technical innovations move well beyond the opposition of human and alien tenuously preserved in the three preceding movies: no longer is a feminised humanity fighting to preserve its life and identity against the overwhelming threats of a lethally efficient alien and a callous system only interested in exploiting resources, bodies and species for profit. Only in superficial, visual, terms are differences displayed: in every other respect the proximity of human, alien and machine has turned into a bewildering interrelationship, a snarled imbrication of genes, behaviours and traits that seems impossible to disentangle. The mirror relation and shared, maternal destiny of human and alien have finally intermingled on screen and in genetic data banks, a crossing from which there seems no return.

The result of the inmixing of alien and human within a machinic matrix, is an end to traditional antitheses: 'the oppositional relation between the human and inhuman has been completely reconfigured to form a series of intersecting potentialities' (Constable 197). Such potential, in terms of representations of monstrosity, suggests that monsters spread more widely, no longer tied to a humanity that has been virtually eclipsed, simulated, it seems, almost to extinction. As the camera homes in on Ripley's tube-bound clone, her familiar voice offers a strange promise to the audience: 'My mommy always said there are no monsters, no real ones, but there are'. The voice of monster's mother dissents from her own mother's reassurances, a voice emanating from the past, telepathetically, or nowhere, to heighten anticipation and anxiety. There are monsters everywhere, not only the ones *Alien* audiences have come to expect: in human bodies, in space, on ships, in laboratories, board rooms, command centres, and, of course, in the voice itself. Ripley, an alien-human hybrid, is the most striking of the new monsters in her various rebirths and her development. Early scenes place particular emphasis on her redundancy and curiosity value as a by-product of the main aim of alien reproduction. Diegetically, in the context of the ongoing serial narrative, these scenes serve to elaborate the continuities and discontinuities of plot and explain how a dead heroine can return to life. But the scenes also work to show off her new corporeal and mental powers, thereby underlining just how non- or post-human she is: possessed of superior physical strength, she also matures at a vastly increased rate. Her body is able to repair itself rapidly: in one scene she thrusts a knife through her own hand and, with little discomfort, withdraws it. As the camera lingers over the wound, it quickly closes. Her education, like that of Frankenstein's monster, displays quick-wittedness, fine linguistic ability and curiosity. She even asks one of the scientists who brought her into the world about her origins. In the mess hall, locked in metal cuffs, she eats slowly studying the utensil in her hand: a scientist holds up his and, in didactic fashion, pronounces the word 'fork'. 'Fuck', she parodies, announcing her inquiry. The scientist is forthcoming: blood samples recovered after her death enabled her to be cloned. 'Did it grow', she continues, referring to the queen: 'she'll breed, you'll die'. The conversation between makers and the remade demonstrates that the past persists in her genetic make-up, a kind of Lamarckian evolution in which memories are retained. She is assured that the situation is not what it was in the days of 'the Company'. The value of the aliens is estimated in more than their military applications: when 'tamed' they provide a source of new alloys or new vaccines. As if she has read

*Frankenstein* in a former life, Ripley punctures his optimism: 'roll over, play dead, heal – you can't teach it tricks'. 'We did you', is the cutting retort.

The facile overconfidence of the military research scientist will soon be demonstrated. Indeed, with the ability, inherited from the alien, to recall the past lives, Ripley also threatens the facility of turning monsters into pets. The monster's mother thus remains tainted with the genetic memories of the monster's arch-opponent, and thus a threat to the success of the project. The commander declares his concern that she may 'take up her old hobbies'. Memory, in another guise, also produces another figure of resistance to the research: having downloaded secret military files from a database, an android sets out to kill Ripley before she can give birth. The android, Call, is another monster, a curious creation made by a prior generation of androids yet programmed with human qualities, compassion being especially prominent. Yet she is a monster to herself, her fellow feeling for an idealised humanity leaves her full of disgust and self-loathing at her own inorganic condition. While she passes very successfully for a human female, she is less effective in respect of her mission: she arrives too late to kill Ripley, her capacity for murder seriously questionable. A compassionate, humane robot makes a very inefficient assassin.

In contrast to Call, there is little humanity or fellow-feeling on display among the human figures in the film. On one hand, soldiers and scientists do the bidding of a technocratic military machine: their callousness and irresponsibility signals how their values and horizons are totally determined by that institution. The crew of misfits that arrive with an illicit cargo of cryogenically frozen living bodies for experimentation work only for their own profit: they are a band of thieves, cutthroats, space pirates with no redeeming qualities. Lecherous, drunken, cruel, ugly in appearance and, by implication, in character, these degraded remnants of humanity make a sorry showing for the species as a whole, offering no reason that it should be saved from the trash-can of evolution. Humanity, it seems, has been discarded by the system it created, another 'meat by-product', like Ripley, of a technoscientific system.

Unlike earlier *Alien* films, the fourth is dominated by 'United Systems Military' (USM) and 'not some greedy corporation'. Intended as a guarantee of the security and integrity of the research ship and the efficient management of the alien creatures, it is, ironically, no more than an indication of misplaced confidence. There is little difference to be seen between Company and military attitudes. Both hold up the alien as the ultimate prize: 'her majesty here is the real pay-off', comments the commander as he argues the case for 'putting her [Ripley] down'. Life is to be controlled, managed, tamed, made to pay, or cursorily discarded. And humans are far less valuable than the alien queen, to be used in all aspects of the breeding process. Humans, indeed, are machines, less than machines, reduced in the technical language of the military-scientific complex, to functional or dysfunctional subunits: Ripley, 'an unexpected benefit of genetic crossing', operates 'at a completely adult capacity', though 'it has connective difficulties'. In its acts and attitudes, the film makes clear, USM assumes the dominant, if conventional, form of institutional or societal monstrosity, the standard against which all others are measured.

Working 'outside regulated space', USM exceeds its own prescriptions; its systemic monstrosity is made plain from the credit sequence: the opening shots offer partial glimpses of failed genetic experiments, pulsating repellent hybrids composed of an odd assortment of human eyes, alien teeth and scissored jaws, stretched pallid skin, long bristles, misplaced limbs, all preserved in huge illuminated jars. These mutated bodies in fragments compose a freak-show signalling the horrifying cruelty of the military-scientific complex. Stasis-bound survivors of another spaceship are used as hosts for further alien reproduction. There is precious little evidence of or hope for humanity in the cavernous labyrinth of the military vessel that is also a breeding-ground of mutants and a museum of scientific atrocities, a floating island of Dr Moreau in space. Given its horrors, it is no wonder that this system finds its ideal counterpart in the alien killing machine. Such is USM's treatment of aliens, however, that even this most horrifying of creatures receives some sympathetic moments. Caged and taught by torture, the alien learns to respect the large red button that delivers painful bursts of freezing gas. On their escape from the cage, the tables are turned, and a guard receives the same treatment at the talons of an alien. The scene emphasises the slow deliberation of the alien's action as it presses the button: it has learnt from humans to savour cruelty, its gestures suggesting a curious pleasure taken in gratuitous vengeance. The monster, as the story develops, learns from and exceeds its creators. Recognising the poetic justice of this monstrous mimicry of human cruelty, moreover, the audience participate in an enjoyment that itself verges on the monstrous. It is, however, the alien queen who receives a more sympathetic presentation, in scenes which return to the monstrosity and abjection of earlier films. The genetic crossing with Ripley has not been kind to her. She has developed a human reproductive system and with it inherited all the agonies of giving birth to live young. Her pre-partum pains echo loudly around the ship. Ripley, hesitating with compassion at the sounds of maternal suffering, is easy prey: grabbed by aliens, she is taken to witness the scene. The pain of the birth is compounded by what comes after: her hideous child, a 'son' and horrible hybrid of human and alien, is an ungrateful little beast. His first act is to smash his mother's skull in a single blow. He turns, like the monstrous female mate imagined by

Frankenstein, from the image of his own kind to a human figure, drooling and leering over his grandmother, Ripley.

*Alien Resurrection* is even more firmly located in a post-human context: set on an experimental military spaceship, the opening scenes of cold scientific sterility, the treatment of human bodies, the ugliness of the human body-traffickers, and even the treatment of cloned aliens, implies that humanity or any transcendent, ideological idealisation of it, is all but erased. This is underlined with the credit sequence showing the results of genetic experimentation in extreme close-ups: part 'unnatural history museum' (Stacey 256) and part circus freak show, the monstrously deformed cloned bodies, neither alien nor human, lay out the stages involved in 'resurrecting' Ripley in order to extract an alien queen. The distorting effects on perception of extreme close-up and the curved glass of the exhibition cases exacerbate the monstrosity. This new techno-military-scientific order is presented as the last gasp of paternal dominance: nature, bodies, gender, all others finally brought under the control of all-powerful rationality that eschews morality, law and humanity in the pursuits of its goals. Significantly, the central computer has been renamed – it is called 'Father'. Its power and control, of course, is as illusory as it is callous. The cloned aliens escape to colonise the ship. Ripley, with the tattoo '8' on her arm, is no more than a 'meat by-product', like 1–7 in the laboratory freak show.

Human and alien are an effect of genetic and machine manipulation: what she 'is' is no longer clear: a 'mother' to the alien queen, a by-product, a monster to be trained like the aliens, her senses, body and mind have adapted into something utterly other. She is not human, though she aligns herself with a ragged band attempting to flee the ship. She is not a machine, though she seems to care for an android sent to kill her. Her and Call's emotional response to the laboratory of failed clones – the still-living no. 7 in particular – 'distinguishes them from unfeeling humans' (Stacey 262). Ripley is not an alien, though she shows some compassion for the queen as she witnesses her labour pains (the alien has been altered genetically in the process of extraction from Ripley, receiving the gift of a human reproductive system) and some feeling as she watches the unpleasant demise of the alien offspring – her 'grandchild' – a male human-alien hybrid. The two heroines left at the end of the film have only their distinctive feminine appearance to recommend them for illusory human identification. Indeed, it is their identifications, their feeling for others, their traces of compassion (programmed or not) and their aesthetic sensibility that distinguish them: on seeing the Earth for the first time (the Earth, rather than the inhabitants who they have saved from alien colonisation), they remark on its beauty.

The multiple crossings, reversals and enfolding of relationships that occur at a genetic level, have different effects in terms of patterns of identification and association in a narrative where species verges on irrelevance. What matters, as links between female figures are established, is pain and feminine identification. These characteristics are all that connect Ripley, Call and the alien queen, as very different excesses (woman; machine; monster) of the military-scientific system that created them. Excess is linked to feeling, to the meaty horrors of corporeal and sexualised existence, to memory, abjection and, even to sovereignty, that is, to all those elements that are palpably beyond the control of the USM project. Yet excess also touches on something unknown, some ungraspable cause, some Thing imponderable, ineffable, elusive: life, but not life as humans know and define it, life in its seething, slimy indestructible and horribly alien form. The scene of alien birth depicts Ripley engulfed by sleek, dark, writhing alien bodies. Yet Ripley is also beyond life, in its human and mortal sense: cloned, neither herself nor an alien, she manifests a sovereignty that derives from having an entirely other relation to death. Beyond death, she is also beyond sexuality. What does she want? Who is she? Not natural, not human, not alien, not woman, not machine: any identity ascribed seems inadequate. Beyond these categories, she also falls between them. A clone and hybrid, she has memories of her human existence; she has a name that is and is not her own, is without place, use or direction, a stranger to herself and a very 'unexpected benefit' to USM. Identity, it seems, is not reducible to genetic factors, no matter how much detail is extracted at a cellular level and objectively made known to a scientific gaze. An individual's 'phenomenal self-experience' is not the key element that continues 'to elude the geneticist'. Rather, the 'fundamental fantasy, the fantasmatic core inaccessible to my conscious experience' forms the underlying cause and knot of subjectivity (Žižek 1999: 312–13). In respect of alien, android and human, this element is not made visible or reduced to knowledge: their fantasmatic core, if they have one, remains undisclosed, unknowable, an absence or dark hole structuring the course of the film. Perhaps it is life in its pure and horrifying instinctual excess; perhaps it is programming gone awry in the multiple, noisy crossings of genetic and machinic connections. Perhaps there is nothing there at all: beyond sex and death, species and gender, existence, empty and evacuated, is embodied in image alone, pure simulation severed from anything that would stabilise identity, a fantasy for others and not themselves.

The alignment of feeling, fabricated, fantastic female figures, indecipherable in themselves, is consolidated through the gendered opposition that takes shape in the course of the film. The opposition is underscored by the renaming of the master computer: once one called out to 'Mother', the Company's disembodied servant serving as the network in which all business was conducted. In the United Systems Military the digital framework is called 'Father'. The irony of these names, whose provenance returns to familial models of human biological and ideological reproduction, lies in way that technology supplanted these traditional functions:

> Father and mother are gone, but their disappearance, far from widening an aleatory freedom for the subject, instead leaves the way clear for a *matrix known as code*. No more mother, no more father: just a matrix. And it is this matrix, this genetic code, which is destined to 'give birth', from now till eternity, in an operational mode from which all chance sexual elements have been expunged.
>
> (Baudrillard 1993b: 115)

The matrix of digital and genetic code, 'Mother' and 'Father' recombined, replicated and replaced, is precisely the world of USM, the machine they serve, and which defines, programmes and manages all existence, giving it form, aims and objectives. The cluster of female figures cohere as the exceptions that embody the horrifying truth of this regime, its nightmare realised in unthinkable form, its calculations and programmes giving birth to a future that is monstrous and repellent.

At the same time, another fantasy rears up from these curiously attractive figures of post-human existence. Female figures, knotted together in their otherness and emptiness, form a screen for the projection of familiar fantasies surrounding the mysteries of feminine sexuality. They promise something more than the system can envisage or contain, their emptiness and excess forming a site of possibilities, attractions and desires whose escape velocity is fuelled by horror and romance alone. Not all, more than, dangerously supplementary to the regime, they embody the possibility of freedom, of a flight from the constraints of a cruel, in-human and patriarchal system: its failure to master the matrix of its own creation and harness its creatures, leaves the knot of otherness as an excess suggesting an Other more fluid, feeling and feminine space. Irigaray's 'awoman', the 'projective map' of phallic fantasy and also site of the diffusions, resistances and transgressions of fluid femininity, is born in the vacuum of outer space (1985: 108). A fantasy, perhaps, but it remains powerful in its effects, projections and identifications. The future, monstrous maybe, is also positively charged, attractive, its femininity disruptively uploaded on to the matrix: it is 'female and dangerous'. Like the system man – or humanity – 'built for his own protection', she now supersedes him (Plant 182–83). The system assumes feminine characteristics in its 'intuitive leaps and cross-connections', in its fluidity, multiplicity, its insurrectionary combinations and parallel dissolution of fixed identities. It gives birth to a new species: 'replicants' (Plant 176–77; 179–80). 'Father's dead, asshole', comments the feminine-identified humane android as a leading USM scientist tries to escape. The latter-day vivisectionist turns in panic, his computer locked down, and a gruesome death inevitable. Father has been taken out by the female android, leaving the alien to finish the job.

USM is destroyed, its digital matrix exploding with the ship. The seeds of another matrix return to Earth. But the world is no longer humanised. With the military machine able to supplant human reproductive processes and write its own code, all pretensions to humanity are discarded: its mastery of the biological matrix and breeding of aliens makes it literally the counterpart of the alien mother that it always held up as its ultimate prize. The indifference of its attitude is matched by the in-difference of its products, reducing and equating (female) alien and human bodies to the same plane as objects to be mutilated, manipulated and manufactured. Cross-breeding extinguishes humanity and, for all the attempts to erase difference, recycles it: the replication of sameness, however, introduces internal deviations and mutations that short-circuit successful cloning and subsequent training so that even 'number 8' manifests a resistance to the system that created her. But the resistance is not that of a heroic humanity or a suffering, abjected femininity become sovereign. Though she looks like a woman, Ripley is far from human: any feeling and compassion she exhibits, attributes usually distinguishing humanity in SF, are reserved for androids and aliens. The world of the film, it seems, is truly posthuman, a future that is thoroughly female, alien and machinic: the species has been virtually bypassed through a technological and alien evolution and, more significant, its qualities and attributes disposed of.

The principle figures of identification may be female in appearance or feminine in terms of association, convention or typical emotional characteristics: a female human-alien hybrid, an android in feminine form, an alien who gives birth. But they are certainly not human. The alien within is both the norm and the surface of identification, all other defining features having been erased or elided, mutated on a plane of indifference. Ripley, except significantly in the way she looks, is an alien-human clone, mother and grandmother to a new species. 'Call', the android in the form of a young woman who plans to save the world by destroying the host body of alien propagation, manifests the most intense human feelings. But, as Ripley notes, on discovering she is a 'robot': 'I should have known – no human being is that humane.' An android designed by machines, she has been programmed to care. With the programming, however, comes a sense of exclusion and self-hate: 'I'm disgusting', Call comments. The alien queen is also changed by genetic mutation and hybridisation: her 'gift' from Ripley is a human reproductive system. It is a painful gift which results, instead of the easy excretion of eggs, in the extenuated and excruciating birth of a living child from her womb, a child that viciously crushes her skull before turning to Ripley – his grandmother – for maternal affection. With the choice of ugly alien or attractive human form, the baby beast turns towards beauty. Abandoned, the child pursues her to be sucked into fragments and globules through a small hole in a depressurised escape craft. This climax refuses straightforwardly explosive models of legitimate expulsion and exudes confused emotions, like those evinced by Ripley when she enters the scene of failed monstrous births: there, amid hideous combinations of dead alien-human body parts she encounters 'number 7', a still living but painfully disproportioned assemblage of mutant limbs with a human head and face pleading to be killed. Ripley torches the laboratory with a flamethrower. At the end, after a maternal hug, she sends her offspring to his death with pain and compassion, a mercy killing drawn out by the anguish in the alienhu-manoid's eyes and Ripley's mouthing of the words 'I'm sorry' as it disinte-grates under pressure.

Pain, compassion, suffering and a 'post-humane' identification with the other add a new twist to the alien series. The 'resurrection' that follows the climactic 'crucifixion' of *Alien 3* discloses relationships more complicated than a symbolic human triumph of over death: humanity almost disappears in the course of the film and there is little sign of a transcendent order estab-lished as a result of reincarnation, little evidence of a sacred mythology recu-perated as a model for human relations. An alien has saved the Earth. Though Ripley ends up saving the world, the salvation is not triumphal, despite having an element of sublimity about it: as Ripley and Call look out at the Earth, which they see for the first time, the sunset or sunrise evokes emotions of wonder: 'it's beautiful'. Significantly, it is Earth, rather than its inhabitants, that is admired. 'You did it, you saved the world', Call goes on, asking 'what happens now': 'I don't know, I'm a stranger here myself', replies Ripley. It is almost as if the return to Earth involves a new colonisa-tion, the birth of new order of humanity inspired by the odd coupling of femalien and femininandroid, both capable of the experiencing their own and others' pain and compassion. A strange post-humanity evinces itself in this feminine-identified compassion: physically hybrid and actually confounding species-identity, their sense of strangeness and alienation, from themselves as much as others, enables uncertain but deeply affective identi-fications: with the genetic basis of identity rendered totally confused, it is not who one is at a corporeal level that seems to count, but how one identifies; not one's own pain that gives an intensity that return's one to oneself, but the other's pain that provides the identificatory link to relationships with others and oneself.

From female abjection and otherness, from corporeal destruction and rebirth, a new subject appears to be resurrected with an ethical, compas-sionate spirit. On the basis of feminine associations and identifications, the film presents the possibility of a new understanding of otherness: the alien, once providing the external threat allowing for the expulsion of internal anxieties caused by a collapsing symbolic order has become too proximate, too close to home. The place of otherness cedes to a generalised sense of strangeness which, in its uncertain, confused identifications, turns hybrid beings away from seeking a stable unified identity and opens, through pain and compassion, onto less structured networks. Ripley and Call do not know what happens next. This strategy differs from conventional developments of the alien theme, like that of another science horror film, *Species* (1995):

> Pitting mysticism against alterity, *Species* solves the problem of a DNA symbolic by imagining the even more potent, precious and powerful functions of the still mysterious human mind, functions that evade digitalization and exceed the machine. *Species*, thus, represents an even more nostalgic and desperate return of the ineffable in the face of the all-too certain.
>
> (Roof 179)

Neither mysticism nor huMan mind is pitted against the alien threat. A certain mystery does exceed digital and genetic programming, the mystery associated, in fantasy, with femininity. The ending attempts to return excess to humanity in its feminised form, an excess which, not of nature, species, body, becomes an idealised image conjuring up the immaterial, eternal transcendence of something like a human spirit, but without humans to embody it. The beauty of (mother) Earth, evoking sensations of wonder and sublimity in the female figures who view it for the first time, guarantees this illusory transcendence. A curious crossing of New Age spiritualism and ecological discourse occurs, with neither framework fitting. What is glimpsed is close to the New Age idea of an evolution to a higher realm: the sight of the world at dawn implies that a 'more than human intelligence' has arrived. This meta-evolutionary perspective depends on merging with the 'global organism': to do that requires the sacrifice of the very 'noumenal Thing' that defines humans and gives them ethical agency, turning them into 'lifeless puppets deprived of human dignity'. Feminalien and feminandriod should be mere puppets but are depicted with dignity and ethics. They have almost given their lives to save the world, implying the anti-anthropocentrism of a deep ecological concern for the planet as a whole, irrespective of species prejudice. But 'Deep Ecology'

> in no way escapes the charge of anthropocentrism: the very demand it addresses to man to sacrifice himself for the interests of the entire biosphere confers on him the exceptional status of universal being; that is, the very apparent humiliation of man to a being whose duty is to

sacrifice himself for the higher aim of preserving the biosphere is the form-of-appearance of its opposite. That is to say, is not the ability to disengage oneself from one's own limited situation and to self-objectivize oneself – to look at oneself as an insignificant part of a larger totality – the highest, exclusive spiritual capacity?

(Žižek 1999: 305–6)

Amid anti-anthropocentrism, humanity returns, universal, spiritual, whole – and machinic at the same time. The android appears as the most human figure, her abjection and self-sacrifice presenting the highest of human values. Yet, these very values have been programmed.

Humanity, its mystery, excess, transcendence, is not guaranteed or resurrected, but is simulated and surpassed by figures that look female, figures that are cloned, programmed and yet appearing to assume a 'nature', an essence, identified with femininity. In *Alien Resurrection*, however, the excess of the machine is not located in the rediscovery of an ineffable femininity associated with childbirth, love and pain (all of which have been genetically or digitally programmed). Such a move would turn representations of abjection into sacred images of suffering and recuperate a messianic maternity as the model of a new, or resurrected, global order. The intensities of emotion emanating from identifications with otherness are tied to the preservation of the image, the maintenance of imaginary feminine figures despite all knowledge of their non-human status. Toned, dark-haired, beautiful in black leatherette, both Call and Ripley survive and, more important, continue to look good. Looking, how one looks, takes place in the very medium in which the look reigns: perhaps there is nothing of more importance in a film produced in a place (Hollywood) where looking good is the overriding imperative. Personal trainers, dieticians and cosmetic surgeons are all conscripted to ensure that the body be enhanced beyond decay and death, to be reborn as pure image, as undying simulation. That is, they are dedicated to the vision machines whose operations parallel the work of digital and genetic coding, the reproduction of the same, as image, information and commodity. There is no transcendence, no resurrection, no difference, only the return of the same, the alienating strangeness of cinematic alternations between attraction and repulsion become a pulse in a network of matricial identifications and technical expenditure. Uncertain of what to do, strangers to themselves, the woman-alien and android fill the screen, waiting for the next episode in the *Alien* series. They are figures of irresolution and projection paused in narrative suspension and expectation of the next repetition in the sequence of cinematic affect. An increasingly digitalised cinematic apparatus, indeed, duplicates cloning, able to repeat, ad infinitum, its series of images, doubles, others and selves. *Alien V*, then, will replicate another Ripley as she (and maybe Call), earthbound renegades, battle with USM and try to destroy her DNA and finally terminate alien experimentation. Ripley, of course, will have to combat yet more of her offspring before killing them and herself. If she is not careful, of course, she will be resurrected again, this time in the service of USM as it tries to deal with another alien outbreak it has been unable to control. Again she will attempt total consummation and obliterate all trace of alien and herself. Somewhere down the line she will have to confront herself in mortal combat: a double of herself will have been produced and unleashed. One, the human-friendly defender, will confront the other, herself, a darker version no doubt magisterially leading an alien invasion . . . On the flat and infinitely expandable plane of the screen, anything is possible.

No longer human in any traditional or conventional sense, these two hybrid entities, Ripley and Call, defined by relationality and process, are, respectively 'feminalien' and 'feminandroid', new and distinct creations. Nonetheless, they are female in appearance, heroic by dint of their looks and identifications if on no other grounds whatsoever. Once predicated on rescuing humanity from imminent extinction, the narrative closures (with miniscule cracks) of the series now move beyond humanist considerations with a feminandroid and feminalien gazing upon the Earth. A beautiful globe, female figures looking and looking good: lines of flight and lines of sight – movements, projections and identifications enabled by code and vision machines shedding all but the semblance of nature, species, gender. The flight of the heroine, her fears, her desires, her fantasies and anxieties, takes off elsewhere: other identificatory possibilities and configurations, posts-, trans-, and hypers-, generating other prospects and projections.

The logic of a particular version of the 'post' – post-human and post-feminist – seems fully realised in *Alien Resurrection*: the categories of human and gender have been rendered redundant, along with all the ideological bases – nature, bodies, feelings, ideals – that support them. From the black hole of horror, gendered identity and subjectivity seems to have achieved escape velocity, flown beyond any material anchor or gravitational force that would pull it back into conventional categorisation. The fourth film in the *Alien* series takes the fight of the heroine beyond norms and conventional structures: it manifests the 'breakdown of traditional models of identity', leaving psychoanalysis and horror conventions 'defunct' (Constable 173). Instead, identity becomes a matter of reconfigurations, of 'intersecting potentialities' (Constable 197). The film puts any idea of the stability of body or identity to flight and follows paths of becoming in which the mingling, couplings and transformation of relations along particular lines of intersection – such as those between Ripley and/as alien – make any identity 'processual', mobile and changeable (Rizzo 333, 342). Here a certain horror remains: the motility of body, subjectivity and identity is 'both a source of freedom and anxiety', and cause of both excitement and dread (Rizzo 335). For Rizzo, the message is positive, emphasising the body's potential to change, adapt and survive. Yet, the double affects of the film involve the viewer in the disturbing process of transformation: the use of generic horror techniques – the visceral effects of music, suspense, distorted images – crosses boundaries between film and viewer, to open up spectating bodies from the inside with sensations that cause corporeal changes (Rizzo 335–36). The parallels between content and apparatus in *Alien IV* are noted by Stacey: 'the monstrous potentiality of cell development in an age of genetic engineering and cloning is given a visual equivalence in the continuously mutating flow of images' (254). This flow, punctuated with an 'overpresence of the abject', foregrounds generic convention and reiterations, placing bodies/genes and identities/images on the same flat, digitally rewritable plane: sameness, normativity, narrative, are all technologically reconfigured as surface effects and affects (Stacey 274). Cell and image duplication lead to an 'excessive sameness' which, because abjection is also foregrounded, cannot be fully expelled to circulate and mutate continuously in the flow of images and simulations (270). Not only does the digitally reconfigured conjunction of image and genetic make-up disturb categories of gender and humanity, its post-human and post-feminist line of flight opens up questions of embodiment, identity and difference and throws them back onto a plane of simulation: otherness finds itself transformed by the becoming normal of abjection, absorbed, almost, in the excessive sameness of images without depth or anchoring context.

Horror, too, is transformed, and gothic along with it. While still evoking effects, the repulsive knot of monstrosity no longer functions as the point where identities dissolve, structures collapse and meanings are confounded: it is no longer the point from which one must recoil in order that sense, system and subjectivity are restored. Instead, it engenders moments of sensation, points of intersection and transformations, a site from which various lines of flight and potentiality become possible. Pulse-re-pulse: this new horror turns on an excess that cannot be expunged but which, in a continual dynamic of attraction and recoil, underlies systems of simulation, sameness, mutation and hybridisation, the very excess that gives them energy and intensity. These couplings of excitement and fear, identification and disgust thus duplicate the process of digital and genetic mutation presented in and by *Alien Resurrection*, rendering the viewing process mobile, affective and unstable, subject only to pulses and (re)pulsions, oscillations of identification and abjection. Bodily sensation and perception are confounded, fixed identities displaced and discarded, in cinematic techniques and digital apparatuses that produce ecstatic flights of identification – Ripley, Call, the Earth, continue to exert an aesthetic attraction – or repulsion: aliens and humans, on the whole have little appeal. The connection between horror and the human is superseded: repulsion from objects of the former (from all that is marked as alien, monstrous, abject) no longer ensures a return to the security of human boundaries. Rather, it causes transformations that reconfigure bodies and identities, letting them fly off in different directions. Or, as the endings of films 3 and 4 (like 1–7, the series has turned into forms of successive if barely related monstrosities) seem to suggest, to fly off, not in some ecstatic ascension, but downwards: Ripley falls back, down into the flames that consume her; the escape craft crash lands on Earth. The movement away from traditional human conventions presented in the combination of genetics, digital images, feminine figure and alien figures, linked to a throwing down and throwing away, a discarding of human body, norms, structures and expectations that is associated with a post-human line of flight which casts off bodies, materiality and context in its transformation to code, virtuality and simulation (Hayles). Humans in 3 and 4 are almost exclusively unappealing: morally if not physically deformed, they are little more than waste products, detritus, rubbish to be disposed of. Lines of flight, lines of fright, lines of sight. If gothic, in modernity, worked to define humanity in relation to and repulsion from otherness and excess configured and contained in figures of monstrosity, post-gothic romance, tracing a line of flight along inhuman trajectories, locates humanity in a redundant lineage: post-modern, post-femininst, post-human . . . post-gothic – a line of shite.

# 6 Resistance is futile: romance and the machine

## Being Borged

It comes from another quadrant of the galaxy, travelling rapidly through space in a giant cube armed with unthinkably powerful weaponry and unbreachable defensive capabilities. Its mission is simple: to assimilate cultures, extracting anything distinctive from their biological or technological make-up. Then, enhanced by its additions, it moves on, leaving devastated worlds in its wake. Relentless, implacable, practically invincible, it is a supremely efficient system of assimilation and destruction. Any resistance is considered vain, as are illusions of freedom or self-determination. Even death has no relevance for it. An indomitable monster, it is body and machine composed of bodies and machines, a meta-cyborganism: the Borg.

The Borg. Though not poetic, the monosyllabic collective noun does it justice. It is singular and multiple, disturbing the categories of a language based on individual speaking subjects. Personal pronouns slide from 'it' to 'they', from 'I' to 'we', as boundaries of individual and group are rendered redundant. 'I am Borg', the one is the many. The Borg is not a race or a species since natural evolution has been supplemented by systematic technological enhancement. The collective is composed of the bodies of various humanoid life-forms that have been assimilated by means of sophisticated biotechnological alterations: limbs are given prosthetic attachments, the functioning of organs improved by technical apparatuses, nervous systems are rewired by microcircuitry and nanotechnological implants. The transformation extends to a cellular level with the rewriting of specific genetic codes. In the process, individual consciousness is transcribed and relocated, becoming part of the single collective mind, a hive mind sustained by an interactive network of subspace signals in which the whole is articulated by incessant instantaneous communicational flows. Interconnectivity is the Borg's strength, allowing rapid adaptation to any alteration in environment or opposition. Yet, for all assimilations of biological and technological

difference, it remains inexorably the same, ever-flexible, constantly adaptable and yet hypostatic, metastable.

Hybrids, homogenised to the high standards of Borg technical specifications, the members ('drones') of the collective, are dressed shabbily in black
with dark rippled body armour protecting their torsos. Black tubes wrap
around chests, shoulders, legs, and disappear into what remains of flesh.
Grey metallic attachments mark the visible skin. One forearm is replaced by
a cumbersome apparatus, a weapon, a tool, somewhat archaic in the
mechanically clockwork turnings and whirrings of its various little probes,
drills, injectors. One eye socket and the surrounding skull are encased by an
array of visual enhancements, telescopic lenses, night sensors, optical scan-
ners or laser projectors. Skin, visible only on one hand and part of the face,
is pallid, hairless, grey-white, drained of any sign of blood or emotion. The
Borg sleep ('regenerate') upright in dark open booths, the eerie glow of dials
brushing the gloom. Movement is regular, if ungainly: the stiff, awkward
gait of drones never evinces any hint of urgency. One dark figure falls and
the others shamble steadily on.

Though the Borg, in function and effect, marks a powerful attempt to
present 'an alterity that is genuinely other', there is something 'old-fash-
ioned' about its form, visually embodying a core contradiction in SF, its
'collision of future and past', its 'prophetic and nostalgic modes' (Roberts
163–65). For all the new technoscientific paraphernalia and rhetoric in
which it is outfitted, the Borg remains very recognisable, its drones familiar
figures dredged up from the vaults of gothic representation. In movement
and appearance, a debt to Boris Karloff's monster is acknowledged: the
deathly pallor of the skin, the uncomfortably reassembled body and the
unwieldy movements suggest something is missing, aesthetically at least, in
the operations of technology on biology. Without emotion, soul or personality, the Borg recalls the zombies from so many B-movie horrors, the living
dead of a Romero film returning to eat human flesh without relish or pleasure. Feeding is vampiric, but without erotic or abhorrent charge: like the
Martians from H. G. Wells' *The War of the Worlds*, sucking blood through
tubes from their human victims, or the machines of *The Matrix*, fuelled by
the electrochemical energy of wired-up bodies, the activity is no more than a
cold necessity. In the process, individuals become mere material or
machines themselves, puppets of instinct, repetitive, mechanical, uniform
automata devoid of freewill, self-consciousness and sentience. In the grey
zone articulating gothic horrors and science fiction, the doubles of humanity
find themselves controlled by powerful technological forces – alien telep-
athy, invasive organisms, remotely operated implants – rather than being
possessed by demons or the turbulent impulses of id. The effect, however,
seems pretty much the same: extreme physical and mental subjugation

rends self from itself, body from body, to the point that identity can never again be called one's own. The 'overmind' from Arthur C. Clarke's fiction is projected into a rationalist utopia beyond the stars and returns with a vengeance as an utterly alien intelligence intent on absorbing bodies, hearts and minds: otherness asks questions of humanity.

Among the horrifying fragments, the monsters, doubles, zombies, automata, aliens and living dead of gothic and science fictions that are sutured and reassembled in the image of the Borg, the motif of the body-snatcher comes to the fore in manifesting anxieties about corporeal integrity and self-control (Seed). The Borg imperative to assimilate, reconfiguring bodies and absorbing minds into a polyphonic whole, further confounds distinctions of mind and body, life and death, individual and social system: minds are not simply erased in the process of turning bodies into puppets of a resolutely alien power, but are conjoined with the whole, agents in its functioning, interactive components of an intelligence rendered less alien. Embodied knowledge, experience, culture and identity are negated on one level but conserved on another in a nightmarish parody of Hegelian dialectical synthesis meeting the post-revolutionary proletarian future of utopian Marxism. Bodysnatching and alien invasion, of course, owe much to Cold War panics about the Red Threat (Jancovich). With the Borg and the fluid interchanges between technology, biology and culture which it materialises, any separation of inside and outside, self and alien, becomes indeterminate: bodysnatched bodies become bodysnatchers in turn on behalf of a mind that is and is more than one's own. Upgraded bodies and a technologically-enhanced collective consciousness meld organism and machine on an informatic and rhizomatic plane, a plane unbounded by unitary organisms, kinship groups, nation-states or political blocs.

Pre-eminent object of modern discipline, site of surveillance, confession, individuation, sexualisation and normalisation, the body functioned as a crucial node in the networks of modernity's power relations (Foucault 1979; 1981). Its imaginary unity serves in the anticipation of psychological and motor coordination and in the symbolic inscription that gives form to subjectivity (Lacan 1977a). Disciplined, imaginary, its integrity and unity, both 'fortress' and 'prison', is always threatened from without and within. To steal, simulate or construct a body is to begin disentangling an entire network of intricate hierarchies and relationships. The monsters of gothic and science fiction, whether idealised or degraded figures, participate in a process of defending or transgressing corporeal borders, marking out the limits of bodies that are individual, social, political. For Joanna Russ, the process begins with *Frankenstein*, its monster the sire of 'every robot, every android, every sentient computer' (126). Having a shared textual origin, she notes, the emergence of both genres is made possible by modernity: science fiction 'draws its beliefs, its material, its great organizing metaphors, its atti-tudes, from a culture that could not exist before the industrial revolution, before science became both an autonomous activity and a way of looking at the world'; *Frankenstein*, too, having supplanted the supernatural machinery of gothic fiction with natural and technological causes, inaugurates one of the 'great myths of the industrial age' (Russ 10; 126). Brian Aldiss concurs, seeing science fiction as having 'diversified' the gothic tale of terror in order to 'encompass those fears generated by change and technological advances which are chief aspects of change' (1973: 53). Modernity fabricates a body simultaneously in tune with and opposed to the rhythms of industrial prog-ress. With science, one of the grand narratives of modernity as Russ suggests, comes progress and change, and with change comes fear, recoil and regres-sion. In the forms of gothic or science fiction, modern culture points its fantastic outlets in both directions.

Traditionally, science fiction heads for the stars, exploring other times and other worlds and racing progress to imagine rational paradises more often than dystopian disasters. This trajectory has been described as the genre's 'expansive mode'. Since the 1960s, however, an 'SF of implosion' turns from the stars and plummets towards the body of Earth. The reversion entails the 'destruction of liberal ideology by autonomous technology'; it falls upon increasingly broken physical and social bodies. At this point, science fiction overlaps with the slash and splatter excesses of popular horror (Csicsery-Ronay 186–88). This is the 'gray area' where hybirds of horror and science fictions (both hybrid forms from the start) coalesce in monstrous fashion (Sobchack 1987: 27). Despite numerous overlaps, science fiction demands a more 'dispassionate' and 'technological view' of violence and destruction (Sontag 428). But *Alien*, for example, entwines a corrupt corpo-rate off-world future with horrifying assaults on bodily integrity, from within as much as without (Creed; Clover). Science fiction, which 'diversified' gothic fears as it romanced rational modernity into outer space, returns to them.

The genre in which implosive science fiction is most evident in its concerns with technology, the body and a wasted socius, is that distinctively 1980s variant, cyberpunk: differences and proximities are delineated in a tone that embraces the implosion of science fiction, reversing the polarities of horror and thrill, turning fear into desire. Cyberpunk still engages with 'body invasion', with 'prosthetic limbs, implanted circuitry, cosmetic surgery, genetic alteration' as well as the 'mind invasion' of interfaces, neurochemistry and artificial intelligence, but it is excited at the idea, cele-brating the dissolution of bodies and borders, surfing on the shockwave of a technocorporate revolution that tears down traditions, institutions, authori-ties. The cyberpunks are the first generation to have grown up in 'in a truly science-fictional world' (Sterling xi–ix). Science, and fiction, has literally imploded. Technology becomes 'visceral', 'pervasive', 'intimate': it crawls beneath the skin and inhabits mental spaces (Sterling xi). Technology's intimacy, combined with the decentralising and fluid surges of new economic imperatives, heralds the emergence of an entirely different order of things. Though cyberpunk abounds with ghosts, demons and monsters, they all appear as technological effects: ghosts are virtual, haunting screens, neural circuits, the dead living on as data; demons are coding algorithms, AIs, acephalic corporate powers; monsters are quotidian and everywhere, the enhanced and mutated bodies of all those inhabiting the wrecked cityscapes and sublime datascapes of cyberpunk's future present. The gothic force, however, is weak, diminishing as the intimate embrace of horror and thrill tightens. A different diversification has occurred in which familiar forms and figures are scattered across so many cultural screens, their recognisable fragments vestiges of fear, hybrids and mutations that are readily assimilable to the consumer-orientated demands of a culture too used to monstrosity and electronically anaesthetised to horror.

*Star Trek*, 'an ongoinging conversation on what it means to be human in a technological and multinational world' (Penley 1997: 17), is curiously situated in respect of generic shifts between expansive and implosive science fiction and the cultural transformations on which they surf. It looks back, but cannot resist a peek at its present and its future. The introduction of the Borg gives form to the disturbance but manifests an ambivalence that refuses any conventional generic assurances. While *Star Trek: the Next Generation* tries to stave off the aesthetics and new economics of cyberpunks and the 1980s – its sets, costumes and machinery could not be visually more different – it also stages an encounter with the new cyberorder in its presentation of the Borg, an imaginary homogenization, a meta-cyborg monstrosity, whose difference and otherness is designed to consolidate a conservative (humanist, liberal, imperial) sameness. The Borg, of course, renders any clear differentiation problematic, opening the project and its projections to anxieties that cannot be easily allayed or expelled. The conservative impulse is strong, nonetheless. Vivian Sobchack notes how the first three *Star Trek* feature films were 'nostalgically backward-looking to earlier visions of the future' (Sobchack 1987: 276). This future passed aligns itself with the 'charming romance' of Gernsbackian science fiction and is endorsed in Jeff Greenwald's account of the international popularity of the *Star Trek: the Next Generation* television series. In the face of the collapse of the NASA space programme, financial cuts and the *Challenger* disaster, the series reawakens dreams of Space Age extraterrestrial romance. With its mission to explore new worlds and discover new civilisations regenerated, with its streamlined starship bursting with every possible labour-saving gadget, with the smug self-assurance of its cosily familial and fiercely individualistic crew, with its federated multiculturalism of safely typed humanoid species, *Star Trek* clings on to a very modern idea of science and fiction. But one longstanding companion to exploration, discovery, adventure, romance and humanistic individualism, of course, is imperialism. Humanist contradictions (between public and private domains, between individual and community) are made evident in the series, but not only do they present a fantasy of united diversities and harmonious differences (another form of 'e pluribus unum'), they 'mask more sinister, imperialist implications of the text's incorporating ethic' (Joyrich 64–65).

Cynthia Fuchs draws the distinction clearly in her discussion of 'The Best of Both Worlds', the double episode split (Picard has just been assimilated – the horror!) between the 1991 and 1992 seasons. The show presents the first full encounter with the Borg: a 'neosocialist cyborg "community"' is opposed to the 'optimistic imperialism' that flies off with the *USS Enterprise* (281). At the time, however, the Soviet bloc was breaking up and, without the resistance of its geopolitical double, optimistic western imperialism began careering in other directions. Greenwald, nonetheless, insists on reading the Borg within a familiar political framework, one in which the lines of us and them, self and other, remain reassuringly in place:

> The Borg are to the 1990s, I suggest, what the Klingons were to the 1960s: a reflection of our political antipodes. When the original *Star Trek* introduced the Klingons, they were the transparent reflection of the Soviet menace: gruff, imperialistic, and ruthless. The Borg, on the other hand, seem to express our misgivings about a more contemporary juggernaut: China.
>
> (253)

The formulation is certainly neat and places appropriate emphasis on the Borg as the key new villain of the piece. But its significance is perhaps too readily explained in a way that misses many of the ramifications of Borg-anxiety. Though China may have emerged as a major power (its recent successful space mission announcing the fact), to locate that power in terms of political blocs (as a 'juggernaut') is to ignore the economic shifts in which power is sustained and circulated in relation to a global corporate market-place rather than nation-states. The formulation also situates otherness at a distance and as the inverted form, the 'reflection', of US imperialism, rendering its threat external to homely borders at a time when transnational capitalism promotes a world trade that overrides such neatly bounded modern notions.

Brannon Braga, one of the producers of *The Next Generation* series as well as the movie, *Star Trek: First Contact*, again featuring the Borg, does not locate the new threat in terms of geopolitical boundaries. His account significantly neglects to place the Borg in a real or imagined realm outside American life and ideology: the threat, indeed, is seen only as an 'antithesis', defined purely in terms of its difference:

> The Borg, to me, represent the antithesis of the American obsession with the individual. We're obsessed with the rights of the individual, and cultivating individualistic children. The Borg are the ultimate threat to such sensibilities. You lose all individuality, and are assimilated into a big hive mind.
>
> (cit. Greenwald 253)

The Borg is not placed on the outside but is defined, in pathologised American terms, as the antithesis of an obsession and, by implication, an entity giving form to something generated internally, an imagined threat projected outwards. The challenge of the Borg discloses a crisis in Judith Butler's 'heterosexual matrix', a crisis prompted by cyborg transgressions in masculine identity, patriarchal integrity and the hierarchical binary system which supports them (Fuchs 282). The Borg, purely negative, purely differential, functions only as the embodied cause of imagined loss: 'multiple losses of choice, individual identity, and morality' (Fuchs 298). But the projection of loss, the imagination of psychological, social, planetary devastations, works in two directions: apocalyptic romances, with their natural or technological disasters, litter science fiction and gothic tales from the start, destructions variously satisfying individualistic or degeneration fantasies or serving as preludes to the recovery or discovery of a better order.

To imagine loss participates in a dynamic of terror and sublimity: overcome by incomprehensible sights, individual senses cannot, initially, cope. But the threat activates, so Edmund Burke (1990) claims, an instinct for self-preservation that reinvigorates the subject, enabling him/her to apprehend imaginatively, in awe and wonder, a system greater than him or herself and feel elevated accordingly. Loss and recuperation are conjoined in sublime terror. Constituted as an object of pure loss, a sublime threat, the Borg activates a familiar form of monstrosity, a figure condensing anxieties in a single object and thereby providing a screen simultaneously enabling their projection and occlusion. Given form, monsters can be exorcised, expelled, destroyed. The imagining of monstrous dissolution activates the energy necessary for limits to be (enjoyably) restored, fantasy returning to its function of supporting the homeostatic circulations of pleasure and desire. As the Borg cube speeds away on its destroying-assimilating beeline to the Terran system and the *Enterprise* limps in pursuit, its acting Captain notes in his log:

'the devastation they could bring is beyond imagination'. The beyond of imagination is precisely its condition, the absence that fires imagination beyond ever-receding horizons, spurring it to greater efforts, further romantic flights in its return to its freshly re-imagined self.

The losses embodied by the Borg are telling: mind absorbed by a collective consciousness, body reduced to the mechanical servitude of living death. Individuality, freewill and autonomy are obliterated. 'Resistance is futile': the Borg proceeds on that basis and makes it so. There is no countenancing of dialogue or exchange, no room for self-representation: 'discussion is irrelevant'. The erasure of the principles underlying humanistic individualism is also spelt out in advance: 'freedom is irrelevant'; 'self-determination is irrelevant'. Even 'death is irrelevant': the inevitable end that guarantees human experience with the consciousness of mortality and selfhood is removed. The Borg thus announces a two-pronged assault aimed at bodies and minds, an attack on both material and ideological levels of existence. This is evident when Picard, captured by the Borg and urged to 'comply' with its demands, declares his intention to resist by refusing to give up his freedom: he will fight to the death. 'Resistance is futile . . . freedom is irrelevant . . . death is irrelevant'. That Picard is prepared to die is not surprising. But the Borg has already anticipated that for which he will die. His defiance to the point of death goes beyond fellow feeling or military duty, beyond material losses of friends, crew, ship, or home planet. Appropriate to the morality he represents in the series, his defiance is framed in terms of an adherence to the very values (freedom, self-determination) the Borg seems to cast readily aside. But these fine principles, the code that definitively seems to separate the Federation from the Borg, are not in themselves quite enough to sustain resistance, too abstract or ideal to bridge the gap between materiality and ideology. The Borg has already specified what it wants: 'we will add your biological and technological distinctiveness to our own. Your culture will adapt to service ours'. They do not want whole bodies, complete technological know-how or, even an entire culture; they simply target that which is most special: 'distinctiveness'. Having taken away a culture's 'distinctiveness', the process of assimilation and adaptation is made easy.

The Borg strategy is not only one of physically assimilating-destroying many lives or crushing the concepts that distinguish a culture. Its sophistication, its unexpectedly diabolical subtlety, directs itself at the obscure thing around which a culture organises itself, the unseen locus of affective bonds, the very difference separating Federation and Borg. 'Distinctiveness' is not quantifiable or calculable in moral, rational or utilitarian terms, but forms the osmazome that gives substance to a sense of culture. 'Distinctiveness', then, is associated with that ill-defined element implied in the equally vague phrase, 'way of life', linked to 'our Thing' which must be defended at all costs, beyond reason, beyond morality, to the death: without it, the Federation are no different from the Borg. What is so horrifying about assimilation (one remains alive, albeit in an altered state of body and consciousness) is that it takes away 'distinctiveness'. In threatening to steal away this strange object, this Thing that gives humanoid culture its particular and peculiar unity, a distinctiveness not in itself distinct, the Borg threatens an unbearable 'theft of enjoyment' (Miller). It is unbearable because it comes so close to home, removing that which is intimate and exterior ('extimate') at the same time. Without it, however, there is only assimilation, unimaginable devastation. Threatening to take away a way of life as well as lives turns the Borg into the most sublime and intimate of threats, a figure of (and in place of) an ultimate dissolution, from within and without, site of the Federation's utter consumption. Reconstituting itself in the face of the Borg threat, then, is an imaginative activity of self-preservation and restoration.

It is strange, given the Borg's firepower (which could easily take Starfleet apart in direct military conflict), that the decision is made to assimilate a single individual before completing the conquest of Earth. But the hive mind is quite subtle, despite the appearance of its drones. It knows what it wants and it knows how to get it. On entering Federation Space, the Borg cube intercepts the *Enterprise*, hailing Picard by name and demanding he surrender himself. He refuses. The Borg kidnaps him. He is altered to become Locutus of Borg, a residually human mouthpiece for an in-human collective. This ingenious tactic is aimed as much at assimilating distinctiveness as it is a battlefield ploy. But it is surely not about making more effective contact with another species: discussion is irrelevant. With Picard, comes the strategic knowledge of Starfleet's most experienced Captain along with the morale-deflating bonus of assimilating so prestigious and authoritative a figure. Picard is certainly distinctive: unlike the *Enterprise*'s previous Captain – the all-American, Kirk – he is of French descent and played by an English Shakespearean actor. He provides the crew not only with impeccable leadership but the rigorous morality of a paternal figure. To see him fully Borged, horrifyingly altered with implants and prosthetics, is one thing; to have him speak for and as the Borg is to pull the plug on the moral authority so central to the series. The effect is disarming in every sense, a palpable vacuum. Is he alive or dead? Does Picard still exist? Being altered, the crew must repeatedly be reminded, means being Borg. Picard has to be considered dead, though the ghost of his presence continues to haunt the crew. Even when recaptured but still wired up to the collective, he looks and speaks as Borg. Distinctiveness, however, cuts both ways: this nodal figure in the Borg plan also provides the point of unravelling. Wired up further, this time to the ship's android, Picard-Locutus provides access to the collective mind and opportunity to defeat it. Significantly, he is active in the process, calling upon some buried, residual trace of humanity to provide the key. The Borg cube is destroyed on the point of destroying Earth.

What is described as a 'futile manoeuvre', recapturing Picard-Locutus, reworks resistance: it is precisely on the basis of futility that resistance becomes possible. Resistance is fertile the ending declares. No matter how overpowering the opposition, the human spirit remains indomitable. Picard's heroic resistance turns on discovering that tiny element – will, spirit, nature, whatever – that refuses to be assimilated, no matter how deeply it is suppressed by technological and alien forces. On the point of obliteration, humanity discovers the power to save itself. Only just, but that is enough: the trace of will, resistance, spirit, the small element remaining when everything else – body, mind, freedom – has been taken away, so the ending of the story assures its audience, provides the basis of victorious recuperation. That little but distinctively indistinct remainder is all that is necessary for a fantasy of human freedom and self-determination to re-erect itself. Implosion is forestalled; expansion can boldly begin again. The Borg has fulfilled its monstrous phantasmatic function: a nostalgic, conservative romance can again soar into outer space. Imagined loss prefigures the glorious return of human values, an intense reanimation of an energy able to reconstitute broken boundaries. The resurrection of a liberal and humanist fantasy requires a casting out of its own demons, an expulsion of anxieties about itself, an otherness of its own making, thus saving itself from implosion. The Borg, an imaginary figure condensing unavowable anxieties, comes too close to home, but fantasy, on the edge of the abyss, recomposes itself to blast unnerving proximity back into the stellar distance from which it is supposed to have come. It'll be back, of course.

Victory over the Borg reasserts recognisable differences and returns to familiar generic patterns. While it appears to offer satisfactory narrative closure, overcoming the 'SF of implosion' and regaining an expansive mode, the closeness of horror lingers on the skin: Picard, though recovering, is marked by Borg implants, the babble of the collective still echoing inside his skull. 'How do you feel?' The first question any on-the-spot TV reporter throws at a victorious sportsperson, an award winner, a crime victim, a disaster survivor (SHaH 2003), is directed to Picard on being released from the control of the collective consciousness: 'almost human', he replies. Though the episode succeeds in repulsing the inhuman Borg horror, recoil engenders a counter-pulse: pulling back drags something of the Borg with it, leaving a residue that disturbs the nostalgic trajectory with a different impulse. Picard forms the key point of Borg-human crossover, remaining Borg after his rescue as he wanders about his old starship. The ramifications of his assimilation are noted by the First Officer: how does one fight an enemy that has taken over a person who 'knows us better than we know ourselves'. If the Borg's success emanates from an ability to continually adapt, then the *Enterprise* has to be even more adaptive: its weaponry and defences must be continually modulated to have any effect, its strategy must be more flexible, its crew must work faster and more efficiently and make continual technological innovations. The 'interdependency' with which Borg and humans mirror each other is highlighted back on the *Enterprise* as Picard remains connected to the collective. The Borg, it seems, like the humans who have rescued one of their own, refuses to cut off a single drone. Both antagonists display a sense of collectivity; both have rendered biology and technology interdependent. The difference of the Federation, the very difference which sustains a human fantasy, is steadily eroded, to the point of rendering questionable its morality and cultural organisation: is not the former, with its imperial divisions of good and evil, or the latter, with its humanoid homogenisation of different species, quite close to the assimilation practised by the Borg? It is difficult to tell the difference between Starfleet's 'assimilationist policy' and its 'distopian counterpart' (Joyrich 65).

Un-familiar, the Borg has crossed a line of differentiation and continues to trouble it. Distinctions between 'self and other, desire and repulsion, culture and nature, death and life' collapse (Fuchs 282). Genders are confounded, as is the difference between individual and group, human and machine. In the crossings and reversals prompted by the Borg, effects associated with the uncanny become visible: the circulations of opposed terms entwining '*unheimlich*' and '*heimlich*', the (re)appearance of what should be hidden, the disturbance of reality and fantasy (Freud 1955); the 'intellectual uncertainty' evoked in discriminating human and machine or the ghostly vacillation across the supposedly impermeable barrier separating life and death (Jentsch; Cixous). The well-documented effects of the uncanny in reversing terms and traversing boundaries are, however, secondary to the decomposition of fantasy that it causes (Lacan 1977c). The figure central in the orchestration of the phantasmatic framework of ideological subjects is the paternal metaphor. Without it, borders collapse, desires and differences slide. Again, the Borg's targeting of Picard is exemplary: his removal from the command centre of Federation operations tears a hole in its psychological, moral and strategic make-up. Though rescued, the paternal figure returns scarred, impeached, tainted, its authority less credible or secure.

The expansive humanist fantasy becomes increasingly porous, subject to pressures it cannot comfortably contain or easily expel. The attempt to hold on, or nostalgically return, to older phantasmatic securities and lines of difference, a regressive movement, is pressed by another momentum in which new relationships emerge. For Sobchack, the interplay of sameness and difference is crucial and informs the tension lying at the heart of the

Federation's encounter with the Borg: in conservative science fictions, the alien is presented in terms of the same, its difference enabling humanism's self-representation and instituting the 'hierarchical relations' appropriate to 'a myth of universal and nonhierarchical homogeneity'. Maintaining a resemblance between aliens and humans 'preserves the subordination of "other worlds, other cultures, other species" to the world, culture and "speciality" of white American culture' so that new American humanism can expand into space 'making it safe for democracy [and] multinational capitalism' (Sobchack 1987: 294–95). *Star Trek*, like the Federation itself, is dominated by representations of species whose physical appearance, traits, cultural codes and characteristics are invariably and recognisably human(oid). The encounter with the Borg, too, operates according to relations of resemblance: the Federation is like the Borg, simile retaining a trace of hierarchical difference. Picard, however, becomes Borg, shifting the difference in the process. For Sobchack, the move from aliens being like humans to being humans constitutes the crucial turn of 'marginal and post-modern SF' transforming 'the reversible and nonhierarchical relations of similitude into a myth of homogenized heterogeneity. That is, nationalism no longer exists as a difference in the culture of multinational capital' (297). Sexual difference is eradicated by the android, identity becomes 'ephemeral'. New relations take shape in a realm of Baudrillardian simulation and indifference, one where metaphor cedes to metonymies, reproduction is replaced by cloning, bodies, nature, families, states rewritten or obliterated by the universality of computer or genetic code. Everything is subjected to the viral logic of transversalism: transsexuality, transeconomics (Baudrillard 1993a; 1993b). And, in the case of the Borg, transhumanity.

While wanting to return to older generic and cultural conventions, *Star Trek: the Next Generation* is dragged forward by the generic pressures of a cyberpunk sensibility and imperatives of a new economic code. The shifting relations of sameness and difference – the move from 'like' to 'is' – threaten the very difference sustaining its expansive fantasy. The tension, moreover, discloses the doubleness of fantasy itself as it shifts from loss to recovery, projection to return. For Sontag, fantasy engages the 'twin specters' of banality and terror, allowing an escape from the former and relief or distraction from the latter, normalising 'what is psychologically unbearable, thereby inuring us to it' in a process of reflecting and allaying anxieties (436). Terror enables an escape from and return to banality, opening onto and closing off objectless anxiety by giving it form and familiarity, directing it into normal channels and letting it solidify through fear and repetition. As a 'distraction', however, fantasy misses its ultimate object, screening it and screening it off, occluding otherness with more palatable, recognisable and reassuring images that sustain an acceptably homogenised difference. The loosely gothic features of the Borg play their part in the nostalgic side of *Star Trek*'s fantasy formation: it is dressed in familiar garb that can be readily recognised and located in terms of a monstrosity romanced within a humanist system of identities and differences. But familiar, normal, images of monstrosity function, in the context of the Borg, as a distraction, an occlusion of and a recoil from other terrors and horrors too unbearable to countenance. Rendered gothic, the Borg can be returned to modernity and the expansive fantasy breathes a sigh of relief. But what flies unseen beneath the wings of nostalgic romance, or lurks in the shadows of familiar gothic representations? What is it that fantasy's distraction tries to avoid? To what, in the internal tensions it exposes, is fantasy drawn? What unacknowledged movement draws it, against its best efforts, in other directions?

## Gothic is irrelevant

The Borg refuses a safe phantasmatic place, passing beyond anything modern culture can face or present. Modernity and the gothic figures that give form to its shadows and darknesses are supplanted, like the sophisticated android, Commander Data. Data is a machine that wants to be human, a tin man, an artificial intelligence that ensures human differences by manifesting a fascination for humanity. He, Locutus notes, 'will be obsolete in the new order'. 'Gothic is irrelevant.' But gothic figures remain visible, working on two levels, one offering a reassuringly repellent image of monstrosity and restoring an older system of fantasy, while the other introduces a different trajectory: disguised in comforting representations it prepares the way for a new order. It works like a disease that creeps into to the bloodstream on the back of a more familiar infection, or like the Kuang virus of Gibson's fiction, penetrating the security protocols of corporate databanks by simulating the codes of everyday transactions. Or like the Terminator: a ruthless metallic killing machine is concealed beneath an organic human skin. 'Your archaic cultures are authority-driven', states the Borg. For that reason a 'human voice', Picard's, is selected, introducing something utterly alien behind a familiar front, a tactic that simulates and undermines authority at the same time. Gothic becomes 'cybergothic', a mode that supplements its modern deployment with the revolutionising imperatives of schizanalysis. Nick Land, citing Deleuze and Guattari, situates cybergothic in relation to machinic movements beyond humanity and history: gothic is part of an 'archaic revival', a 'postmodern sympton' conjuring up 'the final dream of mankind, crashed into retrospection at the encountered edge of history'. Cybergothic presents an 'affirmative telecommercial dystopianism' (Land 1998: 80). It opens onto 'v(amp)iro finance' in which 'vampiric transfusional alliance cuts across descensional filiation, spinning lateral webs of haemocommerce. Reproductive order comes apart in bacterial and intergalactic sex, and libino-economic interchange machinery goes micro-military' (Land 1998: 86–87). Cold steel odor. Archaic structures are used and erased, gothic figures providing the camouflage for a transformation through which human structures are flipped into something entirely and unstoppably machinic.

Land's version of schizanalysis turns on a desire that is thoroughly machinic: it invokes figures from Gibson's fiction along with the dark inhuman doubles of humanity populating films like *Blade Runner* and *The Terminator*. Console cowboys, replicants, terminators all seem like residually human creations but they are less figures of modern scientific progress and more like insurgents from a machinic posthistory: 'the future of runaway processes derides all precedent, even when deploying it as camouflage, and seeming to unfold within its parameters' (Land 1993b: 476). Appearing from another space and another time, the Borg, too, follows the patterns of machinic desire, destroying-assimilating, de- and re-territorialising a universe that once appeared to manifest itself in human terms:

> Machinic desire can seem a little inhuman, as it rips up political cultures, deletes traditions, dissolves subjectivities, and hacks through security apparatuses, tracking a soulless tropism to zero control. This is because what appears to humanity as the history of capitalism is an invasion from the future by an artificial intelligent space that must assemble itself entirely from its enemy's resources.
>
> (Land 1993b: 479)

The Borg, of course, takes whatever bodies or technology it requires from the cultures it assimilates and reassembles the pieces in its own image. Its future is coming. It has already arrived.

Part of the Borg assemblage is drawn from the very fantasy humanity erects in opposition, from the all-too familiar gothic shapes that lumber across space. The Borg is misrecognised, humanity recoils; it is repelled. The proximity of the Borg, the horror it excretes across human skin, takes fantasy to the point of decomposition: 'terminal horror folds back into itself, and the matrix dismantles itself into voodoo' (Land 1998: 86). Horror implodes, dismantling human structures and fantasies, recoil and repulsion too weak to expel the invasive pulse from the future. Horror, it seems, falls short, unable to avoid the void before it or find figures powerful enough to arrest movements of attraction, machinic desire, projection, identification. There is something irresistible about playing in the ruins of human history, something romantic, erotic even, about the enhanced, mutated, prostheticised, engineered, wonderfully monstrous shapes that begin to emerge. In the face of horrific decomposition, fantasy does not confront its limit and retreat in an effort of recuperation: another fantasy, attracted to decomposition, plunges into the fragments, allowing other fantasies to assemble and project themselves forwards.

Terror delivers excitements, possibilities, thrills, exultations: the sublimity it invokes is postmodern rather than modern. Modernity's sublime encountered the unrepresentable as the 'missing contents' of presentation to provide a form that 'because of its recognizable consistency, continues to offer the reader or viewer a matter of solace or pleasure'. It enabled humans to 'share collectively the nostalgia for the unattainable'. The postmodern sublime, in contrast, 'denies itself the solace of good forms' (Lyotard 1984: 81). It 'proceeds "directly" out of market economics', capital and the avant-garde in collusion; it produces an art of the 'immanent sublime, that of alluding to an unpresentable which has nothing edifying about it, but which is inscribed in the infinity of the transformation of "realities"'(Lyotard 1991: 104–5; 129). This transformation is enabled by technosciences working in the service of corporate research and development: its only aim is innovation, optimisation, performance enhancement. Aesthetic enterprise follows the same course: in the space of the unpresentable, infinity of presentations can be realised. Immanent, the sublime is also interiorised: it is not situated in a transcendental space outside and broached by Romantic sensibility in the mountainous grandeur of Nature but unfolds at home and on screens in an 'artificial desktop infinity' (Voller 27). The interiority of the sublime becomes distinctly superficial: its effects bound up with the infinite flickering of images on screens.

Neither horror nor sublimity are what or where they used to be. Fantasy dissolves and precipitates other fantasies, dressed up in, assembled from, the decomposing fragments of the former. Gothic figures remain insofar as they serve in the process of transformation. Instead of horror, which freezes, paralyses, dissolves, as Ann Radcliffe noted, unbounded fantasy launches forward, wanting more. Polarities are reversed, repulsion ceding to attraction in line with the aesthetic and critical mechanisms that already render gothic figures familiar, sympathetic and attractive creatures, worthy of identification and celebration: one must love one's monster/vampire/self. The identification with figures, no longer similar in their difference, but the same, extends to the gothicisation of cyborgs: Frankenstein's monster is the 'first cyborg' (Gray, Mentor and Figueroa-Sarriera 5). History is rewritten from the future and fired back into the past. Rewriting fiction, reorganising lines of history, Mary Shelley's novel turns out to be a prospective story of the advent of cyborgs. Unlike Frankenstein's monster, however, cyborgs do not expect the father-creator to save them (Haraway 1990: 192). Where 'monsters have always defined the limits of community in Western imaginations', cyborgs 'define quite different political possibilities' (Haraway 1990: 213). Some of these possibilities are charted elsewhere by Haraway as she admits, ' I think I am on the side of the vampires, or at least some of them': in new biotechnological scenarios, vampires interrogate kinship and nature, the 'blood ties' of a bloody human history, to open cyborg concerns with race, sexuality and identity (Haraway 1997: 265). Likewise, Anne Rice's vampire-hero, Lestat, 'exemplifies a style of cyborg existence' by evincing the 'pain and complexity' of adapting to a society, lifestyle, language, culture (and species), that is not one's own, thereby posing questions about human and inhuman identity (Stone 178). The identification of and with gothic and cyborg figures renders both increasingly familiar: outsiders and monsters move within a culture they have redefined as banal, normal examples of everyday existence. The gothic horrors and anxieties associated with *Frankenstein* are turned into the cyborg realities of being routinely wired up to machines, undergoing surgical and cosmetic techniques, receiving pros-thetic enhancements and genetic therapies (Clarke 40). The Borg seem less and less unusual. 'High-tech Frankenstein' appears in another everyday activity, a 'figure for humans online' and their 'romance' with aliens, cyborgs and machines (Poster 29–30). The reversal of poles informing the identification and affirmation of monster and cyborg normalises and neutralises traditional horrific antitheses. At the same time, it appears as no more than the surface effect of a thoroughgoing transformation of all the relationships and differences of modernity, a transvaluation in which 'life' is lived in post- or transhuman terms.

The transvaluation has already happened. Humans have already been Borged. Cyborgs, the 'offspring of implosions of subjects and objects and of the natural and the artificial', have got their project well underway, aestheti-cally, subjectively, socially rewiring the planet and all bodies (Haraway 1997: 12). Their 'Manifesto' unequivocally declares: 'by the late twentieth century, our time, a mythic time, we are all chimeras, theorized and fabri-cated hybrids of machine and organism; in short; we are cyborgs' (Haraway 1990: 191). The personal pronoun does not address or interpellate the dispersed community united by modernity as 'humankind', but engages a distributed cyborg collective: 'we live in a society of cyborgs, of machines tightly coupled with "organic" bodies themselves denaturised and reassem-bled, discursively as well as literally under the knife of the surgeon or the hand of the prostheticist' (Gray and Mentor 455). Entwining entities and metaphors, the cyborg institutes itself at two levels simultaneously:

> Manifesting itself as both technological object and discursive formation, it partakes of the power of imagination as well as of the actuality of tech-nology. Cyborgs actually exist. About 10 percent of the current US

population are estimated to be cyborgs in the technical sense, including people with electronic pacemakers, artificial joints, drug-implant systems, implanted corneal lenses, and artificial skin. A much higher percentage participates in occupations that make them into metaphoric cyborgs, including the computer keyboarder joined in a cybernetic circuit with the screen, the neurosurgeon guided by fiber-optic micros-copy during an operation, and the adolescent game-player in the local video-game arcade.

(Hayles 115)

Cyborgs manifest the technological permeation of every relationship, every body, every thing that once appeared natural, organic, biological. Resistance is, indeed, futile.

As a 'hybrid creature of machine and organism, a creature of social reality as well as a creature of fiction', the cyborg envelops fiction and tech-nological reality in the broader waves of social and political transformation (Haraway 1990: 191). Cyberpunk announces the reorganisation of cultural, scientific and economic coordinates and celebrates 'advances' that have 'gotten out of hand', radical, disturbing, upsetting and 'revolutionary' changes that 'can no longer be contained' and are 'surging into culture at large; they are invasive, they are everywhere'. Sterling links these changes to the 'decentralization' and 'fluidity' of Toffler's 'third wave' of economic development. 'Hybrids themselves', possessing 'little patience with borders', cyberpunks embrace the commodities, technologies and modes of organisa-tion (the gadgets, satellite media nets and transnational corporations) that are the 'tools of global integration' (Sterling xi–x). They form the aesthetic arm of a new network of military-corporate innovation and consumer research. Taking 'pleasure in the confusion of boundaries', enjoying 'partiality, irony, intimacy, and perversity', they are already cyborgs them-selves (Haraway 1990: 191–92).

Machines are not separate devices, to be used instrumentally in the service of humans, but, in their use, transform the user: 'what is used as an element in a machine, is in fact an element in the machine' (Wiener 1954: 185). This observation extends from discrete technical objects to entire organisations, 'those machines of flesh and blood which are bureaus and vast laboratories and armies and corporations' (Wiener 1954: 185–86). Machines come to define political structures, even in the Cold War of Wiener's observations:

A sort of *machine à gourverner* is thus now essentially in operation on both sides of the world conflict, although it does not consist in either case of a single machine which makes policy, but rather of a mechanistic technique which is adapted to the exigencies of a machine-like group of men devoted to the formation of policy.

(Wiener 1954: 182)

All of these machines are recoded in terms of the cybernetic and information theory of which Wiener was a pioneer. Social and psychological models, too, are redefined. In *Cybernetics*, Wiener describes Hobbes' Leviathan as a 'Man-State made up of lesser men' and Leibniz's living organism 'as being really a plenum, wherein other living organisms, such as the blood corpuscles, have their life' (1961: 155). One and many, singular and multiple, every organism, in a theory which fuses mathematics, biology and technology on the same plane and in terms of information, appears to have something of the Borg about it. Wiener employs the metaphor of the hive to draw out the interdependency of part and whole in terms of communication:

> all the nervous tissue of the beehive is the nervous tissue of one single bee. How then does the beehive act in unison, and at that in a very variable, adapted, organized unison? Obviously, the secret is in the intercommunication of its members.
>
> (1961: 156)

Wiener notes the difference between individuals, with fixed nervous systems and permanent connections, and communities composed of shifting relations and impermanent connections. The difference between individual and community, with further biotechnological developments in computer networks and cyborg applications, does not last long. Information and intercommunication remains the key, as Wiener stressed: 'any organism is held together in this action by the possession of the means for the acquisition, use, retention, and transmission of information' (1961: 161). While remaining tied to homeostatic models of communication, Wiener goes on to discuss modes of self-reproduction and self-organisation characteristic of the next phase of research. With 'autopoeisis', biological and social organisms are all examined in terms of their capacity to adapt and develop as self-organising, complex systems (Maturana and Varela).

Communications change the world, turning organisms into 'information-processing devices' (Haraway 1990: 208). The cyborgs that emerge are the 'illegitimate offspring of militarism and patriarchal capitalism' (Haraway 1990: 193). Computer networks, the Net encompassing the planet, were developed by DARPA, a military communications system designed with enough interconnections to survive nuclear strikes. The Borg cube works on the same decentralised model, being able to function effectively even if 78 per cent of it is rendered inoperable. Cyborgs, too, emerge from military research: upgraded bodies, enhanced weaponry and battle systems, from cybernetic research into automated anti-aircraft tracking, to the 'Pilot's Associate' that links human to the jet, military application of communications theory is extensive. Whether flying a military fighter or driving a tank, the operator remains wired into a sophisticated battle network made up of circulating information and flickering screens: simulation and warfare blur, warriors of the air, land or sea are tied to their monitors, 'consoldiers' (SHaH 1997). The system into which military personnel are wired becomes a global model. 'C$^3$I' (command, control, communications and intelligence) offers a new mode of distributed, decentralised and adaptable organisation, a network of bodies and machines that reshapes political and corporate structure: the state 'mixes humans, eco-systems, machines and various complex softwares (from laws to the codes that control the nuclear weapons) in one vast cybernetic organism'; capital, fluid, mobile, virtual, replaces 'old body orientation notions of arm's-length suppliers and identifiable territorial corporations' with 'cyborgian notions of transnational webs of licensing, consulting, outsourcing, distributing' (Gray and Mentor 454; 460). The multiplicity of networks entwining life and technology emerges as a singular, universal entity assimilating the planet.

Corporate and economic practices readily adopt, and adapt to, networked, informational models. Technological innovation is embraced with enthusiasm by proponents of the 'new economy', as are metaphors of swarm behaviour and hive mind to indicate how decentralised systems manifest a 'steady weaving together of our lives, minds, and artifacts into a global scale network' (Kelly 1998: 9). Ubiquitous, becoming invisible, distributed, technology employs 'the minimal amount of data to keep all parts of the system aware of one another'; 'swarms need real-time communication' (Kelly 1998: 20–21). Networks, composed of 'organic behaviour in a technological matrix', operate without centre and in the flux of 'sustainable disequilibrium', to 'breed swarm capitalism' (Kelly 1998: 108; 159). The logic of the 'hive mind' accords well with this new form of unbounded capitalism whose emergence and effects are difficult to predict. A 'universal law of vivisystems', defying any restraints, urges corporate expansion and innovation forward:

> higher-level complexities cannot be inferred by lower-level existences. Nothing – no computer or mind, no means of mathematics, physics or philosophy – can unravel the emergent pattern dissolved in the parts without actually playing it out. Only playing out a hive will tell you if the colony is inmixed in the bee.
>
> (Kelly 1994: 16)

What will be, what will have been: the excitable plunge into an unpredict-able future is couched in terms of progress and human potential: 'what is contained in a human that will not emerge until we are all interconnected by waves and politics? The most unexpected things will brew in this bionic hivelike supermind' (Kelly 1994: 16–17). The rhetoric of posthumanism surpasses anything imaginable, relaunching an old science fictional romance of mind beyond matter, beyond mind itself. It is no more than the alibi of swarm capitalism overcoming the checks of nations, states and rational indi-viduals: the 'hive mind' means that there is 'no one in control, and yet an invisible hand governs, a hand that emerges from very dumb members' (Kelly 1994: 16). Biology and technology are made to cohere within a familiar, if more rapid, decentralised and fluid, economic system. It may be comforting to imagine Adam Smith's hand pulling the strings, but the unpredictable, emerging network that is orientated by laissez faire assump-tions of a free and fluid market offers no such assurances.

Swarms, emergent patterns, hive minds, are not guided by modern prin-ciples of rationality, morality or, even, utility. Technoscientific imperatives have replaced older criteria of judgement: the games of corporate research and development departments are directed only to increase efficiency, opti-mise performance and incessantly innovate. Success or failure is determined by the novelty of the moves performed in efficiently reshaping the functions of an organisation or producing a profitable commodity. It is rated only after the innovation has been made, the intervention or invention tagged with the empty commendation of 'quality' or 'excellence' and judged according to ubiquitous performance indicators, forms, questionnaires, benchmarks or league tables that equate all operations and institutions (hospitals, schools, corporations, stocks, universities, football clubs) in the same vapidly effective terms (Lyotard 1984; Readings; Botting; Botting and Wilson). Even for Sontag, the bodysnatcher was a prospective figure, an operative who has 'become far more efficient – the very model of techno-cratic man' (434). The Borg, of course, takes technocratic imperatives further, stating 'we only wish to improve ourselves.' Any reason or end other than assimilation remains unspecified. The Borg's aims and objectives are entirely encompassed by the exponential circularity of assimilation, that is, improvement will enhance performance and maximise efficiency which will serve as an indicator of improvement. Continual improvement accords with the logic of excellence which commands more and more excellent perfor-mances with no other rationale than that of just doing it.

To be outside of this logic is unthinkable, futile. It is a global imperative from which no one is exempt. The Borg's wish is everyone's. It is simple, understated, yet irrefutable: 'we only wish to raise quality of life for all species'. Isn't that how every institutional (governmental, charitable, UN) survey of work, health, poverty, housing, utilities, pay, infrastructutre guarantees itself? The biopower that shifted the sovereign's right of death to the state's right to manage life and populations shifts another gear: 'technobiopower' (Haraway's term) concerns life's quality and directs itself towards immaterial as well as material questions. Who does not want 'quality of life'? (A few villains, smokers for instance, might be cited) Who does not want to be excellent? Quality and excellence are purely affirmative. 'No' has been removed from the vocabulary, erased by the hug of the 'big Yes'. Excellence, held up as the empty standard for everyone to share is interiorised, a marker of the desire articulating the network of bodies and machines: 'administrative procedures should make individuals "want" what the system needs in order to work' (Lyotard 1984: 62). Capitalism, abandoning models of scarcity and need, reverses supply and demand in a move that exploits desire's emptiness, becoming a giving, generous, wasteful mode in which entrepreneurs risk fortunes on the creation of desires, producing goods in advance of demand in other to make new markets and consumers along with products (Goux 1990). Technology speeds up the process: it '*creates* an opportunity for a *demand*, and then fills it' (Kelly 1998: 55). Desire, detached from humanity, is a lubricant of machinic circulations.

The economic and technical capacity to create and recreate desire is crucial to shifts in relations of production and consumption. The new economic order continually insists upon the consumer's pre-eminence in processes of producing, delivering and maintaining the service industry that dominates western cultures. Sales of customised goods and services are upheld by values of trust and loyalty, both of which pertain, not to abstract ideals but to the successful operations of corporations and brands (Fukuyama 1995; Goldman and Papson; Wernick). Consumption is less of a passive, instinctual activity and more of an art, an aesthetic in which desires and values are paraded above things. The other side of the idealised consumer appears in horror movies: George Romero's *Dawn of the Dead*, for example, is set in an out-of-town shopping mall, its zombies drawn irresistibly back to the temple of contemporary consumption to wander the aisles in much the same fashion as they did when they were alive. The movie's setting serves as 'a way of concretely demonstrating the zombification of consumer culture' (Penley 1986: 75). The Borg, however, displays both ends of the consumer economy, the drones visually recalling the living dead while the hive mind orchestrates the process as a whole: 'your culture will adapt to service ours'. 'Your life as it has been is over. From this time forwards you will service us.' Assimilation describes the operations of the service economy: it connects workers and consumers in a global network, all cultures being subjected to the same logic of homogenised circulations, like the range of different goods from all over the world on display at the delicatessen counter of any hypermarket.

Technologically enhanced, consumption moves onto another plane. *Dawn of the Dead* is also invoked in Rob Latham's account of the psychological effects of video-gaming. Gothic associations become bound up in another transformation from the future, a transformation, not only on a large, global scale, but occurring through localised encounters with a variety of small technical objects and commodities. 'Postfuturism' has arrived. The personal computers, digital watches, video games and recorders that were a short time ago luxury items are now an 'integral part of our everyday lives – consuming us as much as we consume them. In the most pervasive and personal way, these electronic artefacts (whose function is representation) both constitute and symbolise the radical alteration of our culture's temporal and spatial consciousness' (Sobchack 1987: 223). This is not an 'invasion' of a 'new electronic space', but a 'pervasion'. Pervasion is 'a condition of kinetic accommodation and dispersal associated with the experience and representation of television, video games and computer terminals' (229). Goods, gadgets, games and a host of screens, those 'machineries of joy' (to use Bradbury's phrase), pervade existence and institute a transformation of the planet and being itself. The consumer is consumed. Informatically and biotechnologically bodies are rewritten and relocated. Recoded 'as information', notes Hayles, bodies 'can not only be sold but fundamentally reconstituted in response to market pressures' (42). Removed from the anchorage of contexts and corporeality, transcribed in informational terms and abstracted onto a virtual, immaterial plane, bodies are rendered (like skills in the vocational training of a 'learning culture') transferable, flexible, adaptable. With microbiology understood in terms of information, genetic science, armed with increasingly sophisticated apparatuses, is equipped not only to understand but also to change the codes of life (Rabinow). Life finds itself 'enterprised up', a phrase embracing *Star Trek* and free market imperatives. The results lead well beyond anything modernity understood as 'nature': 'the species becomes the brand name' (Haraway 1997: 12).

While the global environment may retain the appearance of being a humanised world, its systematic transformation has little time for anything other than the simulation of humanity. Kurt Vonnegut, dismissing the illusions of *Star Trek* and its fans, gently makes the point: 'but computer salesmen, Bill Gates and all that, aren't acknowledging what human beings are and need at all. They don't know, and they don't care. They find human beings *inconvenient*' (cit. Greenwald 166). Cyberpunk puts the case more strongly: humans are little more than 'meat', the lumpy residue of worthless flesh left over after any useful, 'distinctive', information has been uploaded to the digital matrix. Again, the command, control, communication and intelligence network comes into play. As the model of the nervous system itself:

> The agents of the brain might very well be organized hierarchically into nested subroutines with a set of master decision rules, a compositional demon or agent or good-kind-of-homunculus, sitting at the top of a chain of command. It would not be a ghost in the machine, just another set of if-then rules or a neural network that shunts control to the loudest, fastest, or strongest agent one level down.
>
> (Pinker 144)

Ghosts and demons have nothing supernatural about them. They signify only the subroutines and algorithms of normal operations. The skull encases a neural network mirroring and open to the global network, the mind already a hive of sub-commands and 'nested' codes rewritten according to the models of military-corporate $C^3I$. Genetically, too, the same models apply. Information theory was able to reformulate biological and genetic specifications 'through a discourse that resonated with the technosciences of command and control' (Kay 150). 'It's life, Jim, but not as we know it.'

There is little room, perhaps, for either optimism or pessimism in such a context. Both characteristics are tied to the meat or are recalibrated according to the technical standards of a different network, 'philia' and 'phobia' both determined by 'techno-'. Marshall McLuhan's discussion of media notes the extension of 'our central nervous system itself in a global embrace, abolishing both time and space as far as our planet is concerned.' Consciousness will be simulated so that the 'creative process of knowing' can be 'collectively and corporately extended to the whole of human society' (McLuhan, 1964: 3). But extension, like the expansive mode of science fiction, cedes to an implosion in which humans, bodies, societies, are utterly transformed from within as much as without. The onward, upward and outward extension launched by the Space Age goes into reverse with the biotechnological revolution: the boldly explored galaxies, worlds and cultures of outer space are abandoned in favour of an 'intraorganic intro-spection', an 'endocolonization' of the inner spaces of bodies through implants, micromachines and neurostimulants:

> today, indeed, the place *where state-of-the-art technology occurs* is no longer so much the limitless space of an infinitely vast planetary or cosmic environment, but rather the infinitesimal space of our internal organs, of the cells that compose our organs' living matter.
>
> (Virilio 1995: 109–100)

The exploration of space provides 'an alibi for the technical intrusion into an inner world', the illusion of 'extraterrestrial' liberation allowing techno-science to get its 'teeth into a weightless *man-planet* whom nothing can now really protect, neither ethics nor biopolitical morality' (Virilio 1995: 112–13). Neither horror, which carries with it an ethical surge, nor resistance, which maintains a political charge, seem relevant: recoil, romance and identification are channelled in the same network.

In a 'cyborg society' composed of the 'full range of intimate organic-machinic relations' – interfaces, microsurgeries, engineered mice, weapons systems, AI programs – restorative and destructive functions are simply part of the process: limbs and organs can be replaced, bodies can be enhanced, and humans can be degraded in 'the nightmare of the cyberphobes, into the perfect will-less soldier/subjects like the Borg' (Gray, Mentor, Figueroa-Sarriera 3). The difference is slight, inconsequential. Irrelevant, even. The 'same technology' which controls a warplane can also enable the cripple to walk again, or the blind to see: 'there is no choice between utopia and distopia, Good Terminator or Evil Terminator – they are both here'. Resistance is futile, good and bad Borg humming together in the circuits of the hive, with a new ethos of how to adapt and survive: 'perhaps, after all, we just need to learn cyborg family values – good maintenance, technical expertise, pleasures dispersed and multiple, community research and development, improved communication' (Gray and Mentor 465). 'We' are family, 'we' are technicians, 'we' are researchers, 'we' are communicators: 'we' are Borg, already assimilated, already adapted to the indeterminations of a universal, metastable network that is, is not and is more than anything that can be conceived as 'our' own. Embracing the materiality of bodies and machines and the immateriality of codes and values, the network totally envelops every ware, whether soft, hard or wet.

It is perhaps too late to be afraid, very afraid, too late, perhaps, for the resistance that articulates the disciplinary mechanisms and power relations of modernity: 'our dominations don't work by medicalization and normal-ization any more; they work by networking, communications redesign, stress management' (Haraway 1990: 194). Sexual repression has given way to expression, the squeezing out of what was once considered most private, interior and personal (Lotringer). Media and managers draw out what seemed most intrinsically human to spread it across so many screens, balance sheets, forms, tables and charts, all the time dealing with what is now considered inconvenient, recalcitrant, unserviceable. The process is administered with technical precision and professional rigour. The care of customers and clients demands a careful personal touch manifested by another technology, the 'relationship technology' or 'R-tech' that delivers specifically tailored and customised products and services (Kelly 1998:124).

Freedom is irrelevant when the hysterrorisation of consumer choice is replaced by customer service of such personal precision. It knows what you want, more than you do yourself. The Borg, of course, employs the same techniques. Picard, chosen as the 'human voice' of the collective, performs the role of public relations officer and customer services manager. Addressing his first officer from the Borg cube he speaks as Locutus: 'your resistance is hopeless . . . ', there is a pause before the sentence is completed with the addition of ' . . . Number One'. The return to Picard's phrasing and intonation re-establishes their previous relationship of Captain and First Officer, a disarming reminder of the strong and intimate bond between them. It knows, it feels.

Interiority is externalised and transformed in the service of something entirely Other. It is not only the Borg, however, who employs relationship technologies. A prominent role in both cast and crew of *The Next Generation* series is given to a new figure: on the bridge of the *USS Enterprise* a counsellor sits at the left-hand of the Captain. A telepath able to sense the emotional states of crew and aliens, she is perhaps the series' scariest innovation: interiority is penetrated, expressed, excised. Appropriate to a culture obsessed with, imploding on, its Self, so that it engages and proliferates all kinds of therapies and counselling services, the function of a ship's counsellor remains ambivalent in respect of returning to or departing from humanity. Are therapies and counselling services only aimed at restoring or normalising humans, healing the wounds of traumatised, victimised beings? Or do they serve to facilitate adaptation to new codes and patterns of behaviour, insinuating a transferential compliance to the imperatives of a technocratic Other? In this latter aspect, counsellors, therapists, stress managers, emotional intelligence consultants operate as, perhaps unwitting, agents of communication and control, technicians of assimilation and erasure.

The tentacles of the $C^3I$ web spread across and crawl within all bodies and minds, displaying the extensive and intensively diverse reaches of what Gilles Deleuze has called 'control societies'. Replacing discipline and confinement with 'continuous control and instant communication' leads to the ready traversal of modern roles, borders and distinctions: differences between work and education, for instance, disappear, 'giving way to frightful continual training, to continual monitoring of worker-schoolkids or bureaucrat-students' (Deleuze 1995: 175). A learning society emerges as modules and programmes replace courses, continual assessments, vocational and skills training supplanting degrees and knowledge with technical know-how. Distinct entities and institutions cede to the 'modulation' of control, 'a self-transmuting molding continually changing from one moment to the next' (Deleuze 1995: 178–79). Factory production is reconfigured on the model of business and enterprise, introducing 'a deeper level of modulation into all wages, bringing them into a state of constant metastability punctuated by ludicrous challenges, competitions, and seminars' (179). Criteria of performance and excellence apply here, with educators, too, being paid by results. Though control works on modes that are 'short-term and rapidly shifting' it is 'at the same time continuous and unbounded' taking its bearings from the 'universal modulation' of computer networks (181–82). Localised, decentralised, dispersed and yet universal, control fills the vacuum of state regulation and private ownership by instituting a global mode of business and enterprise, of improvement, quality, enhancement, assimilation. Its self-modulating metastability corresponds to the 'sustainable disequilibrium' of swarm capitalism, 'transmutable or transformable coded configurations of a single business where the only people left are administrators' (181). Students and workers already need training in time management. Teachers are already 'managers of learning', counsellors managers of stress. Personnel officers are managers of human resources; homeworkers are trained in domestic management skills. Somewhere, no doubt, sexworkers are already being redefined as managers of pleasure and philosophers managers of thought. Resistance is futile, freedom irrelevant, the choice of no choice at all. Perhaps there remains the option, abandoning all illusions, of seeking out the futility of resistance. But that gesture, too romantic, may already be too late. Otherwise one can, easily enough, sign up for a vocational training module in cyborg family values.

# Bibliography

Adriopolous, Stefan (1999) 'The invisible hand: supernatural agency in political economy and the gothic novel', *English Literary History*, 66: 739–58.

Aldiss, Brian (1973) *Billion Year Spree: the History of Science Fiction*, London: Weidenfeld and Nicholson.

—— (1982) *Frankenstein Unbound*, London: Granada Publishing.

Althusser, Louis (1984) *Essays in Ideology*, London: Verso.

Anon. (1796) 'Review of *The Monk*', *The British Critic*, 7 June: 677.

—— (1797) 'Terrorist novel writing', *Spirit of the Public Journals*, 1: 227–29.

—— (1826) 'Review of *The Last Man*', *The Literary Magnet, or Monthly Journal of Belles Lettres* (new series), 1: 56.

Badley, Linda C. (1996) *Writing Horror and the Body: the Fiction of Stephen King, Clive Barker, and Anne Rice*, Westport, CT: Greenwood Press.

—— (2003) 'Spiritual warfare: postfeminism and the cultural politics of the *Blair Witch* craze', *Intensities*, 3. www.cult-media.com/issue3/Abad.htm (accessed 5 July 2006).

Baldick, Chris (1987) *In Frankenstein's Shadow: Myth Monstrosity and Nineteenth-century Writing*, Oxford: Clarendon.

—— (ed.) (1992) *The Oxford Book of Gothic Tales*, Oxford: Oxford University Press.

Barthes, Roland (1976) *Mythologies*, trans. Annette Lavers, London: Granada.

Bataille, Georges (1955) *Lascaux*, trans. Austryn Wainhouse, Geneva: Skira.

—— (1997) *The Bataille Reader*, Fred Botting and Scott Wilson (eds), Oxford: Blackwell.

Baudrillard, Jean (1983) *Simulations*, New York: Semiotexte.

—— (1987) *The Evil Demon of Images*, trans. Paul Patton and Paul Foss, Sydney: Power Publications.

—— (1988) *America*, trans. Chris Turner, London: Verso.

—— (1990a) *Fatal Strategies*, trans. Philip Beitchman and W. G. J. Niesluchowski, London: Pluto Press.

—— (1990b) *Seduction*, Basingstoke: Macmillan.

—— (1993a) *Symbolic Exchange and Death*, trans. Iain Hamilton Grant, London: Sage.

—— (1993b) *The Transparency of Evil*, trans. James Benedict, London: Verso.

—— (1994) *The Illusion of the End*, trans. Chris Turner, London: Polity.

—— (1996) *The Perfect Crime*, trans. Chris Turner, New York: Verso.

Belsey, Catherine (1994) *Desire*, Oxford: Blackwell.

Benjamin, Walter (1973) *Illuminations*, trans. Harry Zohn, London: Fontana.

—— (1983) *Charles Baudelaire: a Lyric Poet in the Era of High Capitalism*, trans. Harry Zohn, London: Verso.

—— (1999) *The Arcades Project*, trans. Howard Eiland and Kevin McLaughlin, Cambridge, MA: Belknap Press.

Benson, E. F. (1992) 'Negotium perambulans', in Richard Dalby (ed.), *The Collected Ghost Stories of E. F. Benson*, London: Robinson Publishing, 227–38.

Bernstein, Stephen (1999) *Alasdair Gray*, Lewisburg, PA: Bucknell University Press.

Botting, Fred (1997) 'Culture and excellence', *Cultural Values*, 1.2: 139–58.

Botting, Fred and Wilson, Scott (2002) '(This is not a) presentation', *Critical Quarterly*, 44.3: 27–36.

Bowlby, Rachel (1987) 'Promoting Dorian Gray', *Oxford Literary Review*, 9: 147–63.

Boyd, S. J. (1991) 'Black arts: *1982 Janine* and *Something Leather*', in Robert Crawford and Thom Nairn (eds), *The Arts of Alasdair Gray*, Edinburgh: Edinburgh University Press, 108–23.

Braddon, Mary Elizabeth (1896) 'Good Lady Ducayne', *Strand Magazine*, 11: 185–99.

Braidotti, Rosi (2002) *Metamorphoses*, Cambridge: Polity.

Brantlinger, Patrick (1985) 'Imperial gothic: atavism and the occult in the British adventure novel, 1880–1914', *English Literature in Transition (1880–1920)*, 28: 243–52.

Broderick, Damien (1995) *Reading by Starlight: Postmodern Science Fiction*, London: Routledge.

Bruno, Giuliana (1990) 'Ramble city: postmodernism and *Blade Runner*', in Annette Kuhn (ed.), *Alien Zone: Cultural Theory and Contemporary Science Fiction Cinema*, London: Verso, 183–95.

Burke, Edmund (1969) *Reflections on the Revolution in France (1790)*, Conor Cruise O'Brien (ed.), Harmondsworth: Penguin.

—— (1990) *A Philosophical Enquiry*, Adam Phillips (ed.), Oxford: Oxford University Press.

Campbell, Colin (1993) 'Understanding traditional and modern patterns of consumption in eighteenth-century England: a character-action approach', in John Brewer and Roy Porter (eds), *Consumption and the World of Goods*, London: Routledge, 40–57.

Carter, Angela (1982) *The Infernal Desire Machines of Dr Hoffman*, London: Penguin.

Carter, Margaret L. (1997) 'The vampire as alien in contemporary fiction', in Jan Gordon and Veronica Hollinger (eds), *Blood Read: the Vampire as Metaphor in Contemporary Culture*, Philadelphia, PA: University of Pennsylvania Press, 27–44.

Castle, Terry (1995) *The Female Thermometer: Eighteenth-century Culture and the Invention of the Uncanny*, New York: Oxford University Press.

Cavallaro, Dani (2000) *Cyberpunk and Cyberculture*, London: Athlone Press.

Cave, Nick (2001) *The Complete Lyrics 1978–2001*, London: Penguin.

Christensen, Jerome (1994) 'The romantic movement at the end of history', *Critical Inquiry*, 20: 452–76.

Cixous, Hélène (1976) 'Fiction and its phantoms: a reading of Freud's *das Unheimliche* (The "Uncanny")', *New Literary History*, 7: 525–48.

Clarke, Arthur C. (1995) 'Dial "F" for Frankenstein', in Peter Haining (ed.), *The Frankenstein Omnibus*, London: Orion, 681–88.

Clarke, Julie (2002) 'The human/not human in the work of Orlan and Stelarc', in Joanna Zylinska (ed.), *The Cyborg Experiments*, London: Continuum, 33–55.

Clery, E. J. (1995) *The Rise of Supernatural Fiction 1762–1800*, Cambridge: Cambridge University Press.

—— (2000) *Women's Gothic*, Tavistock: Northcote House.

Clery, E. J. and Miles, Robert (2000) *Gothic Documents*, Manchester: Manchester University Press.

Clover, Carol (1989) 'Her body, himself: gender in the slasher film', in *Fantasy and Cinema*, James Donald (ed.), London: BFI publishing, 191–233.

Constable, Catherine (1999) 'Becoming the monster's mother: morphologies of identity in the *Alien* series', in Annette Kuhn (ed.), *Alien Zone II*, London: Verso, 173–200.

Coppock, Vicki, Haydon, Deena and Richter, Ingrid (1995) *The Illusions of 'Post-Feminism'*, London: Taylor & Francis.

Coppola, Francis Ford and Hart, James V. (1992) *Bram Stoker's* Dracula*: The Film and the Legend*, London: Pan Books.

Craft, Christopher (1984) '"Kiss me with those red lips": gender and inversion in Bram Stoker's *Dracula*', *Representations*, 8: 107–33.

Creed, Barbara (1993) *The Monstrous-Feminine*, London: Routledge.

Csicsery-Ronay Jr., Istvan (1991) 'Cyberpunk and neuromanticism', in Larry McCaffrey (ed.), *Storming the Reality Studio*, Durham, NC: Duke University Press, 182–93.

Damrosch, Leo (1989) *Fictions of Reality in the Age of Hume and Johnson*, Madison, WI: University of Wisconsin Press.

Davis, Eric (1993) 'Techgnosis, magic, memory, and the angels of information', *South Atlantic Quarterly*, 92.4: 585–616.

De Rougemont, Denis (1993) *Love in the Western World*, trans. M. Belgion, Princeton, NJ: Princeton University Press.

Deleuze, Gilles (1990) *Logic of Sense*, trans. Mark Lester, London: Athlone.

—— (1995) *Negotiations*, trans. Martin Joughin, New York: Columbia University Press.

—— (2003) *Francis Bacon: the Logic of Sensation*, trans. Daniel W. Smith, London: Continuum.

Deleuze, Gilles and Guattari, Felix (1983) *Anti-Oedipus*, trans. Robert Hurley, Mark Seem and Helen Lane, Minneapolis, MN: University of Minnesota Press.

—— (1988) *A Thousand Plateaus*, trans. Brian Massumi, London: Athlone Press.

—— (1994) *What is Philosophy?*, trans. Graham Burchell and Hugh Tomlinson, London: Verso.

Deleuze, Gilles and Parnet, Claire (1987) *Dialogues II*, trans. Hugh Tomlinson and Barbara Habberjam, London: Continuum.

Derrida, Jacques (1990) 'Some statements and truisms about neologisms, newisms, postisms, parasitisms, and other small seismisms', in David Carroll (ed.), *The States of 'Theory'*, Stanford, CA: Stanford University Press, 63–94.

—— (1992) 'Passages – from traumatism to promise', trans. Peggy Kamuf *et al.*, in Elisabeth Weber (ed.), *Points . . . : Interviews, 1974–1994*, Stanford, CA: Stanford University Press, 372–95.

—— (1994), *Specters of Marx*, trans. Peggy Kamuf, London: Routledge.

Dijkstra, Bram (1986) *Idols of Perversity: Fantasies of Feminine Evil in Fin-de-Siècle Culture*, Oxford: Oxford University Press.

Dika, Vera (1996) 'From Dracula – with love', in Barry Keith Grant (ed.), *The Dread of Difference*, Austin, TX: University of Texas Press, 388–400.

Doane, Janice and Hodges, Devon (1990) 'Undoing feminism: from the preoedipal to postfeminism in Anne Rice's *Vampire Chronicles*', *American Literary History*, 2:3: 422–42.

Doane, Mary Ann (1987) *The Desire to Desire*, Bloomingtom, IN: Indiana University Press.

Dyer, Richard (1988) 'Children of the night: vampirism as homosexuality, homosexuality as vampirism', in Susannah Radstone (ed.), *Sweet Dreams: Sexuality, Gender and Popular Fiction*, London: Lawrence & Wishart, 47–72.

Easlea, Brian (1983) *Fathering the Unthinkable: Masculinity, Scientists and the Nuclear Arms Race*, London: Polity.

Eco, Umberto (1984) *Reflections on the Name of the Rose*, trans. William Weaver, London: Secker and Warburg.

Edwards, Gavin (2000) 'William Godwin's foreign language: stories and families in *Caleb Williams* and *Political Justice*', *Studies in Romanticism*, 39.4: 533–51.

Elam, Diane (1992) *Romancing the Postmodern*, New York: Routledge.

Elsaesser, Thomas (1998) 'Specularity and engulfment: Francis Ford Coppola and *Bram Stoker's Dracula*', in Steve Neale and Murray White (eds), *Contemporary Hollywood Cinema*, New York: Routledge, 191–208.

Ennis, Garth and Dillon, Steve (1998) *Preacher: Dixie Fried*, New York: DC Comics.

Everest, Kelvin and Edwards, Gavin (1982) 'William Godwin's "Caleb Williams": truth and things as they are', in Francis Barker *et al.* (eds), *1789: Reading Writing Revolution*, Colchester: University of Essex, 129–46.

Ferguson, Frances (1984) 'The nuclear sublime', *diacritics*, 14: 4–10.

—— (1992) *Solitude and the Sublime*, New York: Routledge.

Fleenor, Juliann E. (ed.) (1983) *The Female Gothic*, Montreal: Eden Press.

Forry, Steven (1990) *Hideous Progenies*, Philadelphia, PA: University of Pennsylvania Press.

Foucault, Michel (1977) *Language, Counter-Memory, Practice*, trans. Donald F. Bouchard and Sherry Simon, Ithaca, NY: Cornell University Press.

—— (1979) *Discipline and Punish*, trans. Alan Sheridan, Harmondsworth: Penguin.

—— (1981) *The History of Sexuality: Vol. I, An Introduction*, trans. Robert Hurley, Harmondsworth: Penguin.

—— (1987) *The Use of Pleasure*, trans. Robert Hurley, London: Penguin.

Freud, Sigmund (1955) 'The "uncanny"', in *The Standard Edition of the Complete Psychological Works*, Vol. XVII, trans. James Strachey, London: Hogarth Press, 218–52.

—— (1977) 'On the universal tendency to debasement in the sphere of love', in *On Sexuality*, trans. James Strachey, Angela Richards (ed.), Harmondsworth: Penguin, 243–60.

Frye, Northrop (1957) *Anatomy of Criticism*, Princeton, NJ: Princeton University Press.

—— (1976) *Secular Scripture: a Study of the Structure of Romance*, Cambridge, MA: Harvard University Press.

Fuchs, Cynthia J. (1995) '"Death is irrelevant": cyborgs, reproduction, and the future of male hysteria', in Chris Hables Gray (ed.), *The Cyborg Handbook*, London: Routledge, 281–300.

Fukuyama, Francis (1992) *The End of History and the Last Man*, London: Penguin.

—— (1995) *Trust*, London: Hamish Hamilton.

Gelder, Ken (1994) *Reading the Vampire*, London: Routledge.

Gibson, William (1984) *Neuromancer*, London: HarperCollins.

—— (1986) *Burning Chrome*, London: HarperCollins.

—— (1996) *Idoru*, London: Penguin.

Glazer, Miryam (1989) '"What is within is now seen without": romanticism, neuro-manticism, and the death of the imagination in William Gibson's fictive world', *Journal of Popular Culture*, 23: 155–64.

Glover, David (1993) 'Travels in Romania: myths of origins, myths of blood', *Discourse*, 16: 126–44.

Godwin, William (1985) *Enquiry Concerning Political Justice* (1793), Isaac Kramnick (ed.), Harmondsworth: Penguin.

—— (1988), *Caleb Williams* (1794), Maurice Hindle (ed.), Harmondsworth: Penguin.

Goldberg, Jonathan (1995) 'Recalling totalities: the mirrored stages of Arnold Schwarzenegger', in Chris Hables Gray (ed.), *The Cyborg Handbook*, New York: Routledge, 233–55.

Goldman, Robert and Papson, Stephen (1998) *Nike Culture*, London: Sage.

Goldsmith, Steven (1993) *Unbuilding Jerusalem: Apocalypse and Romantic Representation*, Ithaca, NJ: Cornell University Press.

Goux, Jean-Joseph (1990) 'General economy and postmodern capitalism', *Yale French Studies*, 78: 206–24.

—— (1998) 'Subversion and consensus: proletarians, women, artists', in Jean-Joseph Goux and Philip R. Wood (eds), *Terror and Consensus*, Stanford, CA: Stanford University Press, 37–51.

Graham, Kenneth W. (1990) *The Politics of Narrative*, New York: AMS Press.

Gray, Alasdair (1981), *Lanark*, Edinburgh: Canongate Books.

—— (1992) *Poor Things*, London: Bloomsbury.

Gray, Chris Hables and Mentor, Steven (1995) 'The cyborg body politic: version 1.2', in Chris Hables Gray (ed.), *The Cyborg Handbook*, New York: Routledge, 453–66.

Gray, Chris Hables, Mentor, Steven and Figueroa-Sarriera, Heidi J. (1995) 'Cyborg-ology', in Chris Hables Gray (ed.), *The Cyborg Handbook*, New York: Routledge, 1–14.

Greenberg, Harvey R. (1991) 'Reimagining the gargoyle: psychoanalytic notes on *Alien*', in Constance Penley *et al.* (eds), *Close Encounters*, Minneapolis, MN: University of Minnesota Press, 83–104.

Greenwald, Jeff (1998) *Future Perfect: How* Star Trek *Conquered Planet Earth*, Harmondsworth: Penguin.

Grosz, Elizabeth (2000) 'Deleuze's Bergson: duration, the virtual and a politics of the future', in Ian Buchanan and Claire Colebrook (eds), *Deleuze and Feminist Theory*, Edinburgh: Edinburgh University Press, 214–34.

Hables Gray, Chris (1997) 'The ethics and politics of cyborg embodiment: citizenship as a hypervalue', *Cultural Values*, 1.2: 252–58.

Haining, Peter (ed.) (1995) *The Frankenstein Omnibus*, London: Orion.

Halberstam, Judith (1995) *Skin Shows*, Durham, NC: Duke University Press.

Hamilton, Paul (1995) 'Wordsworth and the shapes of theory', *News from Nowhere: Theory and Politics of Romanticism*, 1: 11–21.

Haraway, Donna (1990) 'A manifesto for cyborgs: science, technology and socialist feminism in the 1980s', in Linda J. Nicholson (ed.), *Feminism/Postmodernism*, New York: Routledge, 190–233.

—— (1997) *Modest_Witness@Second_Millenium*, London: Routledge.

Hayles, N. Katherine (1999) *How We Became Posthuman*, Chicago, IL: University of Chicago Press.

Heath, Stephen (1982) *The Sexual Fix*, London: Macmillan.

Henderson, Andrea (1994) '"An embarrassing subject": use value and exchange value in early gothic characterization', in Mary Favret and Nicola J. Watson (eds), *At the Limits of Romanticism*, Bloomington, IN: Indiana University Press, 225–45.

Hogle, Jerrold E. (1979) 'The texture of self in Godwin's *Things as They Are*', *Boundary* 2: 261–81.

—— (1994) 'The ghost of the counterfeit in the genesis of the gothic', in Allan Lloyd Smith and Victor Sage (eds), *Gothick Origins and Innovations*, Amsterdam: Rodopi, 23–33.

—— (1998a) '*Frankenstein* as neo-gothic: from the ghost of the counterfeit to the monster of abjection', in Tillotama Rajan and Julia M. Wright (eds), *Romanticism, History and the Possibilities of Genre*, Cambridge: Cambridge University Press, 176–210.

—— (1998b) 'Stoker's counterfeit gothic: *Dracula* and theatricality at the dawn of simulation', in William Hughes and Andrew Smith (eds), *Bram Stoker: History, Psychoanalysis and the Gothic*, Basingstoke: Macmillan.

—— (2004) '"Gothic" romance: its origins and cultural functions', in Corinne Saunders (ed.), *Companion to Romance*, Oxford: Blackwell, 216–32.

Hollinger, Veronica (1990) 'Cybernetic deconstructions: cyberpunk and postmodernism', *Mosaic*, 23.2: 29–44.

—— (1997) 'Fantasies of absence: the postmodern vampire', in Jan Gordon and Veronica Hollinger (eds), *Blood Read: the Vampire as Metaphor in Contemporary Culture*, Philadelphia, PA: University of Pennsylvania Press, 199–212.

Hurley, Kelly (1996) *The Gothic Body*, Cambridge: Cambridge University Press.

Huxley, Aldous (1955) *Brave New World*, Harmondsworth: Penguin.

Huyssen, Andreas (1981–82) 'The vamp and the machine: technology and sexuality in Fritz Lang's *Metropolis*', *New German Critique*, 24–25: 221–37.

Irigaray, Luce (1985) *This Sex Which Is Not One*, trans. Catherine Porter with Carolyn Burke, New York: Columbia University Press.

—— (1993) *An Ethics of Sexual Difference*, trans. Carolyn Burke and Gillian C. Gill, London: Athlone.

Jackson, Rosemary (1981) *Fantasy: the Literature of Subversion*. London: Methuen.

Jameson, Fredric (1975) 'Magical narratives: romance as genre', *New Literary History*, 7: 135–63.

—— (1984) 'Postmodernism, or the cultural logic of late capitalism', *New Left Review*, 146: 53–92.

—— (1991) *Postmodernism, or, The Logic of Late Capitalism*, London: Verso.

Jancovich, Mark (1996) *Rational Fears: American Horror in the 1950s*, Manchester: Manchester University Press.

Jenstsch, Ernst (1995 [1906]) 'On the Psychology of the Uncanny', trans. Roy Sellars, *Angelaki*, 2.1: 7–16.

Jervis, John (1998) *Exploring the Modern*, Oxford: Blackwell.

Johnson, Barbara (1993) 'The Last Man', in Audrey Fisch *et al.* (eds), *The Other Mary Shelley*, Oxford: Oxford University Press.

Joyrich, Lynne (1996) 'Feminist enterprise? *Star Trek: The Next Generation* and the occupation of femininity', *Cinema Journal*, 35.2: 61–84.

Kaczvinsky, Donald P. (2001) '"Making up for lost time": Scotland, stories and the self in Alasdair Gray's *Poor Things*', *Contemporary Literature* XLII, 4: 775–99.

Kaplan, Cora (1986) '*The Thorn Birds*: fiction, fantasy, femininity', in James Donald and Victor Burgin (eds), *Formations of Fantasy*, London: Methuen, 142–66.

Katz, Jon (1995) 'The age of Paine', *Wired*, 1.01: 64–69.

Kavanagh, James H. (1990) 'Feminism, humanism and science in *Alien*', in Annette Kuhn (ed.), *Alien Zone*, London: Verso, 73–81.

Kay, Lily E. (2000) *Who Wrote the Book of Life? A History of the Genetic Code*, Stanford, CA: Stanford University Press.

Kelly, Kevin (1994) *Out of Control: the New Biology of Machines*, London: Fourth Estate.

—— (1998) *New Rules for the New Economy*, London: Fourth Estate.

Ketterer, David (1974) *New Worlds for Old: the Apocalyptic Imagination, Science Fiction, and American Literature*, Bloomington, IN: Indiana University Press.

King, Maureen (1993) 'Contemporary women writers and the "new evil": the vampires of Anne Rice and Suzy McKee Charnas', *Journal of the Fantastic in the Arts*, 5.3: 75–84.

Kittler, Friedrich (1997) *Essays: Literature Media Information Systems*, John Johnston (ed.), The Netherlands: G + B Arts International.

Klancher, Jon (1998) 'Godwin and the genre reformers: on necessity and contingency in romantic narrative theory', in Tilottama Rajan and Julia M. Wright (eds), *Romanticism, History and the Possibilities of Genre*, Cambridge: Cambridge University Press, 21–38.

Kliger, Samuel (1952) *The Goths in England: a Study in Seventeenth and Eighteenth Century Thought*, Cambridge, MA: Harvard University Press.

Kojève, Alexandre (1969) *Introduction to the Reading of Hegel*, trans. James Nichols Jr., New York: Basic Books.

Kristeva, Julia (1982) *Powers of Horror*, trans. Leon S. Roudiez, New York: Columbia University Press.

—— (1987) *Tales of Love*, trans. Leon S. Roudiez, New York: Columbia University Press.

Lacan, Jacques (1977a) *Ecrits*, trans. Alan Sheridan, London: Tavistock.

—— (1977b) *The Four Fundamental Concepts of Psychoanalysis*, trans. Alan Sheridan, London: Penguin.

—— (1977c) 'Desire and the interpretation of desire in *Hamlet*', *Yale French Studies*, 55/56: 11–52.

—— (1982) 'Seminar of 21 January 1975', in Juliet Mitchell and Jacqueline Rose (eds), *Feminine Sexuality*, London: Macmillan, 162–71.

—— (1992) *The Ethics of Psychoanalysis*, trans. Dennis Porter, London: Routledge.

—— (1993), *The Psychoses: the Seminar of Jacques Lacan Book III 1955–56*, trans. Russell Grigg, London: Routledge.

—— (1998) *Encore: the Seminar of Jacques Lacan Book XX Encore 1972–1973*, trans. Bruce Fink, New York: Norton.

Lacoue-Labarthe, Philippe and Nancy, Jean-Luc (1988) *The Literary Absolute: the Theory of Literature in German Romanticism*, trans. Paul Barnard and Caroline Lester, New York: State University of New York Press.

Land, Nick (1993a), 'Circuitries', *PLI*: 217–35.

—— (1993b), 'Machinic desire', *Textual Practice*, 7.1: 471–82.

—— (1998) 'Cybergothic', in Joan Broadhurst Dixon and Eric J. Cassidy (eds), *Virtual Futures*, New York: Routledge, 79–87.

Lapsley, Rob and Westlake, Michael (1993) 'From *Casablanca* to *Pretty Woman*', in Antony Easthope (ed.), *Contemporary Film Theory*, London: Longman, 179–203.

Latham, Rob (1997) 'Consuming youth: the lost boys cruise mallworld', in Jan Gordon and Veronica Hollinger (eds), *Blood Read: the Vampire as Metaphor in Contemporary Culture*, Philadelphia, PA: University of Pennsylvania Press, 129–47.

Leary, Timothy (1991), 'The cyberpunk: the individual as reality pilot', in Larry McCaffrey (ed.), *Storming the Reality Studio*, Durham, NC: Duke University Press, 245–58.

Lecercle, Jean-Jacques (1989) 'Répétition and vérité dans *Caleb Williams*', *Tropismes*, 4: 73–96.

LeFanu, Sarah (1988) *In the Chinks of the World Machine: Feminism and Science Fiction*, London: The Women's Press.

Levy, Stephen (1992) *Artificial Life*, London: Jonathan Cape.

Lieberman, Rhonda (1993) 'Shopping disorders', in Brian Massumi (ed.), *The Politics of Everyday Fear*, Minneapolis, MN: University of Minnesota Press, 245–65.

Light, Alison (1984), '"Returning to Manderley": romance fiction, sexuality, class', *Feminist Review*, 16: 7–23.

Lotringer, Sylvère (1988) *Overexposed*, London: Paladin.

Lupton, Deborah (1994) 'Panic computing: the viral metaphor and computer technology', *Cultural Studies*, 8.3: 556–68.

Lyotard, Jean-François (1984) *The Postmodern Condition*, trans. Geoff Bennington and Brian Massumi, Manchester: Manchester University Press.

—— (1991) *The Inhuman*, trans. Geoff Bennington and Rachel Bowlby, Oxford: Polity Press.

—— (1994) *Lessons on the Analytic of the Sublime*, trans. Elizabeth Rottenberg, Stanford, CA: Stanford University Press.

Machen, Arthur (1894) *The Great God Pan*, London: John Lane.

—— (1977) 'The novel of the white powder', in Charles Fowkes (ed.), *The Best Ghost Stories*, London: Hamlyn, 224–37.

McKendrick Neil, Brewer, John and Plumb, J. H. (1982) *The Birth of a Consumer Society*, London: Europa.

McLuhan, Marshall (1964) *Understanding Media*, London: Routledge and Kegan Paul.

Markley, Robert (ed.) (1996) *Virtual Realities and Their Discontents*, Baltimore, MD: Johns Hopkins University Press, 1–10.

Marshal, William (1999) 'Wafers of death', in *Terror Tales*, Whitby: Black Crow Press, 17–64.

Marx, Karl (1943) *The Eighteenth Brumaire of Louis Napoleon*, in *Karl Marx: Selected Writings*, Vol. 2, V. Adoratsky (ed.), London: Lawrence & Wishart, 311–426.

—— (1973) *Grundrisse*, trans. Martin Nicolaus, Harmondsworth: Penguin.

—— (1976) *Capital*, Vol. I, trans. Ben Fowkes, Harmondsworth: Penguin.

Massé, Michelle A. (1992) *In the Name of Love*, Ithaca, NY: Cornell University Press.

Matthias, T. J. (1805) *The Pursuits of Literature*, 13th edn, London: Thomas Becket.

Maturana, Humberto R. and Varela, Francisco J. (1980) *Autopoiesis and Cognition*, Dordrecht, Holland: D. Reidel Publishing.

Merleau-Ponty, Maurice (1968) *The Visible and the Invisible*, trans. Alphonso Lingis, Evanston, IL: Northwestern University Press.

Miles, Robert (1995) *Ann Radcliffe: the Great Enchantress*, Manchester: Manchester University Press.

Miller, Jacques-Alain (1988) 'Extimité', *Prose Studies*, 11.3: 121–31.

Mitchell, Juliet and Rose, Jacqueline (eds) (1982) *Feminine Sexuality: Jacques Lacan and the école freudienne*, Basingstoke: Macmillan.

Modleski, Tania (1982) *Loving with a Vengeance*, New York: Routledge.

Moers, Ellen (1978), *Literary Women*, London: Allen Lane.

Negra, Diane (2004) 'Quality postfeminism?', *Genders* 3, www.genders.org/g39/g39_negra.html (accessed 2 June 2006).

Newton, Judith (1990) 'Feminism and anxiety in *Alien*', in Annette Kuhn (ed.), *Alien Zone*, London: Verso, 82–87.

Nicholls, Bill (1988) 'The work of culture in an age of cybernetic systems', *Screen*, 29.1: 278–89.

Nicholls, Peter (1976) 'Science fiction: the monsters and the critics', in Peter Nicholls (ed.), *Science Fiction at Large*, London: Gollancz, 159–83.

Nicholson, Linda J. (ed.) (1990) *Feminism/Postmodernism*, New York: Routledge.

O'Flinn, Paul (1995) 'Production and reproduction: the case of *Frankenstein*', in Fred Botting (ed.), *Frankenstein: New Casebooks*, Basingstoke: Macmillan, 21–47.

Olsen, Lance (1991) 'The shadow of spirit in William Gibson's *Matrix* trilogy', *Extrapolation*, 32.3: 278–89.

Parrinder, Patrick (1980) *Science Fiction*, London: Methuen.

Paulson, William R. (1988) *The Noise of Culture: Literary Texts in a World of Information*, Ithaca, NY: Cornell University Press.

Pearce, Lynne (2007) *Romance Writing*, Cambridge: Polity Press.

Penley, Constance (1986) 'Time travel, primal scene, and the critical dystopia', *Camera Obscura*, 15: 67–84.

—— (1997) *NASA/Trek*, New York: Verso.

Peters, Tom and Waterman, Robert H. (1982) *In Search of* Excellence, London: Harper and Row.

Philmus, Robert M. (1970) *Into the Unknown: the Evolution of Science Fiction from Francis Godwin to H. G. Wells*, Berkeley, CA: University of California Press.

Pick, Daniel (1984) '"Terrors of the night": *Dracula* and "degeneration" in the late nineteenth century', *Critical Quarterly*, 30: 71–87.

Pinker, Steven (1997) *How the Mind Works*, London: Allen Lane.

Plant, Sadie (1995) 'The future looms: weaving women and cybernetics', in Mike Featherstone and Rob Burrows (eds), *Cyberspace/Cyberbodies/Cyberpunk: Cultures of Technological Embodiment*, London: Sage, 45–64.

Platt, C. (1995) 'Superhumanism: interview with Hans Moravec', *Wired*, 1.06.

Poe, Edgar Allan (1967) *Selected Writings*, David Galloway (ed.), Harmondsworth: Penguin.

Poovey, Mary (1979) 'Ideology and *The Mysteries of Udolpho*', *Criticism*, 21.4: 307–30.

Porter, Roy (1993) 'Consumption: disease of the consumer society?', in John Brewer and Roy Porter (eds), *Consumption and the World of Goods*, London: Routledge, 58–81.

Poster, Mark (2002) 'High-tech Frankenstein, or Heidegger meets Stelarc', in Joanna Zylinska (ed.), *The Cyborg Experiments*, London: Continuum, 15–32.

Priest, Christopher (1979) 'British science fiction', in Patrick Parrinder (ed.), *Science Fiction: a Critical Guide*, London: Longman, 187–98.

Punter, David (1996) *The Literature of Terror*, Vol. II, London: Longman.

—— (1998) *Gothic Pathologies*, Basingstoke: Macmillan.

—— (1999) 'Heartlands: contemporary Scottish gothic', *Gothic Studies*, 1.1: 101–18.

Rabinow, Paul (1992) 'Artificiality and enlightenment: from sociobiology to bio-sociality', in Jonathan Crary and Sanford Kwinter (eds), *Incorporations*, New York: Zone, 234–42.

Radcliffe, Ann (1826) 'On the supernatural in poetry', *New Monthly Magazine*, 16: 145–52.

Radway, Janice (1984) *Reading the Romance*, Chapel Hill, NC: University of North Carolina Press.

Readings, Bill (1993) 'For a heteronomous cultural politics: the university, culture and the state', *Oxford Literary Review*, 15: 163–99.

Rice, Anne (1977) *Interview with the Vampire*, London: Futura.

—— (1995) *The Vampire Lestat*, New York: Warner Books.

—— (1999) 'Interview', *Gothic Studies*, 1.2: 169–81.

Rizzo, Teresa (2004) 'The *Alien* series: a Deleuzian perspective', *Women: a Cultural Review*, 15.3: 330–44.

Roberts, Adam (2000) *Science Fiction*, London: Routledge.

Roof, Judith (1996) *Reproductions of Reproduction*, London: Routledge.

Rucker, Rudy (1992) 'On the edge of the Pacific', in Rudy Rucker, R. U. Sirius and Queen Mu (eds), *Mondo 2000: User's Guide to the New Edge*, New York: HarperCollins.

—— (1994) 'Wetware', in *Live Robots*, New York: Avon Books.

Rushkoff, Douglas (1994) *Cyberia*, London: HarperCollins.

Russ, Joanna (1995) *To Write Like a Woman: Essays in Feminism and Science Fiction*, Bloomington, IN: Indiana University Press.

Seed, David (1996) 'Alien invasions by bodysnatchers and related creatures', in Victor Sage and Allan Lloyd Smith (eds), *Modern Gothic*, Manchester: Manchester University Press.

Senf, Carole A. (1982) '*Dracula*: Stoker's response to the new woman', *Victorian Studies*, 26:

Serres, Michel (1995) *Angels: a Modern Myth*, trans. F. Cowper, Paris: Flammarion.

SHaH (1997) 'Incorporating the impossible: a general economy of the future present', *Cultural Values*, 1.2: 178–204.

—— (2003) 'How it feels', in Jane Arthurs and Iain Grant (eds), *Crash Cultures*, Bristol: Intellect, 23–34.

Shelley, Mary (1969) *Frankenstein; or, the Modern Prometheus*, M. K. Joseph (ed.), Oxford: Oxford University Press.

—— (1974) *Frankenstein; or the Modern Prometheus: the 1818 Text*, James Rieger (ed.), Chicago, IL: University of Chicago Press.

—— (1994) *The Last Man*, Morton D. Paley (ed.), Oxford: Oxford University Press.

Shelley, Percy Bysshe (1923) *The Complete Poetical Works*, Thomas Hutchinson (ed.), London: Oxford University Press.

Shippey, Tom (1992) 'Semiotic ghosts and ghostliness in the work of Bruce Sterling', in Tom Shippey (ed.), *Fiction 2000: Cyberpunk and the Future of Narrative*, Athens, GA: University of Georgia Press, 208–20.

Sobchack, Vivian (1987) *Screening Space*, 2nd edn, New Brunswick, NJ: Rutgers University Press.

—— (1993) 'New age mutant ninja hackers: reading *Mondo 2000*', *South Atlantic Quarterly*, 92.4: 569–84.

Sontag, Susan (1974) 'The imagination of disaster', in Gerald Mast and Marshall Cohen (eds), *Film Theory and Criticism*, New York: Oxford University Press, 422–37.

Spark, Muriel (1951) *Child of Light: a Reassessment of Mary Wollstonecraft Shelley*, Hadleigh, Essex: Tower Bridge.

Sponsler, Claire (1993) 'Beyond the ruins: the geopolitics of urban decay and cybernetic play', *Science Fiction Studies*, 20.2: 251–65.

Stacey, Jackie (2003) '"She is not herself": the deviant relations of *Alien Resurrection*', *Screen*, 44.3: 251–76.

Stephenson, Neal (1993) *Snow Crash*, London: Penguin.

Sterling, Bruce (ed.) (1994) *Mirrorshades*, London: HarperCollins.

Stevenson, Randall (1991) 'Alasdair Gray and the postmodern', in Robert Crawford and Thom Nairn (eds), *The Arts of Alasdair Gray*, Edinburgh: Edinburgh University Press, 48–63.

Stevenson, Robert Louis (1979) *The Strange Case of Dr Jekyll and Mr Hyde and Other Stories*, Jenny Calder (ed.), Harmondsworth: Penguin.

Stoker, Bram (1993) *Dracula*, Maurice Hindle (ed.), Harmondsworth: Penguin.

Stone, A. R. (1995) *The War of Desire and Technology at the Close of the Mechanical Age*, Cambridge, MA: MIT Press.

Styles, John (1993) 'Manufacturing, consumption and design in eighteenth-century England', in John Brewer and Roy Porter (eds), *Consumption and the World of Goods*, London: Routledge, 527–54.

Suvin, Darko (1979) *Metamorphoses of Science Fiction*, New Haven, CT: Yale University Press.

Telotte, J. P. (1990) 'The doubles of fantasy and desire', in Annette Kuhn (ed.), *Alien Zone: Cultural Theory and Contemporary Science Fiction Cinema*, London: Verso, 152–59.

Tomc, Sandra (1997) 'Dieting and damnation: Anne Rice's *Interview with the Vampire*', in Jan Gordon and Veronica Hollinger (eds), *Blood Read: the Vampire as Metaphor in Contemporary Culture*, Philadelphia, PA: University of Pennsylvania Press, 95–113.

Turney, Jon (1998) *Frankenstein's Footsteps: Science, Genetics and Popular Culture*, New Haven, CT: Yale University Press.

Twain, Mark (1981) *Life on the Mississippi*, New York: Bantam Books.

Twitchell, James (1988) 'The vampire myth', in Margaret L. Carter (ed.), *Dracula: the Vampire and the Critics*, Ann Arbor, MI: UMI Research Press, 109–15.

Vernon, Polly (2007) 'Interview with the vampire', *Observer Magazine*, 13 May: 14–18.

Virilio, Paul (1995) *The Art of the Motor*, trans. Julie Rose, Minneapolis, MN: University of Minnesota Press.

—— (1997) *Open Sky*, trans. Julie Rose, London: Verso.

—— (2000) *A Landscape of Events*, trans. Julie Rose, Cambridge, MA: MIT Press.

Vlasopolos, Anca (1983) '*Frankenstein*'s hidden skeletons: the psycho-politics of oppression', *Science Fiction Studies*, 10: 125–36.

Voller, Jack (1993) 'Neuromanticism: cyberspace and the sublime', *Extrapolation*, 34.1: 18–29.

Volney, C. F. (1979) *A New Translation of Volney's Ruins*, trans. R. D. Richardson, New York: Garland.

Walpole, Horace (1982) *The Castle of Otranto: a Gothic Story*, W. S. Lewis (ed.), Oxford: Oxford University Press.

Waugh, Patricia (1992) *Practising Postmodernism, Reading Modernism*, London: Edward Arnold.

Weiskel, Thomas (1976) *The Romantic Sublime: Studies in the Structure and Psychology of Transcendence*, Baltimore, MD: Johns Hopkins University Press.

Wells, H. G. (1958) *The Time Machine*, in *Selected Short Stories*, Harmondsworth; Penguin.

—— (1966). *Experiment in Autobiography*, 2 vols, London: Victor Gollancz and the Cresset Press.

—— (1988) *War of the Worlds*, London: Planet Three Publishing.

—— (1993) *The Island of Dr Moreau*, London: Everyman.

Wernick, Andrew (1991) *Promotional Culture*, London: Sage.

White, Mimi (1989) 'Representing romance: reading/writing/fantasy and the "liberated" heroine of recent Hollywood films', *Cinema Journal*, 28.3: 41–56.

Wicke, Jennifer (1992) 'Vampiric typewriting: Dracula and its media', *English Literary History*, 59: 467–93.

Wiener, Norbert (1954) *The Human Use of Human Beings: Cybernetics and Society*, London: Eyre and Spottiswoode

—— (1961) *Cybernetics*, 2nd edn, New York: MIT Press and John Wiley & Sons.

Williams, Ioan (ed.) (1970) *Novel and Romance 1700–1800: a Documentary Record*, London: Routledge.

Williams, Raymond (1979) 'Utopia and science fiction', in Patrick Parrinder (ed.), *Science Fiction: a Critical Guide*, London: Longman, 52–64.

Wilt, Judith (1981) 'The imperial mouth: imperialism, the gothic and science fiction', *Journal of Popular Culture*, 14: 618–28.

Wollstonecraft, Mary (1989) *A Vindication of the Rights of Men* (1790), in *The Works of Mary Wollstonecraft*, Vol. 5, Janet Todd and Marilyn Butler (eds), London: Pickering.

Wood, Robin (1996) 'Burying the undead: the use and obsolescence of Count Dracula', in Barry Keith Grant (ed.), *The Dread of Difference*, Austin, TX: University of Texas Press, 364–78.

Wordsworth, William (1920) *The Poetical Works*, Thomas Hutchinson (ed.), London: Oxford University Press.

—— (1933) *The Prelude (Text of 1805)*, Ernest de Selincourt (ed.), London: Oxford University Press.

Wright, Elizabeth (2000) *Lacan and Postfeminism*, Cambridge: Icon.

Zanger, Jules (1997) 'Metaphor into metonymy: the vampire next door', in Jan Gordon and Veronica Hollinger (eds), *Blood Read: the Vampire as Metaphor in Contemporary Culture*, Philadelphia, PA: University of Pennsylvania Press, 17–26.

Žižek, Slavoj (1989) *The Sublime Object of Ideology*, New York: Verso.

—— (1993) *Tarrying with the Negative*, Durham, NC: Duke University Press.

—— (1994) *The Metastases of Enjoyment*, New York: Verso.

—— (1996) *The Indivisible Remainder*, London: Verso.

—— (1997) *The Plague of Fantasies*, London: Verso.

—— (1999) *The Žižek Reader*, Elizabeth and Edmond Wright (eds), Oxford: Blackwell.

—— (2000) *The Fragile Absolute*, London: Verso.

# Index